Sociolinguistics in Deaf Communities

THE SOCIOLINGUISTICS IN DEAF COMMUNITIES SERIES

VOLUME 1

Sociolinguistics

in Deaf Communities

Ceil Lucas, Editor

GALLAUDET UNIVERSITY PRESS

Washington, D.C.

53⁰⁰

ASL+COLL
LUCAS
S

Sociolinguistics in Deaf Communities

A Series Edited by Ceil Lucas

Gallaudet University Press

Washington, D.C. 20002

© 1995 by Gallaudet University

All rights reserved

Published 1995. Second printing 1996

Printed in the United States of America

ISBN 1-56368-036-X

ISSN 1080-5494

The paper used in this publication meets the minimum requirements of American National Standard for Information Sciences—Permanence of Paper for Printed Library Materials, ANSI Z39.48-1984. ∞

Contents

Contributors

Jeffrey E. Davis
Sign Language Interpreting
   Preparation Program
Miami-Dade Community College
Miami, Florida

Barbara Gerner de García
Department of Educational
   Foundations and Research
Gallaudet University
Washington, D.C.

Kathy Jankowski
Superintendent
Central North Carolina School for
   the Deaf
Greensboro, North Carolina

Arlene B. Kelly
Culture and Communication
   Studies Program
Gallaudet University
Washington, D.C.

Mary Ann La Bue
Graduate School of Education
Harvard University
Cambridge, Massachusetts

Ceil Lucas
Department of Linguistics and
   Interpreting
Gallaudet University
Washington, D.C.

Dominique Machabée
LSQ Research Group
University of Quebec at Montreal
Montreal, Canada

Liza Martinez
Department of Linguistics and
   Interpreting
Gallaudet University
Washington, D.C.

Melanie Metzger
Department of Linguistics
Georgetown University
Washington, D.C.

Stephen M. Nover
Language, Reading and Culture
   Program
University of Arizona
Tucson, Arizona

Samuel Supalla
Sign Language/Deaf Studies
   Program
University of Arizona
Tucson, Arizona

Introduction

When I think about the concept of sociolinguistics in Deaf communities, I consistently see an image of a powerful explosion: all over the world, as self-awareness and self-empowerment grow in Deaf communities, issues in all areas of sociolinguistics are emerging. The occurrence and distribution of sign languages throughout the world, their interaction with spoken languages, and the accompanying language choices users make; language policy and planning in education, in interpreting, and in the media; the teaching of sign languages as second languages; linguistic and sociolinguistic variation within sign languages; the structure of sign language discourse; language attitudes in Deaf communities—these are some of the sociolinguistic issues that are demanding attention. And valuable research attention is being paid to all of these issues by researchers both deaf and hearing in many different countries.

One goal of this series to to provide, in one yearly volume, an ongoing forum for current data-based research on the various aspects of sociolinguistics in Deaf communities. Another goal is for the research in each volume to be of a truly international nature, representative of the world's Deaf communities. Some volumes will focus on one single topic, whereas others such as this first one will contain papers on a variety of topics. I am assisted in the selection of the papers by an editorial board that is also of an international nature.

In this first volume, the selection of papers shows the variety and range of sociolinguistics issues currently facing Deaf communities: the nature of sociolinguistic variation within ASL, fingerspelling in LSQ (Langue des Signes Québécoise), the acquisition of fingerspelling in ASL, language use by a Navajo family with deaf children, language policy, classroom practice and multiculturalism in deaf education, aspects of ASL discourse and of the discourse of sign language used by Deaf Filipinos, and the nature and role of rhetorical language in Deaf social movements.

It is my hope that this volume and the ones to follow it will help us gain a clear understanding of the richness and complexity of sociolinguistics in Deaf communities.

I am grateful to the contributors and to the members of the advisory board for their hard work in getting this volume together and in getting the series started. I also gratefully acknowledge Ivey Pittle Wallace, Managing Editor of Gallaudet University Press, whose patience, humor, and sheer hard work have made this series possible.

C. Lucas
Washington, D.C.

Part I **Variation**

Sociolinguistic Variation in ASL:

The Case of DEAF

Ceil Lucas

Since William C. Stokoe's pioneering work in the 1960s, it has been recognized that natural sign languages are autonomous linguistic systems, structurally independent of the spoken languages with which they may coexist in any given community. This recognition has been followed by extensive research into different aspects of ASL structure and accompanied by the recognition that, as natural sign languages are full-fledged autonomous linguistic systems shared by communities of users, the sociolinguistics of sign languages can be described in ways that parallel the description of the sociolinguistics of spoken languages. In particular, as concerns sociolinguistic variation, we can assume that the kind of interaction between linguistic forms and immediate linguistic environment and between social factors and linguistic forms that has been described extensively in spoken language communities—beginning with Fischer (1958), developed by Labov (1966), Shuy, Wolfram, and Riley (1968), and Wolfram (1969), and continued by many researchers, including Sankoff and Cedergren (1971), Cedergren (1973), Trudgill (1974), Rickford (1979), L. Milroy (1980, 1987), and J. Milroy (1992), to name but a few—also obtains in the Deaf community.

Indeed, there have been some investigations of sociolinguistic variation in ASL, but such investigations have generally been limited to small numbers of informants, have been based on data collected with a wide variety of methods, and have looked at a disparate collection of linguis-

Deaf with a capital *D* will be used here to indicate those who consider themselves culturally Deaf and members of the Deaf community.

I wish to acknowledge the very valuable assistance provided by Greg Guy, Walt Wolfram, Ralph Fasold, Stephen E. Brown, and John Rickford in the preparation of this paper. I also wish to thank Lois Lenderman for preparing the sign drawings.

tic features. The result is that, as yet, we do not begin to have a complete picture of what kinds of internal and external constraints might be at work in ASL variability. Padden and Humphries (1988, 2) describe "a particular group of deaf people who share a language—American Sign Language (ASL)—and a culture. The members of this group reside in the United States and Canada, have inherited their sign language, use it as a primary means of communication among themselves, and hold a set of beliefs about themselves and their connection to the larger society. . . . This . . . is not simply a camaraderie with others who have a similar physical condition, but is, like many other cultures in the traditional sense of the term, historically created and actively transmitted across generations."

Certainly, then, there is an evergrowing awareness among its users of the existence and use of a language that is independent and different from the majority language, English, and there is awareness of sociolinguistic variation within ASL. However, there are many aspects of that variation that have yet to be explored. In terms of linguistic structure, most of the studies to date focus on lexical variation, with some studies of phonological variation, and very few of morphological or syntactic variation. In terms of social factors, the major focus has been on regional variation, with some attention paid to ethnicity, age, gender, and factors that play a particular role in the Deaf community, such as audiological status of parents, age at which sign language was learned, and educational background. There are no studies that examine the interaction of socioeconomic status and variation in a systematic way. So, for example, while there is a widespread perception among ASL users that there are "grassroots" Deaf people (Jacobs 1980) whose educational backgrounds, employment patterns, and life experiences are different from middle-class Deaf professionals, and that while both groups use ASL, there is systematic variation between the two groups; the sociolinguistic reality of these perceptions has yet to be explored. In this regard, Padden and Humphries (1988, 4) state that "Even within the population of Deaf people who use ASL, not surprisingly, there is enormous diversity. Large communities of Deaf people in Boston, Chicago, Los Angeles, and Edmonton, Alberta . . . have their own distinctive identities. Within these local communities there are smaller groups organized by class, profession, ethnicity, or race, each of which has yet another set of distinct characteristics."

This paper will provide a brief overview of research on sociolinguistic variation in ASL and will examine the issue of internal constraints on ASL variables through an analysis of the sign DEAF.

RESEARCH ON SOCIOLINGUISTIC VARIATION

As I mentioned earlier, there have been some investigations of sociolinguistic variation in ASL. These studies have looked at phonological variation, lexical variation, and morphosyntactic variation. As of this writing, only three studies have looked specifically at internal constraints on variation in terms of factor groups and weightings, and a number of studies look at external constraints, but not always in quantitative terms. In the area of phonological variation, Battison, Markowicz, and Woodward (1975) examined variation in thumb extension in some signs. The social factors determining the selection of the thirty-nine signers participating in the study were whether or not the informant had deaf parents, the age at which the signer learned to sign (before or after age six), and gender. Informants provided intuitive responses concerning whether they would extend their thumb in certain signs, in addition to being asked to sign ten sentences under three conditions: as if to a deaf friend, as if to a hearing teacher, and in a practice situation. Informants were asked to practice the sentences and were videotaped doing so without their knowledge. In terms of linguistic constraints on thumb extension, six features were reported to distinguish the signs being investigated, including indexic (i.e., whether the sign is contiguous to its referent), bending of fingers, midfinger extension, twisting movement, whether the sign is on the face, and whether the sign is made in the center of one of four major areas of the body. From these features, the most heavily weighted environments were determined, and a rule was proposed incorporating the constraints. Woodward, Erting, and Oliver (1976) examined face-to-hand variation—that is, certain signs that are made on the face in some geographic regions are made on the hands in other geographic regions, including MOVIE, RABBIT, LEMON, COLOR, SILLY, PEACH, and PEANUT. Questionnaire data from forty-five informants indicated that New Orleans signers produced signs on the face that Atlanta signers produced on the hands. Woodward and De Santis (1977b) researched variation in one-handed and two-handed versions of the same signs produced on the face (such as CAT, CHINESE, COW, and FAMOUS) also by means of a questionnaire. The phonological features that seemed to be conditioning the variation (in order of heaviest weighting) include outward movement of the sign, high facial location as opposed to low facial location, and complex movement. They claimed that signs that tended to become one-handed were those having one or more of the following features: no outward movement, made in the salient facial area, made lower on the face, and with complex movement. They reported that Southerners use two-handed forms more than non-Southerners, older signers use two-handed signs more than younger signers, and that African American signers tended to use these same older two-handed signs on the face more often than white signers of the same age. De Santis (1977) examined variation in signs that can be produced on the hands or at the elbow, such as HELP and PUNISH, and reported more male informants using the hand version and more females using the elbow version. Data included some videotapes of free conversation and responses to a questionnaire.

An early study of lexical variation in ASL was done by Croneberg (1965), who used a 134-item sign vocabulary list to examine variation in Virginia, North Carolina, Maine, New Hampshire, and Vermont. He describes the difference between what he calls horizontal and vertical variation ("horizontal variation is what is popularly known as dialect variation, differences in the speech of groups of people living in different geographical areas. Vertical variation occurs in the speech of groups that are separated by social stratification." [p. 314]), provides examples of regional variation, and states that while some informal observations of vertical variation in the deaf community have been made, "no studies comparable to this brief regional survey have been made of vertical sociolinguistic variation" (p. 317). Croneberg discusses the central role of residential schools as centers of dialect innovation and regional distinctiveness and observes that, whereas both Virginia and North Carolina emerged as dialect areas distinct from each other, there was a considerable overlap between the New England states and a substantial amount of idiolectal variation. Shroyer and Shroyer (1984) also looked at lexical variation. They collected data on 130 words (the criterion for the inclusion of a word being the existence of three signs for the same word) from thirty-eight white signers in twenty-five states.

Lexical differences between African American signing and white signing have been explored by Woodward (1976), Aramburo (1989), and Guggenheim (1992). Each of the three studies explores a small number of lexical variants based on a limited number of informants; Woodward's data came from direct elicitation as well as spontaneous language production, whereas Aramburo and Guggenheim observed lexical variation during the course of structured but informal interviews. A frequently articulated perspective that there exists a variety of African American signing that differs markedly from white signing in all areas of structure (and not just lexically) has yet to be explored empirically. However, as of this writing, Woodward is conducting an NEH-funded project, the goal of which is to produce a dictionary of Black Southern signing and a database of free conversation.

Finally, some small-scale studies of lexical variation have looked at gender differences (Mansfield 1993), differences in the use of signs for sexual behavior (Bridges 1992), variation related to signers' socioeconomic status (Shapiro 1993), and lexical variation in the signing produced by interpreters for deaf-blind people (Collins 1993). (It should be noted that lexical variation has been explored in sign languages other than ASL; see, for example, Deuchar 1984, Woll 1981, and Kyle and Woll 1985, on British Sign Language; Collins-Ahlgren 1991 on New Zealand Sign Language; Schermer 1990 on Dutch Sign Language; Boyes-Braem 1985 on Swiss German Sign Language and Swiss French Sign Language; Radutzky 1992 on Italian Sign Language; and Campos 1994 on Brazilian Sign Language.)

Morphological and syntactic variation in ASL have been explored mainly by Woodward. Woodward (1973a, 1973b, 1974) and Woodward and De Santis (1977a) explored the variable use of three morphosyntactic rules: negative incorporation, agent-beneficiary directionality, and verb reduplication (all Woodward's terms). Negative incorporation is a rule whereby negation is indicated in a verb by outward movement, as in DON'T-WANT, DON'T-KNOW, and DON'T-LIKE as opposed to WANT, KNOW, and LIKE. What Woodward refers to as agent-beneficiary directionality seems to be the use of space to show verb agreement, and verb reduplication is the movement of the verb as a function of aspect, as in STUDY-CONTINU-ALLY or STUDY-REGULARLY. Data for the study of these three aspects of ASL syntax were gathered from 141 informants, including 132 white signers and 9 African American signers. Other social variables included whether or not the informant was deaf, whether or not the informant's parents were deaf, age at which the informant had learned ASL, whether or not the informant had attended college, and gender. Informants were shown examples of the variables in question and were asked to indicate on a questionnaire whether or not they used the forms presented. The overall results showed that the deaf informants who had learned to sign before age six and who had deaf parents used the form of the rules being investigated that were closer to ASL. Finally, a more recent study by Metzger (1992) explores variable pronoun usage in ASL and, based on a limited corpus, reports variability between the use of the index finger and the thumb for the third person pronoun.

IMPORTANT ISSUES

These studies raise several important issues. One concerns our linguistic understanding of ASL structure. We have learned a great deal about the linguistic structure of ASL in the years since the first studies of variation in ASL were done in the early 1970s. Naturally, a central concern of any variation study is to clearly define the linguistic variables being examined and to make sure that they are variable in the first place. It is not clear, for example, that the rules of negative incorporation, agent-beneficiary directionality, and verb reduplication in Woodward's studies are actually variable in a native signer's use of ASL. The apparent variability of these rules merits re-examination, as it may simply have been an artifact of combining data from native and nonnative signers. For example, in terms of agent-beneficiary directionality, it may be that directionality is obligatory—it is basically the way that agreement with subject and object is shown and is not optional. Failure to use space properly in these verbs would seem to result not in a variable form but in an ungrammatical one. Woodward's findings for the social variables support this observation: "deaf people, people with deaf parents, and people who learned signs before the age of six patterned in lects that approach 'pure' ASL more closely, and hearing people, people with hearing parents, and people who learned signs after the age of six patterned in lects that do not approach ASL closely" (1973a, 309).

Furthermore, the fundamental perspective on the structure of signs has changed dramatically since the earliest studies of variation were conducted. Stokoe's (1960) perspective, which clearly shaped sign language studies from 1960 until quite recently, held that signs are composed of three basic parts or parameters (the location at which the sign is produced, the handshape, and the movement) and that unlike the sequentially produced segments of spoken languages, these parts are produced simultaneously. In a more recent perspective developed by Liddell and Johnson (1989), signs are viewed as composed of movement and hold segments, sequentially produced, somewhat analogous to the consonants and vowels of spoken languages. I recognize that there is considerable ongoing debate as to the nature of the segments in question. (See, for example, Coulter 1992, Sandler 1992, Perlmutter 1992, and Uyechi 1994.) In this paper, I will work within the Liddell and Johnson framework because, as Liddell (1992) amply demonstrates, it allows not only for the efficient description of any individual sign but also for an accurate account of phonological processes such as assimilation, metathesis, epenthesis, and segment deletion—processes that play central roles in variation.

Clearly, our understanding of the nature of ASL structure will have direct bearing on the identification and description of the internal constraints on variation. As Fasold (1990, 244) points out, "a substantial amount of work in variation analysis . . . involves variation and change in its 'nuts and bolts' linguistic context." Focus on the linguistic context entails understanding the relationship between the variable in question and the environment in which it occurs. At this point, we have a fairly clear picture of the nature of variability in spoken languages. We know what might be variable and what constraints might look like. We know that variables may include structural categories (e.g., third person singular -s), alloforms (e.g., plural -s), processes (e.g., consonant cluster reduction), co-occurrence relations (e.g., negative concord), item permutation (e.g., placement of adverbs), or lexical choices (lexical items or function words). And we know that the internal constraints upon variables may be sequential (e.g., preceding or following environment), compositional (feature of the variable in question), or functional (e.g., the morphological status of the variable). They may also relate to structural incorporation (e.g., syntactic environment, such as following noun phrase or adjective phrase) or frequency of occurrence. And we know that a number of different constraints may operate on a given variable.

As for sign languages, we are just beginning to form an idea of what might be variable and what constraints on variability might be. The earlier studies show us mainly phonological and lexical variables, and the internal constraints described are of the compositional nature, i.e., features of the variable signs themselves. For example, in the thumb extension study by Battison et al. (1976), constraints on thumb extension include whether the other fingers in the sign are bent, whether there is twisting in the sign, and so forth. We need to learn a lot more about what the constraints on variability may be besides the compositional ones. Furthermore, although we can expect that some of the variables and constraints upon them may be analogous to those in spoken languages, the fundamental differences between sign and spoken language structures may result in differences in the kinds of variables and the constraints upon them. For example, Wolfram (1974) and Guy (1990) have both found that one constraint on *t/d* deletion in word-final consonant clusters is whether the *t* or *d* is a past tense morpheme, that is, an affix. Now, research on sign language structure has begun to reveal that sign languages make significantly less use of affixation, so the morphological status of the variable segment would not be a good candidate for a constraint. Indeed, individual segments may not turn out to be variable in the way they have been shown to be in many spoken languages. The search for variables and constraints will have to take into account the morphological structure of sign languages, which tends to be highly synthetic and basically distinct from the morphological structure of spoken languages.

THE PILOT STUDY

In the remainder of this paper, I will simply try to approach the issue of ASL variables and constraints upon them by focussing on one sign that exhibits variable location, the sign DEAF. That is, I will focus on what appears to be phonological variation. As I stated earlier, I work within the Liddell and Johnson framework, within which the basic form of the sign is viewed as a sequence of a hold segment, a movement segment, and a hold segment (HMH). Each segment includes an articulatory bundle that includes the features of handshape, location, palm orientation, and nonmanual signals (facial expression). Figure 1a illustrates the basic form of the sign in this framework, and figure 1b provides an illustration of this form of the sign. It has a "1" handshape, and the palm is generally oriented inward. In its citation form—the oldest form of the sign and

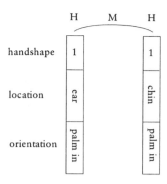

FIGURE Ia. *DEAF*

the form that appears in dictionaries—the sign begins just below the ear and ends near the corner of the mouth. The sign thus has two locations. However, a second variant of this sign begins at the corner of the mouth and moves upward to the ear, and a third variant simply contacts the lower cheek. Figures 1c and 1d provide illustrations of these forms of the sign.

The ear-to-chin version of the sign is the citation form. If we consider that the structure of this sign is a hold, a movement, and a hold (HMH), we can say that the chin-to-ear version shows the process of metathesis, whereby the first and last segments are inverted. The contact-cheek version consists of a movement and a hold (MH). Now, the issue is what motivates the production of a particular variant. The ear-to-chin variant and the chin-to-ear variant each have two locations and, because what varies is indeed the location, it makes sense to look for something in the environment having to do with location. For example, one might say that the location of the preceding or following sign might determine where the sign DEAF begins, at the chin or at the ear. In fact, Liddell and Johnson, in their discussion of metathesis, state:

> A number of signs exchange the initial sequence of segments with a sequence of final segments in certain contexts that appear to be purely phonological. The sign DEAF is typical of such metathesizing signs. [The ear to chin] form of the sign typically occurs immediately following signs produced in higher facial areas. . . . However, if DEAF is immediately preceded by a sign in the lower facial regions (and perhaps other lower areas), the initial two segments are exchanged with the final two segments. (1989, 244–45)

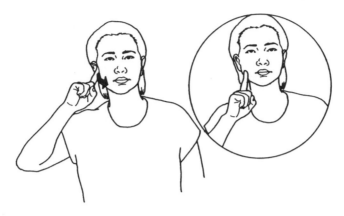

FIGURE 1b. *DEAF ear* ⟶ *chin*

FIGURE 1c. *DEAF chin* ⟶ *ear*

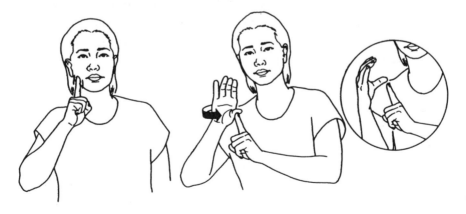

FIGURE 1d. *DEAF CULTURE contact cheek*

Note that their transcription of the sign is MHMMH as opposed to HMH, but the issue is the same. They do not consider the contact cheek form of the sign.

In this investigation, I wanted to determine the constraints on the variability of DEAF to see if indeed the location of the preceding and following sign plays a role. I also wanted to subject the data to a Varbrul analysis in order to obtain some idea of the respective weightings of the constraints identified. Varbrul (a computer program developed by Cedergren and Sankoff in 1974) has been used extensively to analyze variation in spoken languages. The investigation has two parts, a pilot study conducted at the LSA Institute at Ohio State University during the summer of 1993 and an analysis conducted in the fall of 1993. In the pilot study, not knowing what factors might turn out to be important, I tried to identify as many factors as possible that might play a role. The data for the pilot study consisted of videotapes of five native users of ASL in formal situations, either presenting lectures to a group or participating in television interviews. There were three women and two men. I considered first of all the syntactic function of the sign DEAF itself: it can function as an adjective, as in DEAF COMMUNITY or DEAF WORLD; it can function as a predicate, as in PRO.I DEAF ("I am deaf"); and it can function as a noun, as in DEAF UNDERSTAND. As I collected my data for the pilot, I noticed that the sign occurred frequently in what might be termed "fixed phrases," such as DEAF PEOPLE, DEAF WORLD, and so forth, so I initially included that as a factor. I then focussed on the preceding and following environments of the sign. Not knowing what important factors might be, I decided to follow a spoken language model and consider the preceding and following segments. In the framework I use, that means considering whether the preceding and following segment is a movement, a hold, or a pause. For example, in the phrase SEE DEAF PEOPLE, the preceding sign ends in a hold, and the following sign begins with a movement. I then considered the location of the preceding and following sign, that is, where the preceding sign ends and where the following sign begins. For example, in the phrase KNOW DEAF COMMUNITY, the preceding sign KNOW is produced on the forehead and the following sign COMMUNITY is produced at midchest. This information is very important, given the earlier claims that the form of the sign DEAF is determined by the location of the preceding sign. I expected preceding and following location to be important factors. In the example KNOW DEAF COMMUNITY, one would expect the sign DEAF to be produced from ear to chin, given the location of the sign KNOW. This would be in contrast with the phrase DIS-APPOINT DEAF COMMUNITY, for example, in which DISAPPOINT is produced on the chin, and one might therefore expect DEAF to be produced from chin to ear.

I also considered the syntactic function of the preceding and following sign—specifically, is it a noun, a verb, an adjective, a pronoun, a determiner, or a discourse marker of some kind? I noted whether the preceding and following sign used the same hand as the hand used for DEAF. Finally, I noted whether the preceding and following events were signs or fingerspelling. I suspected that this was far too many factors, but I wanted to make sure that I had not left anything out. I had 213 examples of the sign, all produced by native users of ASL. I used the MacVarb program (a version of Varbrul) developed by Greg Guy, counting the production of the sign from chin to ear or contacting the cheek as applications of the rule. For readers who are not familiar with it, the function of the Varbrul program is to estimate (based on observed data) factor values or probabilities for each environmental factor: a numerical measure of each factor's influence on the occurrence of the linguistic variables under investigation (Guy 1989). The values range between 0 and 1. A factor with a weighting greater than 0.500 is said to favor the application of the rule being examined. Factors with values less than 0.500 disfavor the rule, while factors with values at 0.500 are said to have no effect. The "rule" in this case is the production of the sign from chin-to-ear or as contact-cheek, as opposed to ear-to-chin. The factors found in the pilot study are shown in table 1.

Pilot Study Results

The results of the pilot study were somewhat surprising. As can be seen, occurrence in a fixed phrase seemed to have no effect; the same holds for the segmental status of the preceding and following segment and the syntactic function of the preceding and following sign. For that factor, a preceding adverb and a following noun seem to disfavor the occurrence of chin-to-ear or contact cheek, but no other factor seems to have any effect. The most surprising result of the pilot study was that preceding and following location seem to play only a modest role. The most important factor seemed to be the syntactic function of the sign DEAF itself, with adjective clearly favoring the application and predicate and noun disfavoring it.

TABLE 1. *Results from the Pilot Study: Non-ear-to-chin*
Realizations of DEAF

Factor Group	Weighting
Syntactic function	
adjective	0.76
predicate	0.37
noun	0.35
Fixed phrase	
fixed	0.52
not fixed	0.48
Preceding segment	
movement	0.51
hold	0.47
pause	0.52
Location of preceding sign	
chin	0.50
ear	0.50
Syntactic function of preceding sign	
noun	0.46
verb	0.53
adverb	0.29
adjective	0.64
pronoun	0.52
other	0.57
Following segment	
movement	0.50
hold	0.50
Location of following sign	
chin	0.54
ear	0.46
Syntactic function of following sign	
noun	0.35
verb	0.51
adverb	0.46
adjective	0.48
pronoun	0.59
other	0.60

The results of the pilot led me to collect more data and to refine my factor groups. I also realized that all of my pilot examples were from formal settings, in which the signer is lecturing or appearing in a formal television interview, so I decided to consider the effect of style as well. I collected more formal examples and added 250 examples taken from informal settings, for a total of 486 tokens. It should be pointed out, of course, that data collection involving sign languages necessarily involves a videocamera and all of the attendant methodological and ethical considerations. It seems that the videocamera will always be more intrusive than the audiorecorder used for spoken language interviews and that audiotaped interviews may achieve an informality that may never be possible with videotaped interviews. Rickford (email communication 1993) observes that he and his research colleagues have found videotape to be more formalizing than audiorecording for spoken language studies as well. Specifically describing his data collection experience with Foxy Boston, he says that his overall impression from the videotaping session was that "she was much more formal and less vernacular than in any of the previous four audiorecording sessions, even though she had a best friend along and interacted with her throughout the session." The mechanics of accomplishing informal videotaped interviews definitely deserves the continuing attention of sign language researchers. For present purposes, the informal interviews, albeit videotaped, were clearly different in style from the formal events.

In terms of refining my factor groups, I reduced them to four: syntactic function of the sign DEAF, location of preceding and following sign, and style. I ran the MacVarb program again, this time including the step-up/step-down procedure. The results can be seen in table 2.

Data Analysis

Once again, we see that the most important factor is the syntactic function of the sign DEAF, with adjective favoring the application of the rule, noun disfavoring it, and predicate having a modest to neutral effect. And again, preceding and following location have, if anything, a modest effect, as does style. The step-up/step-down procedure tests all of the factor groups for significance, first by adding them one at a time to the

TABLE 2. *Results from October 1993 Study:*
Non-ear-to-chin Realizations of DEAF

Factor Group	Weighting
Syntactic Function	
adjective	0.63
predicate	0.49
noun	0.39
Location of preceding sign	
chin	0.54
ear	0.46
Location of following sign	
chin	0.55
ear	0.45
Style	
formal	0.46
informal	0.54

Note. Step-down procedure threw out all factor groups as
insignificant except for syntactic function, significant at 0.000

analysis (step-up) and then by subtracting them one at a time (step-down), each time testing whether the inclusion of a given factor group in the analysis produces a statistically significant improvement in the fit between the estimated probabilities and the observed data. The program uses .05 as the criterion for significance, with the result of .25 being suggestive of significance. In the step-up procedure, the significance for the respective factor groups is seen in table 3.

Preceding and following location are not significant, then, whereas syntactic function and style are. In the step-down procedure, three factor

TABLE 3. *Results of Step-up/Step-down Procedure*

Factor Group	Significance
Syntactic function	0.000
Preceding location	0.494
Following location	0.575
Style	0.047

groups were discarded as not being significant: preceding and following location and style, leaving syntactic function with a significance of 0.000.

What do we make of these results? At the very least, the claims about the location of the preceding and following signs probably need to be re-examined. This can be illustrated with two examples from the data, seen in figure 2:

In the first example, the signer signs SEE chin→ear PRESIDENT. Both SEE and PRESIDENT are produced well above chin level, close to or above the ear. If preceding location were a factor, one might predict that DEAF would be signed from ear to chin. In the second example, chin→ear PRIDE, if the following location were a factor, one might predict that DEAF would be signed from ear to chin. Yet in both examples, the sign is produced from chin to ear. Now, the present study is limited to 486 tokens, and it may be that with the addition of more tokens, preceding and fol-

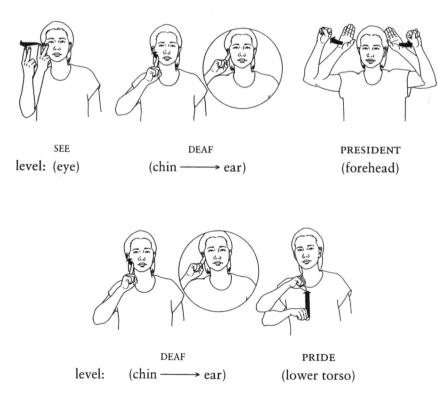

SEE   DEAF   PRESIDENT
level: (eye)   (chin ⟶ ear)   (forehead)

DEAF   PRIDE
level: (chin ⟶ ear)   (lower torso)

FIGURE 2. *Two examples showing that preceding and following location are not significant.*

lowing location would emerge more strongly as factors. However, there is something else of interest about DEAF: there exist at least twelve other signs with phonological structure like that of DEAF (i.e., consisting of a hold, a movement and a hold, with the first hold being produced in a location above or below the second hold, either directly above or below or diagonally above or below). Of these twelve, only two clearly permit the metathesis that we see in DEAF. They are HEAD and MOTHER^FATHER ("parents"). Of the remaining ten, there is some question as to whether HOME permits metathesis (Liddell and Johnson claim that it does, whereas there is disagreement among Deaf informants as to whether it does or not), and DORM, INDIAN, YESTERDAY, POWER, IMPROVE, BODY, KING, PRINCE, and CHRIST do not allow it.

It may be worth investigating whether we are dealing with a case of lexical diffusion here, with the change initiating in commonly occurring signs such as DEAF, MOTHER^FATHER, and HEAD. Instead, it may be a case of phonologically regular variation within a subset of items that Wolfram describes as "phonological regularity within a morphemically-defined set." He gives as an example the subset of English plurals that has a regressive assimilation rule of voiceless fricatives to voiced ones (e.g., knife, knives) compared with other items that aren't subjected to this regular variation (email communication, September 1993).

With the DEAF data, it is important to notice that DEAF is a frequently used sign that also occurs in many collocations such as DEAF COMMUNITY, DEAF WORLD, DEAF PEOPLE, DEAF CULTURE, and so forth. This characteristic of DEAF may help account for the favoring of chin-to-ear and contact-cheek when DEAF is functioning as an adjective, particularly in the contact-cheek form.

Indeed, as Diane Brentari pointed out in a conversation with the author (September 1994), it might be argued that the adjective form of the contact-cheek DEAF is basically the first half of a compound sign, when it occurs with the signs CULTURE, RESIDENTIAL SCHOOL, COMMUNITY, FAMILY, CLUB, MAN, PARENTS, BLIND, PERSON, and PEOPLE, all examples from the data. That is, these are essentially compound constructions in which lexicalization has occurred. Following Liddell and Johnson's (1989) account of compound formation in ASL, part of that lexicalization may include retaining the initial contacting hold in the first sign of the compound while deleting the other segments that make up the sign. So the contact-cheek version of DEAF might be the result of structural reduction occurring in the compounding process. In fact, almost all (41/48 informal and 4/5 formal) of the examples of DEAF-contact-cheek with an adjective function occur in what appear to be established constructions (i.e., compounds).

But that observation leads to two others. First, if contact-cheek is the result of reduction, it would have to be the reduction of the chin-to-ear form. Were it the reduction of the ear-to-chin form, we would expect it to be produced near the ear (i.e., retaining the first contact hold) but it is not. It is always produced near the corner of the mouth. Secondly, not all contact-cheek forms occur as adjectives in compounds.

The data on the relative frequency of all forms are also useful here in understanding the results: out of 486 tokens examined, 170 were ear-to-chin, 229 were chin-to-ear, and 87 were contact-cheek. Of the contact-cheek forms, 53 of the 87 occurred as adjectives, whereas 30 were nouns, and only 4 were predicates. How do we account for the 30 noun and 4 predicate contact-cheek forms that do not occur in compound constructions? An examination of the examples does not reveal any striking patterns. The contact-cheek variants occur mostly as subjects of sentences with a variety of verbs and predicates (LOOK-AT, CAN, FINE, FEEL, etc.), but many of these verbs and predicates occur with the ear-to-chin and chin-to-ear variants as well. One distinction is that the contact-cheek variant does not seem to occur as a direct object or as the object of a preposition. The fact that it only occurs as a subject may suggest that it occurs for emphasis. As a predicate, contact-cheek occurred twice in the data with a pronoun subject and twice with a noun subject.

Lexicalization in compounds would account for the contact-cheek form. It would not account for the choice of chin-to-ear over ear-to-chin. One possible explanation for the apparent preference of chin-to-ear over ear-to-chin might have to do with general constraints on the formation of signs. As I mentioned earlier, although there are a number of signs with the structure of chin-to-ear, most of these signs do not allow metathesis. It may be that the movement from chin to ear is the preferred one and that the ear-to-chin form of DEAF is a marked one, even though it is the citation form of the sign. With the chin-to-ear (and contact-cheek, which may start out as chin-to-ear), it may be that the language is trying to bring the citation form in line with other signs having that phonological structure. One hypothesis to account for the discrepancy between DEAF as an adjective and DEAF as a noun or predicate might be that the gradual change to the chin-to-ear or contact-cheek forms began in environments where DEAF occurs most frequently (i.e., as an adjective), and it is slowly spreading to environments where the sign functions as a noun or as a predicate. This would seem to be a kind of lexical diffusion.

Another possible explanation might have to do with possible differences in the pragmatics of nouns and predicates as opposed to adjectives. That is, DEAF occurs as a noun and as a predicate less frequently than as an adjective, and the use of DEAF as a noun or predicate may be marked. Examples are sentences such as DEAF UNDERSTAND (noun; "Deaf people understand.") or PRO.1 DEAF (predicate; "I am deaf."), in which the sign DEAF might be emphasized or stressed, thus motivating the more marked ear-to-chin variant. Clearly, the different distribution of nouns and predicates versus adjectives deserves more research.

The present study might indeed benefit from more tokens. However, I would also like to investigate variability that occurs in large classes of signs. Thumb extension, for example, seems to be a rule that applies to a large number of signs, as does pinky extension. Examination of such variability may provide a clearer picture of constraints on phonological variation in ASL. And it may turn out that some phonological features allow more variation that others, implying that hand configuration is more susceptible to variation than is location. However, it is important to notice that although many signs with the phonological structure of DEAF do not allow metathesis, there is a class of signs that has two locations: signs that are similar to DEAF but different in one important detail. The signs RESTAURANT, FLOWER, HONEYMOON, ARIZONA, CONGRESS, and NAVY, for example, do allow metathesis. The difference seems to be that, unlike DEAF and other signs like it, the locations in these signs are on a horizontal plane as opposed to the vertical one of DEAF. It is not necessarily the case, then, that location is not variable. What seem to be common sense intuitions about the possible effects of preceding and following location are not borne out by a close examination of the variable data. Variable location may have to do with the specific structure of the sign; other factors that we cannot as yet fully explain, such as the grammatical status or word-class of the variable, may have regular and significant effects that we might not have predicted from intuitions. The present study shows that what at first glance may appear to be a rule with straightforward phonological constraints, i.e., metathesis governed by preceding and following location, may indeed require re-examination.

REFERENCES

Aramburo, A. 1989. Sociolinguistic aspects of the Black Deaf community. In *The sociolinguistics of the Deaf community*, ed. C. Lucas, 103–119. San Diego: Academic Press.

Battison, R., H. Markowicz, and J. Woodward. 1975. A good rule of thumb: Variable phonology in American Sign Language. In *Analyzing variation in language*, ed. R. W. Fasold and R. Shuy. Washington, D.C.: Georgetown University Press.

Boyes-Braem, P. 1985. Studying sign language dialects. In *SLR 1983: Proceedings of the Third International Symposium on Sign Language Research, Rome, June 22–26, 1983*, ed. W. Stokoe and V. Volterra, 247–253. Silver Spring, Md.: Linstock Press.

_____.1994. An overview of current sign language projects in Switzerland. In *The Deaf Way: Perspectives from the international conference on Deaf culture*, ed. C. Erting, R. Johnson, D. Smith, and B. Snider, 382–386.

Bridges, B. 1992. *Gender variation with sex signs*. Unpublished manuscript. Gallaudet University Department of Linguistics and Interpreting, Washington, D.C.

Campos de Abreu, A. 1994. The deaf social life in Brazil. In *The Deaf Way: Perspectives from the international conference on Deaf culture*, ed. C. Erting, R. Johnson, D. Smith, and B. Snider, 114–116. Washington, D.C.: Gallaudet University Press.

Cedergren, H. 1973. On the nature of variable constraints. In *New ways of analyzing variation in English*, ed. C.J. Bailey and R.W. Shuy, 13–22. Washington, D.C.: Georgetown University Press.

Cedergren, H., and D. Sankoff. 1974. Variable rules: Performance as a statistical reflection of competence. *Language* 50:333–355.

Collins, S. 1993. Deaf-blind interpreting: The structure of ASL and the interpreting process. In *Communication Forum 1993*, ed. E. A. Winston. Washington, D.C.: Gallaudet University School of Communication.

Collins-Ahlgren, M. 1991. Variation in New Zealand Sign Language. Paper presented at NWAVE XX conference, Georgetown University, Washington, D.C.

Coulter, G. 1990. Emphatic stress in ASL. In *Theoretical issues in sign language research, volume I: Linguistics*, ed. S. Fischer and P. Siple, 109–125. Chicago: University of Chicago Press.

———, ed. 1992. *Phonetics and phonology, volume 3: Current issues in ASL phonology*. San Diego: Academic Press.

Croneberg, C. 1965. The linguistic community. In *A dictionary of American Sign Language,* ed. W. Stokoe, D. Casterline, and C. Croneberg. Washington, D.C.: Gallaudet College Press.

De Santis, S. 1977. Elbow to hand shift in French and American sign languages. Paper presented at the annual NWAVE conference, Georgetown University, Washington, D.C.

Deuchar, M. 1984. *British Sign Language*. London: Routledge and Kegan Paul.

Fasold, R. 1990. *Sociolinguistics of language*. Oxford: Basil Blackwell.

Fischer, J. 1958. Social influences on the choice of a linguistic variant. *Word* 14:47–56.

Guggenheim, L. 1992. Ethnic variation in ASL: The signing of African Americans and how it is influenced by conversational topic. Unpublished manuscript, Gallaudet University Department of Linguistics and Interpreting, Washington, D.C.

Guy, G. 1989. *MacVarb application and user documentation*. Stanford, Calif.: Stanford University, Linguistics Department.

———. 1990. Explanation in a variable phonology: -t, d deletion. Paper presented at NWAVE XIX conference, University of Pennsylvania, Philadelphia.

Jacobs, L. 1980. *A Deaf adult speaks out*. Washington, D.C.: Gallaudet University Press.

Kyle, J., and B. Woll. 1985. *Sign language: The study of Deaf people and their language*. Cambridge: Cambridge University Press.

Labov, W. 1966. *The social stratification of English in New York City*. Washington, D.C.: Center for Applied Linguistics.

———.1969. Contraction, deletion, and inherent variability of the English copula. *Language* 45(4):715–762.

———.1972. *Sociolinguistic patterns*. Philadelphia: University of Pennsylvania Press.

Liddell, S.K. 1992. Holds and positions: Comparing two models of segmentation in ASL. In *Phonetics and phonology*, ed. G. Coulter, 189–211. San Diego: Academic Press.

Liddell, S.K., and R.E. Johnson. 1989. American Sign Language: The phonological base. *Sign Language Studies* 64:195–278.

———. In press. *Aspects of the phonology and morphology of American Sign Language*. San Diego: Academic Press.

Lucas, C., and C. Valli. 1992. *Language contact in the American Deaf community*. San Diego: Academic Press.

LeMaster, B. 1990. The maintenance and loss of female and male signs in the Dublin Deaf community. Ph.D. diss., UCLA.

Mansfield, D. 1993. Gender differences in ASL: A sociolinguistic study of sign choices by Deaf native signers. In *Communication forum 1993*, ed. E. A. Winston. Washington, D.C.: Gallaudet University School of Communication.

Metzger, M. 1992. Pronoun variation in formal and informal discourse.

Unpublished manuscript, Gallaudet University Department of Linguistics and Interpreting, Washington, D.C..

Milroy, J. 1992. *Linguistic variation and change: On the historical sociolinguistics of English.* Oxford: Basil Blackwell.

Milroy, L. 1980. (1987, 2d ed.) *Language and social networks.* Oxford: Basil Blackwell.

Padden, C., and T. Humphries. 1988. *Deaf in America: Voices from a culture.* Cambridge, Mass.: Harvard University Press.

Perlmutter, D. 1992. Sonority and syllable structure in American Sign Language. In *Phonetics and phonology,* ed. G. Coulter, 227–261. San Diego: Academic Press.

Radutzky, E., ed. 1992. *Dizionario bilingue elementare della Lingua Italiana dei Segni.* Rome: Edizioni Kappa.

Rickford, J. 1979. Variation in a Creole continuum: Quantitative and implicational approaches. Ph.D. diss. University of Pennsylvania.

Sandler, W. 1992. Linearization of phonological tiers in ASL. In *Phonetics and phonology,* ed. G. Coulter, 103–129. San Diego: Academic Press.

Sankoff, G., and H. Cedergren. 1971. Some results of a sociolinguistic study of Montreal French. In *Linguistic diversity in Canadian society,* ed. R. Darnell. Edmonton: Linguistic Research.

Schein, J.D. 1987. The demography of deafness. In *Understanding deafness socially,* ed. P.C. Higgins and J.E. Nash, 3–28. Springfield, Ill.: Thomas.

Schein, J.D., and M. Delk. 1974. *The deaf population of the United States.* Silver Spring, Md.: National Association of the Deaf.

Schermer, T. 1985. Analysis of natural discourse of deaf adults in the Netherlands: Observations on Dutch Sign Language. In *Proceedings of the Third International Symposium on Sign Language Research,* ed. W. Stokoe and V. Volterra, 281–288. Silver Spring, Md.: Linstok Press.

Schermer, T.M. 1990. *In search of a language: Influences from spoken Dutch on sign language of the Netherlands.* Delft: Eburon.

Shapiro, E. 1993. Socioeconomic variation in American Sign Language. Unpublished manuscript, Department of Linguistics and Interpreting, Gallaudet University, Washington, D.C.

Shroyer, E., and S. Shroyer. 1984. *Signs across America.* Washington. D.C.: Gallaudet College Press.

Shuy, R., W. Wolfram, and W. Riley. 1968. *Field techniques in an urban language study.* Washington, D.C.: Center for Applied Linguistics.

Stokoe, W.C. 1960. Sign language structure: An outline of visual communication systems of the American Deaf. *Studies in linguistics: Occasional papers 8.* Buffalo, N.Y.: University of Buffalo. (rev. ed., 1978. Silver Spring, Md.: Linstock Press)

Trudgill, P. 1974. *The social differentiation of English in Norwich*. London: Cambridge University Press.

Uyechi, L. 1994. Visual phonology. Ph. D. diss., Stanford University.

Wilbur, R., and B. Schick. 1987. The effects of linguistic stress on sign movement in ASL. *Language and Speech* 20:301–323.

Wilcox, S., and P. Wilcox. 1991. *Learning the SEE: American Sign Language as a second language*. Englewood Cliffs, N.J.: Prentice Hall.

Wolfram, W. 1969. *A sociolinguistic description of Detroit Negro speech*. Washington, D.C.: Center for Applied Linguistics.

———. 1974. *Sociolinguistic aspects of assimilation*. Arlington, Va.: Center for Applied Linguistics.

———. 1981. *Dialects and American English*. Englewood Cliffs, N.J.: Prentice Hall.

———. 1991. The linguistic variable: Fact and fantasy. *American Speech* 66(1):22–32.

Woll, B. 1981. Borrowing and change in BSL. Paper represented at the Linguistics Association of Great Britain Annual Meeting, York.

Woodward, J. 1973a. Implicational lects on the deaf diglossic continuum. Ph.D. diss. Georgetown University.

———.1973b. Interrule implication in American Sign Language. *Sign Language Studies* 3:47–56.

———.1973c. Some observations on sociolinguistic variation and American Sign Language. *Kansas Journal of Sociology* 9(2):191–200.

———.1974. A report on Montana-Washington implicational research. *Sign Language Studies* 4: 77–101.

———. 1975. Variation in American Sign Language syntax: Agent-beneficiary directionality. In *Analyzing variation in language,* ed. R. Shuy and R. Fasold, 303–311. Washington, D.C.: Georgetown University Press.

———. 1976. Black southern signing. *Language in Society* 5(2):211–218.

Woodward, J., and S. De Santis. 1977a. Negative incorporation in French and American sign languages. *Languages in Society* 6(3):379–388.

———. 1977b. Two to one it happens: Dynamic phonology in two sign languages. *Sign Language Studies* 17:329–346.

Woodward, J., and C. Erting. 1975. Synchronic variation and historical change in American Sign Language. *Language Sciences* 37:9–12.

Woodward, J., C. Erting, and S. Oliver. 1976. Facing and hand(l)ing variation in American Sign Language. *Sign Language Studies* 10:43–52.

Yau, S., and J. He. 1990. How do deaf children get their name signs during their first month in school? In *SLR '87: Papers from the Fourth International Symposium on Sign Language Research*, ed. W. H. Edmondson and F. Karlsson, 243–254. Hamburg: Signum Press.

Part 2 **Language Contact**

Description and Status of Initialized

Signs in Quebec Sign Language

Dominique Machabée

The first idea for this work was triggered by the observation that there exists a relationship between the handshape of some signs in Quebec Sign Language (henceforth LSQ) and the first letter of the equivalent written French word. This phenomenon, also observable in other sign languages, is called initialization. It quickly became evident that little has been published on this subject. It is also clear that initialization is given a particular status (oralization and fingerspelling are commonly discussed outcomes of language contact, whereas initialization is generally neglected). The main goal of this work is to describe these signs and verify the extent to which initialized signs are used by Deaf people. Another issue to be addressed has to do with the notion of borrowing and can be summarized by the following questions: can initialization represent a form of lexical borrowing from French, and can the existant definitions used when talking of borrowing between oral languages apply to this particular contact phenomenon? Finally, I will propose an explanation for the status of initialized signs.

A brief survey of different notions of borrowing will be followed by a review of the literature on fingerspelling and initialization. Then, data from LSQ will be analysed from two points of view: one related to form, the other to meaning. The question of integration of initialized signs in LSQ will be then addressed. Finally, two proposals on the status of initialized signs will be proposed.

The research for this paper was done in Colette Dubuisson's research group on Quebec Sign Language, supported by a grant from the CRSH and the MESS. I thank Linda Lelièvre and Michel Lelièvre for their helpful participation in my work and wish to emphasize the great amount of patience they demonstrated.
The term Deaf with a capital *D* will be used in this chapter to indicate those who consider themselves culturally Deaf and members of the Deaf community.

THEORETICAL PRELIMINARIES

The Status of the Term "Borrowing"

Since we know that Deaf communities are usually considered to be bilingual (Davis 1989, Hansen 1990, Lacerte 1991, and Lucas and Valli 1989), we can expect to find lexical borrowing from the majority oral language in the signed language. In this work, I will attempt to clarify the status of initialized signs. First of all, it is important to note from the start that this work does not presume to take part in theoretical debates on the different manifestations of language contact; it will limit itself to a distinction between two notions, namely code-switching and borrowing. Because the object of study is limited to single lexical items, I will thus speak of one-item code-switching or borrowing. The main distinctions between these notions are of frequency and linguistic integration. This work will present two different analyses of the possible status of initialized signs, each treating initialized signs differently. One analysis is based on the theoretical position that code-switching and borrowing are two distinct phenomena (Sankoff, Poplack, and Vanniarajan, 1990), whereas the other supposes that code-switching and borrowing are on a continuum (Myers-Scotton 1992).

A distinction between different types of borrowing will be useful. According to Haugen (1950), lexical borrowing, which is the imitation of a model from a donor language (L2) by a borrowing language (L1), can take the form of loanwords, loanblends, and loanshifts. Loanwords present morphemic importation from L2 without replacement of L2 morphemes by L1 morphemes. Haugen presents several examples. First is the American English *shivaree*, from the French word *charivari*. Here, the morphemes are imported from L2, French, and there was phonemic substitution but no morphemic substitution. Loanblends present both morphemic substitution and importation, as illustrated by the Pennsylvania German word [blaUmǝpaI], from the English *plum pie*, where the morpheme [paI] is imported, but the native morpheme [blaUmǝ] has been substituted for *plum*. Finally, loanshifts present only morphemic substitution, represented by such words as *gratte-ciel* (French) and *rascacielos* (Spanish), from the English *skyscraper*, in which there is no importation of morphemes, only substitution.

The possibility of adopting the notion of nonce borrowing, proposed by Poplack, Sankoff, and Miller (1988), will also be taken into consid-

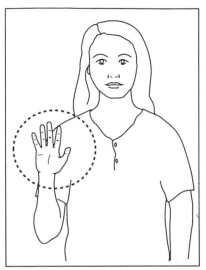

FIGURE 1. *Fingerspelling space*

eration. This category explains the presence of linguistically integrated items that do not respond to the criterion of frequency for loans.

Fingerspelling

This section will briefly review the literature on fingerspelling since this phenomenon appears to be closely related to initialization. However, the fingerspelling system of LSQ will first be introduced.

The manual alphabet of LSQ is identical to that of ASL. It is one-handed and is composed of the same handshapes (see appendix A); the fingerspelling space is the same (see figure 1).[1]

Fingerspelling was extensively studied by Battison (1978). He suggested that it is a result of the influence of English on ASL. It can be used to mark meaning distinctions that do not exist in ASL and that are not conveyed by the context. According to Battison, fingerspelled words can become loansigns when they are restructured. In LSQ, Desouvrey et al. (1992) show that fingerspelled words can be lexicalized (mainly by representing the first letter and a medial letter). It seems, however, that this phenomenon is much less frequent in LSQ than it is in ASL.

Battison (1978) believes restructured fingerspellings are borrowings from English. Davis (1989) takes the position that fingerspelling is not

1. Drawings found in this work are from Carole Pilon.

lexical borrowing in the strictest sense since a lexical item is not borrowed into another language as in a relationship between two phonological systems. Rather, the relationship takes place between the orthography of English and ASL phonology. Davis qualifies fingerspelling as an ASL phonological event. For the same reason, Lucas and Valli (1992, 43) do not consider fingerspelling to be borrowing. According to these authors, fingerspelling is a unique outcome of language contact. They consider it not to be an outcome of contact between a sign language and a spoken language *but rather between a sign language and the orthographic system used to represent that spoken language.*

Initialized Signs in the Literature

Many authors mention the existence of these signs in different sign languages (ASL, British Sign Language (henceforth, BSL), French Sign Language (henceforth, LSF), and others), but few of them elaborate. First, an overview of the different definitions of initialized signs will follow. It will be shown that those could point out only two different possibilities: namely, initialization can be the result either of a fingerspelling reduction or of differentiation of an existing sign.

Battison (1978, 58) defines initialized signs as follows: "Initialized signs (or initial dez signs, or initial handshape signs) are those whose handshapes correspond (via fingerspelling) to the first letter of the English word which commonly translates the sign." For Battison, initialization ("incorporating a handshape into the sign to stand for the (usually first) letter of the English word equivalent") is clearly an artificial influence of English on ASL, whereas fingerspelling is a natural influence. Woodward (1979) also considers initialized signs to be like authentic ASL signs, which are modified in order to have their handshape represent the first letter of the corresponding English word. Supalla (1990), in a paper on name signs, also gives a definition of initialized signs. Citing the signs DRINK and WATER, he says the second one is an initialized sign if the handshape of DRINK has been replaced by /W/. He doesn't consider his name sign (made with an /S/ handshape contacting both sides of the chin) to be an initialized sign because it is not based on an ASL sign. These conceptions of initialized signs are somewhat restrictive because, to be considered initialized, a sign must be derived from an existing sign.

Stokoe et al. (1976, xxv) define initialized signs (or loansigns) as "coinages to translate a particular English word and have as dez the manual alphabet configuration for the first letter of that word. Although this is an open class and still used in coinage of new signs, it is by no means an innovation." In fact, it is well known now that some ASL initialized signs can be traced back to the eighteenth century. Elsewhere, Stokoe et al. (p. iv$_b$) write that "these signs [initial-dez signs] are virtually abbreviations of a finger-spelled word. The dez forming the first letter of the word makes a slight movement unlike a genuine sign, in neutral space or perhaps in a more marked tab region." This definition of initialized signs is different from those given by Battison (1978), Woodward (1979), and Supalla (1990), for whom these signs are a modification of an existing sign.

Bellugi and Newkirk (1981), working on ASL, clearly distinguish between two different origins of initialized signs. Some originate from a handshape, to which a movement and place of articulation are added (for example, signs representing colours). Others are made by differentiation of an existing sign. They cite as an example the initialized sign MODULATION, which was created in their laboratory by modifying the handshape of the sign CHANGE.

For Swisher and McKee (1989), the ease of initialization is affected by the nature of the manual alphabet in use. For example, in BSL, which has a two-handed alphabet, initialization, even if present, is less frequent. There is, in this case, less overlapping between the alphabet and the natural handshapes. Kyle and Woll (1985), while working on BSL, mention common initialized signs from ASL in which the handshape of an existing sign is changed to correspond to the first letter of its English counterpart. According to them, in BSL, some signs develop differently: "signs like GOLD in BSL have developed from the opposite direction. The older form of GOLD, for example, is a simple •g•. The movement found in the modern sign GOLD (which is the same as in signs such as BRIGHT and SUN^2 is a later addition and serves to distinguish GOLD from signs such as GOVERNMENT (•g•g•) or AUGUST (•g•g•)."^{3} According to Kyle and Woll, these

2. According to Kyle and Woll, the older form of the sign GOLD was made using the handshape •g• in neutral space (note that this alphabet is two-handed, and that •g• is made with two closed fists, one resting on the other). The modern sign starts the same way but is completed by a separation of the hands while the fists open.

3. In Kyle and Woll's notation system, •g•g• means that the initial handshape is repeated, that is, the contact between the two hands forming the letter •g• is repeated.

signs seem to be a result of a fingerspelling reduction to which a movement is added.

These different definitions can be summarized in the following way: initialized signs are the result of either a fingerspelling reduction or a change of handshape in an existing noninitialized sign. Furthermore, Kyle and Woll propose that in BSL some signs might result from an addition of movement to a sign that was simply a fingerspelling reduction. In the following sections, the data found in LSQ will be described. It will be demonstrated that these three definitions are applicable to LSQ initialized signs. However, some LSQ signs do not fit any of these definitions.

METHODOLOGICAL CONSIDERATIONS

Data Base

Data were extracted from three different sources described in the following sections.

VIDEOTAPED CONVERSATIONS

The source of data most important is a thirty-hour corpus of videotaped conversations recorded in 1988, in which participants expressed themselves on a variety of topics of their choice. This recording was made in four sessions and involved ten participants. Participants were selected on the basis of their knowledge of LSQ by a Deaf person who later monitored free group interactions. Groups were later formed, taking into consideration their acquaintance with one another. Each participant knew the monitor; we expected this to reduce the degree of discomfort this kind of session might generate. Three sessions lasted about two hours, and one lasted three hours. Each participant was filmed by an individual camera while another camera filmed overall views.

Participants

The video corpus is composed of ten participants. The monitor took part in all sessions. The participants ranged in age from 22 to 31, and the average age was 26.2 years old. Half the participants have a high school education (or almost), three of them have a college diploma, and two are at university level. None of the signers has Deaf parents, but two of them have Deaf brothers or sisters.[4] Eight of them were born in the Montreal region, and all have a certain knowledge of French as a second language.

OTHER SOURCES

Signs were also found in a dictionary of LSQ (Bourcier and Roy, 1985) and in day-to-day exchanges with Deaf informants. For all signs taken from the dictionary, I consulted the Deaf informants in order to ensure that these signs were quite familiar to them and could theoretically be used by other Deaf people.

Informants

The work was undertaken with five different informants, four of whom have Deaf parents. All of them considered LSQ as their first language. Three were consulted only during a preliminary stage of the research, whereas two were active throughout our work. These latter informants, a thirty-one-year-old woman and a twenty-two-year-old man, grew up in Montreal and have Deaf parents.

Historical Considerations

Very little information is available on LSQ. Certain information in Abbé Lambert's (1865) dictionary of LSF proved useful in identifying a number of initialized signs. For example, the sign •N•OM[5] (*name*) was considered to be initialized on the grounds of historical information. In LSF, this sign is described by Abbé Lambert: "Frapper de l'index de la m. d. sur celui de la m. g., avec l'expression de chercher ou demander le nom."[6]

---

4. The fact that none of the signers was born of Deaf parents is not surprising due to the fact that about ninety percent of Deaf children are born of hearing parents.

5. Initialized signs are noted using dots to identify the hand configuration that links it to the letter of the equivalent word in French. Here, the glosses are not translated in English in order to preserve the link between the handshape of the sign and the French word. When necessary, the English translation is parenthesized.

6. "With the index finger of the right hand, contact the index finger of the left hand, with the expression of searching for or asking for a name."

Sternberg (1981) writes that the organization of the hands represents "the *x* used by illiterates in writing their names." It appeared to us, on the basis of this information, that the only possible explanation of the change is initialization. I therefore treated the sign •N•OM as an initialized sign.

Data Collection

From our various sources, we first collected all the signs that could possibly be of initialized origin, that is, all the signs for which the handshape corresponds to the first letter of an equivalent written French word. In the case of videorecordings, an informant with a good knowledge of French examined the whole corpus and noted these signs. We obtained 398 possible initialized signs in this way.

All these potentially initialized signs were presented to Deaf informants, who were asked to give their native intuitions on the possibility of an initialized origin. The answers were often unanimous, allowing us to have a good idea of the signs that were commonly felt to be initialized or noninitialized. The intuition of the informants demonstrated, for example, that most of the signs with an /R/ handshape were considered to be initialized, whereas the signs with an /A/ handshape were rarely felt to be initialized. On the basis of the informants' intuition, I developed different criteria in order to differentiate between signs related to initialization and those in which the handshape/letter equivalence could be due only to chance.

Signs articulated in the fingerspelling area were clearly initialized (110 different signs). Criteria were necessary to determine the status of the other signs (288 different signs). The following letters (or handshapes) were represented: A, B, C, D, E, F, G, H, I, J, L, M, N, O, P, R, S, T, U, V, and W. I proceeded in a different manner depending on the letter. The signs with an /A/, /B/, /G/ (or/l/), or /S/ handshape, which are common in LSQ, frequently correspond to the first letter of a French word only by chance. All the signs having one of these handshapes were eliminated unless they corresponded to one of the following criteria:

1. The sign is part of a group of initialized signs. For example, the sign •S•OCIÉTÉ (*society*) was considered initialized because of the other initialized signs formationally identical except for their handshape.
2. The sign is based on another sign that is not initialized. For

example, the sign •S•OUTIEN[7] (*support*) is based on the sign AIDE (*help*).

3. We have historical information on the origin of the sign. For example, the sign •M•ILLE (*thousand*), in LSF (Lambert 1865), was identical to the modern LSQ sign, except for the handshape, which was /M/.

Signs with /D/ and /M/ handshapes were also treated the same way. These handshapes are more easily associated with the handshapes of the manual alphabet, but they can frequently be transformed by a variable rule into /G/ (or /1/) and /B^ /.[8] Knowing this, signs with a /G/ or /B ^ / handshape that corresponded to French words starting with the letters *D* or *M* were retained as possibly initialized.

For the signs with one of the other handshapes (/C/, /E/, /F/, /H/, /I/, /J/, /L/, /N/, /O/, /P/, /R/, /T/, /U/, /V/, or /W/), I adopted different criteria. These handshapes are, to a different degree, less common in LSQ. The chances of having a correspondence between handshape and first letter only by chance are smaller. I therefore retained these signs for analysis unless one of the following criteria indicated that they were not initialized:

1. The sign is in fact an extension of another sign, whether initialized or not. For example, the sign •P•ERSONNE (*person*), to which a movement is added, gives LE MONDE (*people*), POPULATION, or PUBLIC (*public*). They are distinguished by oralization. I did not include POPULATION and PUBLIC in my list since they are derived from •P•ERSONNE and have no direct link with initialization. Another example is the sign INGÉNIEUR (*engineer*), which is made with two /I/ handshapes; it is not an initialized sign since it is derived from the sign MESURER (*to measure),* from which it is distinguished only by movement.

2. If an iconic explanation was available, I rejected the sign even if it could also be explained by initialization. For example, the /F/ handshape in the sign •F•RÈRE (*monk*) can be analysed as a classifier representing the buttons on a monk's robe (figure 2).

3. If we had no indication of initialization for a sign and if the in-

7. See the transcription symbols section for the significance of the boldface type.

8. The latter handshape is a /B/ handshape that is bent.

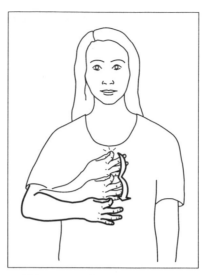

FIGURE 2. *F*RÈRE

formants did not feel that the sign was of initialized origin, I rejected the sign.

This first stage of classification by handshape was made on a generally intuitive basis, relying to a large extent on the informants' responses. The first group of handshapes I identified (/A/, /B/, /D/, /G/, (or /1/), /M/, and /S/) corresponds quite well to the unmarked handshapes identified by Battison (1978) (/A/, /S/, /B/, /5/, /G/, /C/, and /O/). The handshape /5/ is obviously without interest for our purposes. I added /D/ and /M/ handshapes, which, in context, can frequently change to /G/ and /B^/ handshapes. Battison also considers /C/ and /O/ handshapes to be unmarked, whereas I analyzed them in the second list. In a conversation, Christopher Miller (1992) stated that these handshapes are different from the /A/, /B/, /S/, and /G/ handshapes in two ways. First, they are neither totally closed nor totally open. Second, in LSQ, these handshapes have a different behaviour with respect to the dominance condition which states that only the unmarked configurations can appear on the nondominant hand if both hands within a sign do not have the same handshape. In LSQ, /C/, and /O/ can appear on the nondominant hand only if they have morphemic status (for example, when they are classifiers), whereas the other unmarked handshapes are less constrained.

To summarize, the signs with the handshapes /C/, /E/, /F/, /H/, /I/, /J/, /L/, /N/, /O/, /P/, /R/, /T/, /U/, and /V/ were all retained as initialized unless one of the preceding analytical criteria was applicable. The signs having an /A/, /B/, /D/, /G/, /M/, or /S/ handshape were all rejected unless one of the selection criteria was applicable.

The criteria applied to our possible initialized signs probably eliminated some signs that are in fact initialized, but I felt these criteria were necessary to minimize the possibility of including noninitialized signs in our corpus. After the application of these criteria, 93 signs were rejected. The initial corpus of 288 signs (excluding the 110 that are signed in the fingerspelling space) is thus reduced to 195 initialized signs. The total corpus is composed of 305 different signs.

It is important to notice that not all the initialized signs retained here are widespread. Some clearly are, but others are not and can even be viewed as idiosyncratic. The type of work undertaken in this paper does not allow us to clearly distinguish initialized signs according to their frequency. Nevertheless, the informants' native intuition might enable us to partially understand this phenomen. The important point in this work is to determine whether initialization is really used by Deaf people. The fact that some initialized signs appear to be idiosyncratic is also important.

Transcription Symbols Used in Glosses

In order to distinguish between the different signs or tokens of sign, I use numbers and letters in subscript. For example, if for a given concept there exist different signs, I attribute a distinct subscript number to each ($SIGN_1$, $SIGN_2$, etc.). If, for the same sign, we have tokens that are slightly different in their formation (for example, if the orientation is different), I distinguish between these tokens with a letter ($SIGN_{1a}$, $SIGN_{1b}$, etc.). If we have only one sign and one token (or many identical tokens) for a concept, the sign has no subscript. Most of the signs were observed on video. Signs observed in daily exchanges or found in the LSQ dictionary are always written in bold face characters.

DATA ANALYSIS

An Analysis Based on Form

If we consider structural factors such as place of articulation, orientation, and movement, we notice that initialized signs can be separated into three groups, the first two of which seem to have greater significance.

Class I Signs

Class I signs (ninety-one signs) share a characteristic restricted manner of formation since they seem to be related to fingerspelling. They are formed with a handshape representing the first letter of a French written word. To this handshape is added a restricted set of places of articulation and movements.

Place of Articulation

Signs of class I can be made in two places of articulation: fingerspelling space and neutral space. Fingerspelling space is characteristic of these signs, which are articulated in that space most of the time. A few signs are made in neutral space. For example, signs that can be made with one or two hands are always made in neutral space when made with two hands. Others, which would be made in fingerspelling space in a citation form, can be made in neutral space, depending on context. For example, in •v•ENDREDI SOIR (*Friday evening*) the signer did not articulate •v•ENDREDI in fingerspelling space and SOIR in neutral space. He preferred to articulate the first sign in neutral space, shifting his dominant hand to the same spatial position as the sign SOIR.

Two signs observed on the video were articulated outside their normal location. One is a token of the sign •G•RIS (*gray*), which, in context, is two-handed and signed on both sides of the head. The context is the following: BARBE •G•RIS CHEVEUX (*beard, gray, hair*). The former is two-handed and is made near the chin, whereas the latter is also two-handed but made near the hair. For reasons of efficiency or economy, the sign •G•RIS, which was made in between, is made with two hands and in the same place of articulation as CHEVEUX. In the second example, instead of signing RIDEAUX (*curtains*, figure 3) and afterward the sign •B•LEU (which is usually made in fingerspelling space), the signer makes the sign RIDEAUX with /B/ handshapes and oralizes *bleu*. Moreover, the first part of the path movement is accompanied by the movement normally found in •B•LEU (a twisting movement of the forearm). However, let us remember that a large majority of class I signs are made either in fingerspelling or neutral space.

Movement

Signs of class I also have specific movements that generally have a common feature: the absence of path movement (here called internal movements). Most of the handshapes (whether articulated in fingerspelling or

FIGURE 3. *RIDEAUX*

neutral space) are accompanied by a side-to-side movement (↔). The up-and-down movement (↑↓)is a variant of the first and is found with the horizontal handshapes (/G/ and /H/). A circular movement is found in the signs •B•EIGE and •R•OSE₂ (*pink*), which are commonly made with this movement (for the latter, see figure 4). Six other signs were made with a circular movement (•É•DUCATEUR₁ᵦ, • I•NFRAROUGE, •R•ÉFÉRENCE₁ᵦ, •R•ÉPUTATION₁ₐ, ULTRA-•V•IOLET, AND •V•ITAMINE₁c), but the movement can be of another type. Other tokens (•É•DUCATEUR₁ₐ, •R•ÉFÉRENCE₁ₐ, •R•ÉPUTATION₁ᵦ, and •V•ITAMINE₁ᵦ) had a side-to-side movement. The sign •V•ITAMINE₁ₐ simply had no movement. A twisting movement of the forearm (ω) is commonly found in •B•LEU, •B•LEUET, (*blueberry*), •J•AUNE (*yellow*), •J•EU/•J•OUER (*toy/to play*), and •J•EUDI (*Thursday*). Three other movements can be found, each in only one sign. The twisting movement away from the signer (∝) is found in the sign •R•OSE₁ (*pink*), and flexion of the finger's first interphalangeal joints (δ) accompanies the sign •V•EUF (*widower*). The last movement is found in the sign •M•ERCREDI₂ (*Wednesday*); it is a swinging movement rather than a side-to-side movement. This movement distinguishes •M•ERCREDI from the sign •M•ARDI₁ (*Tuesday*), which has a straight side-to-side movement.[9] Movements other than side-

9. Synonyms of these two signs allow a distinction using the second letter as handshape: M•A•RDI et M•E•RCREDI (they then have a straight side-to-side movement).

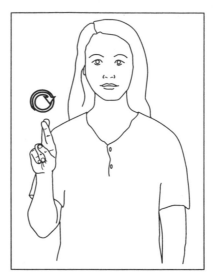

FIGURE 4. •R•OSE$_2$

to-side and up-and-down are usually found in widespread signs, such as colour signs and signs for days of the week. Path movements can occasionally be found but only when there is morphological modification (see p. 53 for further explanation).

A few class I signs that have two handshapes can bear a transition movement. In •S•ERVICE •S•OCIAL (*social service*), •S•OUS-•S•OL (*basement*), and •T•RONC •C•OMMUN (*core curriculum*), the second handshape is separated from the first by a small rightward movement. Frequently, movement was also absent from the signs of class I. Even though the citation form always has a movement, in context it was observed that twenty-nine percent of the class I signs had no movement at all.[10]

CLASS II SIGNS

Class II signs have the same characteristics as noninitialized LSQ signs. They can be executed in different places of articulation and have many different possible movement types. They may simply have an internal movement and can also be articulated in neutral space, but they never have both of these characteristics, which are exclusive to class I signs.

---

10. Of the 91 signs of class I, we observed a total of 160 tokens, 47 of them having no movement in context.

Place of Articulation

Class II signs have many possible places of articulation: neutral space, body (torso and chest), head (forehead, temple, cheek, chin, nose, and mouth), arm, and nondominant hand. These places of articulation can be combined with each other. For example, the sign •P•ARENTS[11] first contacts the right temple and, after a downward movement, there is another contact on the right side of the chin.

Movement

Some signs can have only a contacting movement, whether on the nondominant hand or on another place on the body. The movement can also be a path movement away from or toward the signer, upward or downward, to the left or right. When the sign is made with two hands, the movement can be alternating, either upward and downward or downward and upward, away from or towards the signer. Movement can also take the form of an arc movement away from or toward the signer or downward. I also found circular movements and twisting movements of the wrist.

These movements are combined with the different places of articulation. For example, the circular movement can be made away from the signer, in neutral space, near the temple, near the nondominant hand, near the cheek, or around the nondominant hand. The alternating movement of the hands can be made in neutral space, in contact with the chest or near the mouth. There are multiple combinations of places of articulation and movements in class II. This class thus cannot be defined by a closed set of possibilities as class I was.

Class III Signs

This class contains nineteen signs that are made with an initialized handshape in fingerspelling space (like class I signs) but are followed by a sign. This type of sign is probably uncommon but not totally unusual inasmuch as a few of these signs were observed in the LSQ dictionary (Bourcier and Roy 1985). Of the nineteen signs of this class, only one is composed of an initialization in fingerspelling space, followed by a sign that is also initialized (•I•NTERNATIONAL₂). The signer produces an /I/

---

11. This sign, even if known to most LSQ signers, does not appear to be widespread. Nevertheless, it was observed in our video data.

handshape in the fingerspelling space, which moves to produce the initialized sign of class II, •I•NTERNATIONAL. The first handshape, articulated
in the fingerspelling space, therefore appears to be redundant.

The eighteen remaining signs all have a noninitialized sign as a second part, but redundancy is also present in these signs. For example, the
sign •I•NFORMATEUR (*informant*) presents a handshape in fingerspelling
space that does not add any information, since the signer articulates /I/
in fingerspelling space and afterwards articulates the sign INFORMATION,
followed by the person suffix. Other signs show interesting creations. For
example, the sign •E•XPLOITATION, which seems clearly to have been created on the spur of the moment, is made with an /E/ handshape in
fingerspelling space, followed by the sign PROFITER *(to take advantage of)*.
Furthermore, the sign •P•OLLUTION₂ is made with a /P/ handshape followed
by the sign SALE (*dirty*). Another sign, •É•COLOGIE (*ecology*), also likely
created on the spur of the moment, is first made with an /E/¹² handshape
in the fingerspelling space, followed by the sign ÉCOLE (*school*). This sign
is accompanied by the oralization of the French word, *écologie*. The signer
then repeats the sign ÉCOLE and completes by fingerspelling L-O-G-I-E.

This class of signs, of little quantative importance, will not be described
in further detail.

An Analysis Based on Meaning

An analysis based on meaning shows that form is often related to
meaning. In other cases the signs seems arbitrary. Whether or not we find
a link between form and meaning, we will see that many signs can be
grouped in families.

MOTIVATED SIGNS

I will call the signs showing a link between form and meaning *motivated signs*.¹³ Some are constructed with classifiers, such as •L•OI (*law*),
where the nondominant hand has a /B/ handshape (classifier for a flat
surface—in this case, representing paper), and the dominant hand has

---

12. The characters bearing an accent are always initialized as if there were
no accent. There are no "manual codes" to represent the accents.

13. I prefer this term rather than *iconic signs* because it is more general; it
clearly includes signs that have, for example, a metaphorical relation with the
meaning.

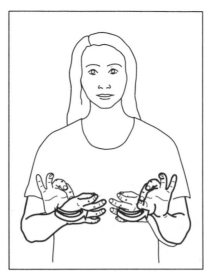

FIGURE 5. •F•ESTIVAL

an /L/ handshape. Other signs have a symbolic place of articulation (the sign •É•MOTION, made on the chest; •C•ONCEPT, on the temple, and •R•ESTAURANT, near the mouth). Other signs refer to physical features of the referent, such as •R•OMAIN (*Roman*) where the handshape traces the form of a Roman military helmet above the head, and •R•AT, where the handshape, placed before the nose and accompanied by a bending movement of the fingers, represents the muzzle of a rat.

Other signs have a form/meaning link that is less evident. For example, the movement of the sign •P•IRE (*worst*) seems to refer to the metaphor that places positive upward and negative downward. The rhythm of the signs •F•ESTIVAL and •P•ARTY suggests the idea of celebration (figure 5).

Signs from class I obviously never have a form/meaning link since they are formed only by a handshape made in the fingerspelling space, to which is added an internal movement. About one third of the signs of class II appear to be arbitrary synchronically, but this appearance of arbitrariness should not exclude the possibility of historical motivation.

SIGNS BASED ON AN EXISTING SIGN

Signs can also be created on the basis of a semantic link with an existing sign. When a sign is said to be based on an existing sign, it is identical to a noninitialized sign (except for the handshape) and is semantically related to this sign. Ten signs of class II are based on an existing sign

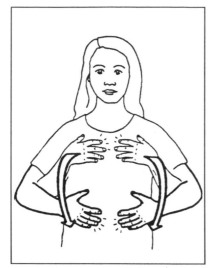 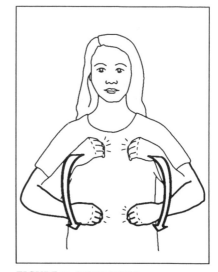

FIGURE 6. *CORPS*   FIGURE 7. •O•*RGANISME*

that have exactly the same meaning. In this case, there is no lexical creation but only a change of handshape. These signs represent only five
percent of class II data. Most of the signs based on an existing sign show
a distinctive meaning (fifty-seven signs were identified, twenty-nine percent of the class II data). For example, the sign CORPS (*body*) served as a
base to create the initialized signs •O•RGANISME (*organism*), •H•UMAIN$_I$ (*human), and* •P•HYSIQUE$_I$ (*physical*); see figures 6 and 7. The base sign CORPS
is clearly motivated, but in other cases, the base sign appears arbitrary.
These signs, created on the basis of an existing sign, form sign families,
which are described below.

SIGN FAMILIES

Sign families consist of two or more signs.[14] Some are formed on the
basis of a noninitialized sign, but other families group only initialized
signs. These signs can be either motivated or unmotivated. Signs from
class I are evidently nonmotivated and, despite their limited structural
possibilities, can be grouped in families. Signs from class II have many
structural possibilities and can be based on an existing sign or not and
can also be motivated or not.

---

14. Initialized signs based on an existing sign with an identical meaning were
not counted as members of a family. These are more likely variants of the same
sign.

Class I Sign Families

All class I signs are formed in an identical way: they present a handshape generally oriented as in fingerspelling, an internal movement (usually a side-to-side movement), and are made in fingerspelling or neutral space.[15] Nevertheless, some of them can be grouped into families classified according to meaning: kinship signs (•C•OUSIN, •N•EVEU [nephew]/ •N•IÈCE, •O•NCLE [uncle], •P•ARENTÉ [relatives], and •T•ANTE [aunt]), color signs (•B•LEU [blue], •G•RIS [grey], •J•AUNE [yellow], •R•OSE$_1$ [pink], •R•OSE$_2$, •V•ERT [green], and •V•IOLET$_2$ [purple]), and signs indicating days of the week. Apart from meaning, these signs can be grouped into families on the basis of a consistent type of behaviour. Signs denoting kinship terms can be made with one or two hands; color signs have structural characteristics (particular movements) that distinguish them from other signs of class I; and signs indicating days of the week can be morphologically modified (see p. 53).

Class II Sign Families

Many sign families are observed in class II. Signs from each family are made in an identical way except for the handshape. A family can include as many as twelve signs, but most of them contain only two or three signs. However, all these families are capable of expansion.

A large family, also found in both ASL and Australian Sign Language, is based on the sign GROUP (this base sign is nonexistent in LSQ). The signs extracted from our data are: •A•SSOCIATION, •A•TELIER (workshop) •C•OMMUNAUTÉ (community), •C•OMITÉ (committee), •D•ÉPARTEMENT (department), •É•QUIPE (team), •É•TAT (state), •F•AMILLE (family), •G•ROUPE (group), O•R•GANISATION (organization), •R•ÉUNION (meeting), •S•OCIÉTÉ (society).[16] Another sign family consists of the following signs: PHRASE (sentence), •D•ÉCODEUR (decoder), •G•RAMMAIRE (grammar), •L•ANGAGE (language), •L•ANGUE (language), •L•INGUISTIQUE (linguistics). The sign PHRASE is not initialized but is probably the sign on which the initialized signs are based. The signs CORPS, •P•HYSIQUE, and •O•RGANISME, already mentioned, are other examples.

15. More than 94 percent of the class I tokens are accompanied by oralization, which distinguishes them from each other.

16. Not all these signs are equally well established. That is, the signs •A•TELIER, •C•OMITÉ, AND •É•TAT are not frequently used. They were observed either in videos or the LSQ dictionary.

Forty-four families containing 110 of the 195 total signs were identified in class II. These families represent a productive means of lexical creation in LSQ. In effect, although most of the families consist of only a few signs, none is a closed class.

Links between LSQ and ASL

The initialized signs identified in our data are always related to French, but they may also have a link with some ASL signs. In effect, many LSQ initialized signs are also found in ASL (whether in an identical or similar form). Some of them may have had a common origin, such as color signs. For others, we can assume that a model may have been borrowed from ASL, the handshape later being adapted to the equivalent written French word.

More than 60 percent of class II signs appear to be based on existing signs. I therefore verified that these initialized signs that lacked a noninitialized base sign were not simply borrowed from ASL initialized signs (which could be based on ASL noninitialized signs). It was observed that many signs appear to be native to LSQ to the extent that some of them are not based on a noninitialized sign. I maintain that not all class II signs are based on an existing noninitialized sign. Moreover, if initialized signs often present a feature common in ASL signs, initialization is without doubt a means of lexical creation that is productive in LSQ.

Conclusion

Initialization appears to be a phenomenon that is noteworthy in LSQ. Many different signs were observed, repeatedly in some cases. Signs are realized either in fingerspelling or neutral space, accompanied by an internal movement or no movement at all (class I signs), or the same way as natural LSQ signs (class II signs). In this latter case, signs are often created on the basis of an already existing noninitialized sign, but they sometimes appear to be constructed simply using the lexical creation means of LSQ. Many of these might be inspired by ASL's initialized signs, but this explanation applies to only some of them. Therefore, we can conclude that initialized signs in LSQ appear to be made using the lexical creation means of LSQ, not just as an imitation of an existing sign.

At the beginning of this paper, we considered whether initialization is a result of contact with the oral language and whether it is really used by Deaf people in practice, and if such was the case, whether it could be construed as borrowing. Borrowing is commonly defined as a copy by L1 of a model from L2. It is usually distinguished from code-switching by different factors, both linguistic and sociolinguistic. At a linguistic level, a borrowed element is usually integrated into L1 phonologically, morphologically, or syntactically. Borrowing is also expected to be widespread, unlike code-switching. The following sections will briefly examine the integration of initialized signs in LSQ, from both a sociolinguistic and a linguistic viewpoint.

Sociolinguistic Integration of Initialized Signs

The total number of initialized signs in our data was 305 (91 class I signs, 195 class II signs, and 19 class III signs). However, the total number of tokens observed was 733 (160 class I signs, 551 class II signs, and 22 class III signs). This means that some signs are used more than once. It was hypothesized that looking at these repetitions, using our informants' intuition, could help identify some widespread initialized signs that will be later examined on the basis of their linguistic integration.

WIDESPREAD USE OF INITIALIZED SIGNS

It is certainly imprudent, in a work using limited data, to talk of the frequency of initialized signs. Nevertheless, our data can probably give us an indication of the frequency of a few signs. In other words, if a sign is observed to occur again and again in different conversations and is used by different signers, then it may be an established sign. The opposite is not necessarily true: a sign that is not recurrent in our corpus might nevertheless be very common in LSQ. In order to obtain some idea of the number of signs in our corpus that are recurrent in LSQ, I decided on an arbitrary and conservative criterion. This criterion states that if a sign in our data is used by three or more different signers in different conversations, then it can be considered widespread.

Not all class I signs were observed in the LSQ88 corpus. Eighty were observed, while eleven were extracted from the dictionary or observed in day-to-day exchanges. Table 1 shows the frequency of these eighty

TABLE 1. *Number of Tokens of Class I*

Number of Signs	Number of Tokens
50	1
13	2
6	3
3	4
2	5
1	6
3	7
1	9
1	10

signs. Once the criterion was applied, only ten signs could be considered widespread. These signs are •G•RIS (*grey*), •O•NCLE (*uncle*), •C•OUSIN, •D•IMANCHE (*Sunday*), •V•ERT (*green*), •S•ERVICE •S•OCIAL (*social services*), •B•LEU (*blue*), •V•ENDREDI (*Friday*), •J•EU/•J•OUER (*toy/to play*), and •S•ECONDAIRE (*secondary education*). These signs were all identified by our informants as widespread signs.

Out of the 195 signs of class II, 152 were observed on videotapes, and 43 were observed in daily exchanges or in the dictionary. The number of tokens observed for the 152 signs ranges from one to twenty-three. Table 2 gives the details.

After the application of our criterion, thirty-four signs of class II could be said to be widespread. These signs[17] are: •P•ROFESSIONNEL$_I$, •R•ÉFLÉCHIR, •A•SSOCIATION, •M•ILLE, •P•AYS$_I$, •R•ELIGION$_I$, •U•NIVERSITÉ$_I$, •I•TALIEN, •G•ROUPE, •N•ORD, •N•ORMAL, •P•ERMETTRE, •R•ESPECT, •S•UD, •O•PINION, •I•MPOSSIBLE, •L•OI, •N•ATUREL$_I$, •R•AISON, •C•LUB DE NUIT, •J•AMAIS, •R•ÉPONDRE, •P•OLITIQUE, •L•ANGUE, •P•ERSONNE, •C•ARACTÈRE$_I$, •F•AMILLE, •V•IN, •C•OMMUNIQUER, •V•RAI$_I$, •C•ULTURE, •I•DÉE, •F•RANÇAIS, and •N•OM. Many signs identified as widespread by our informants do not appear in the preceding lists. For example, among class I signs, signs for days of the week are clearly wide-

17. Respectively, *professional, reflect upon, association, thousand, country, religion, university, Italian, group, north, normal, to allow, respect, south, opinion, impossible, law, natural, reason, nightclub, never, to answer, politics, language, person, temperament, family, wine, to communicate, true, culture, idea, French,* and *name.*

TABLE 2. *Number of Tokens of Class II Signs*

Number of Signs	Number of Tokens
68	1
25	2
13	3
12	4
2	5
8	6
4	7
4	8
3	9
1	10
2	11
1	12
2	13
1	14
2	15
2	17
1	18
1	23

spread. Only chance can explain the fact that we find •D•IMANCHE (*Sunday*) but not •S•AMEDI (*Saturday*). In fact, although this kind of procedure can help us identify some widespread signs, our informants' intuition was necessary to formulate a more precise idea of which signs are clearly widespread and which are clearly idiosyncratic. A large gray area still remains, but it is beyond the scope of this work.

Nonestablished Initialized Signs

This aspect of initialized signs is not clarified by our data. Nevertheless, consulting our informants on this question gives us an idea of the number of signs that are nonestablished or at least idiosyncratic. Approximately 25 percent of class I signs and 10 percent of class II signs appear to be nonestablished initialized signs.

Degrees of Integration

It appears that initialized signs exhibit different degrees of integration into LSQ. Some are well integrated, are no doubt part of the lexicon, and have no noninitialized synonyms (at least, none that are widespread). These include signs such as •L•UNDI (*Monday*), •C•ULTURE, •R•ÉPONDRE (*to answer*). On another level we find signs that are common but have a noninitialized synonym (the latter possibly more commonly used), such as •D•ICTIONNAIRE / DICTIONNAIRE (*dictionary*). On a third level, we find a gray area: signs are usually known by signers but are generally not accepted as "true LSQ," such as the sign •P•ARENTS.[18] On a fourth level, we find initialized signs that are idiosyncratic, such as •É•LECTRON, •Î•LE (*island*), •M•ONDIAL (*worldwide*) from class II; and •C•HÂTEAU (*castle*) and •F•ARINE (*flour*) from class I. These signs, when from class II, are generally created by modifying a base sign that has the same or related meaning. For example, •É•VOLUTION is signed the same way as its noninitialized synonym except for the handshapes, which are changed to /E/. Also, •M•ONDIAL is made just as the other signs related in meaning (MONDE, (*world*), GÉOGRAPHIE (*geography*), and •I•NTERNATIONAL$_I$), but with an /M/ handshape.

What clearly emerges from this is that initialization is one of a number of lexical resources available to signers. In many cases, the concept can also be rendered by another noninitialized sign. Some initialized signs are widespread and sometimes have no synonym (at least none that is widespread). Others are clearly idiosyncratic and generally have a widespread noninitialized synonym. Between these two extremes, some signs are known to our consultants but are not widely used by signers. In such cases, we usually note the existence of another sign or another way to express the concept. For example, the signs •F•RAISE (*strawberry*) and •F•RAMBOISE (*raspberry*) from class I, are less frequently used than another sign that can be glossed SMALL OBJECT. This sign is used to refer to many different concepts, such as *wheat, blueberry, beans, strawberry, raspberry, seed,* and *pill,* and is accompanied by oralization that serves to specify the meaning.

Linguistic Integration of Initialized Signs

For established initialized signs, a certain degree of linguistic integra-

18. Here, in accordance with Battison (1978), we would talk about "artificial signs." In effect, signers seem to consider these signs as part of Signed French. They are usually rejected by Deaf people; nevertheless, these signs were observed in discourse, a fundamental criterion for them to be included in our corpus.

tion is observed. This section will be restricted to morphological and syntactic integration: phonological integration will be discussed later in the chapter (see p. 56–57).

Established initialized signs were looked at with an informant in order to determine if they could be integrated into LSQ morphological structure.[19]

NOUNS

Most of the initialized signs are nouns. It appears that they can frequently be modified for plurality in a number of ways: repetition of the sign, repetition superimposed on an arc movement, two-handed signing for a usually one-handed sign, etc.[20] Many signs can also have qualitative modifications to express qualities such as *big, small, tall, short, nice, ugly, good,* and *no good.* These changes can be obtained by movement modifications and facial expression: shorter movement to express *small,* and larger movement to express *big,* etc.

Signs for days of the week (class I) can undergo well-known modifications based on time lines to express different meanings such as *last Monday, Monday two weeks ago, next Monday, Monday in two weeks, every Monday, each Monday* (see figures 8 and 9).

ADJECTIVES

Adjectives can be modified to mark degree. For example, modifying the movement of the sign •I•MPOSSIBLE (larger, more tense, and faster) and the facial expression will amplify the degree of impossibility. Color signs can be modified to mark the intensity of the color. For example, modifying the movement, rhythm, and facial expression of •J•AUNE (*yellow*) derives meanings such as *dark yellow* or *acid yellow.* Adjectives often have a predicative role; for example, •V•ERT (*green*) can be signed with a large side-to-side movement, meaning *it's green all over.* Adjectives can also be repeated on an arc to qualify referents. Finally, some adjectives seem to allow a change to mark temporal aspect. For example, •J•ALOUX (*jealous*) can be repeated and the rhythm of movement can be broken to signify *again and again.*

19. Because this work was done with one informant only, it does not claim to be comprehensive. Nevertheless, it will give an idea of the possibilities of morphological integration.

20. Facial expression plays a very important role in all modifications.

FIGURE 8. *"last Monday"*

FIGURE 9. *"Monday two weeks ago"*

VERBS

Like many verbs of LSQ, initialized verbs can be modified to mark their arguments, number, and aspect. If the verb is signed on the body, it cannot be inflected for its arguments. I will discuss here two examples of initialized signs that undergo this type of inflection.

The sign •R•ÉFLÉCHIR (*to reflect upon*) is anchored on the body and can be modified to mark temporal aspect (for example, *again and again, for a long time*), temporal focus (*to start to*), and manner (*easily, with difficulty*). These modifications are made by a change in movement (size and rhythm) accompanied by facial expression. A sign such as •C•RITIQUER (*to criticize*), nonanchored on the body, undergoes the same modifications, but it also marks its arguments (by hand orientation and movement direction; see figures 10 and 11), its number (by repetition of the sign), and its distributional aspect (repetition of the sign at different points on an arc movement).

Fingerspelling and Initialization

According to Battison (1978), fingerspelling is an outcome of the influence of English on ASL. When fingerspellings are restructured, Battison calls them loanwords. For Davis (1989), fingerspelling is part of ASL and while clearly an outcome of language contact, does not represent lexical

FIGURE 10. *I-•C•RITIQUER-2* "*I criticize you*"

FIGURE 11. *2-•C•RITIQUER-1* "*You criticize me*"

borrowing because the systems involved are the phonological system of the signed language on one hand and the orthographic system of the spoken language on the other, instead of two phonological systems. Similarly, Lucas and Valli (1992) write that fingerspelling can't be strictly associated with borrowing. It is a particular outcome of language contact, where a language represents but does not borrow the orthography of another.

The fact that we are examining languages in different modalities should allow us to question whether we can strictly apply the definitions of borrowing elaborated for pairs of oral languages. The distinctions could result from the difference in modality. If borrowing is possible only between two phonological systems, then there are few possibilities for lexical borrowing between a signed and a spoken language (except perhaps some oralizations and semantic borrowing). [See editor's note on p. 59.] Knowing that the phonological system of oral language is not easily accessible to Deaf people, we can think of fingerspelling as a parallel system that is used to convey phonological material of the oral language, based on written forms of oral language and functioning as a bridge between the two phonological systems.

For Battison (1978), initialization is an artifical influence of English on ASL. Other authors give cursory mention of or ignore this process.

Yet, we have seen that initialization is not a negligible process inasmuch as it is used by Deaf people themselves. Initialization might have been inspired by hearing people in contact with Deaf people, such as teachers. However, it has clearly been adopted—at least partly—by Deaf people, who even use it as a productive means of lexical creation.

Stokoe et al. (1976) define initialized signs as a reduction of fingerspelled words. In effect, class I signs have characteristics that are structurally comparable to those of fingerspelling—place of articulation and orientation. Instead of using fingerspelling, a signer produces only the first letter (context and oralization completing the information). An internal movement is then added to complete the sign. Many signs of this class, just like fingerspellings, are not recurrent. Others have become established without modifications. A few others may undergo changes that incorporate them in LSQ. They are moved to neutral space, and a movement is added (for example, •H•ANDICAPÉ (*handicapped*) and •R•OCK'N'ROLL, which are similar to class I signs but are made in neutral space with a small path movement added and a change in orientation).

Most of the signs of class II are made a different way. A French lexical item can be fingerspelled or initialized in fingerspelling space, but if a signer wants to create a sign, one way is to create an initialized sign using an existing sign or simply to use the ordinary means of sign creation available in LSQ. Here, the link with fingerspelling is more tenuous, consisting only of the handshape. There does not appear to be a line of evolution between the signs of both classes, whereby class I signs are transformed into class II signs (except for a few signs described above). It appears that class II signs are formed using the usual morphological processes and rarely simply by modifying a class I sign.

Phonological Integration

Phonological integration is not an easy question to deal with since the languages we are examining are so different from each other. If we conceive of fingerspelling as an interface between the written form of the oral language and the signed language, we can see initialization as a way to transpose elements of the oral language via the orthographic representation into the signed language. Unless we talk of semantic borrowing, elements from the oral language must always undergo a certain degree of phonological integration in order to be articulated manually. This integration will vary in degrees according to the type of sign; class I signs would be minimally integrated, whereas class II signs would be more integrated.

Conclusion

It is clear that to talk of initialized signs as a phenomenon of code-switching or borrowing is impossible if we strictly apply the definitions constructed to analyse contact between oral languages. The fact that we are studying languages so essentially different as a manual and an oral language has as a result that borrowing—in its strictest sense—is impossible in the manual mode (unless we talk of semantic loans). An enlarged definition of borrowing—which takes into account the fact that the handshapes representing the writing system are the nearest we can get to the phonology of the oral language in a manual mode—will permit us to view initialization as a possible borrowing process between signed languages and oral languages.

HYPOTHESES ON THE STATUS OF INITIALIZED SIGNS

This section presents two different analyses of the possible status of initialized signs, each treating class II signs differently. The first analysis is based on the theoretical position that code-switching and borrowing are two distinct phenomena (following Sankoff, Poplack, and Vanni-arajan, 1990), whereas the other supposes that code-switching and borrowing are on a continuum (following Myers-Scotton, 1992).

First Analysis

In the first analysis, I propose that nonestablished class I signs that have many similarities with fingerspelled words (they usually have the same hand orientation and the same place of articulation, and only an internal movement is added) also have the status of code-switches. For example, the signer produced the sign •C•HÂTEAU (*castle*) in the following context:

C'EST-ÇA •C•HÂTEAU$_I$ CHIC I-REGARDER-3$_I$

"Mhm, I looked around, the castle was neat."

The signer could use the usual noninitialized sign for *castle*, but instead he started in LSQ, switched to produce •C•HÂTEAU in fingerspelling space, and finished in LSQ. Such a sign appears to us to be a code-switch. Established class I signs appear more likely to be borrowings.

Class II signs can be analyzed as loanblends. One part, the handshape, is "borrowed," while the rest is LSQ material. They are well integrated in LSQ and can be well-established LSQ signs. The existence of idiosyncratic class II signs suggests we adopt the category of nonce loans (as defined by Poplack, Sankoff, and Miller [1988]), since they do not correspond to the criterion of recurrence for true loans.

The fact that code-switches and borrowing are distinct phenomena for Sankoff, Poplack, and Vanniarajan (1990) may provide an explanation of the fact that class I and II signs are quite different. But it makes it difficult to explain how we can find established signs in class I if this is not a code-switching/borrowing continuum. We also cannot explain the fact that a few signs of class II appear to be from class I (such as •H•ANDICAPÉ).

Second Analysis

In this analysis, I adopt the point of view according to which nonce borrowings do not exist and for which code-switches and borrowings are on a continuum. Class I signs would then be code-switches if they are not recurrent but will become integrated borrowings if established. Some of them can have a movement added and be moved to neutral space, then becoming class II signs (•H•ANDICAPÉ$_1$). However, signs from class II would be analyzed differently. These signs use an element from the oral language to create a sign on an LSQ model. For class I signs, the principal element of the sign is the handshape, which is inspired from the orthographic system used to represent the oral language, while the internal movement added only serves to make a minimally acceptable sign. Moreover, class I signs are not created on the model of natural LSQ signs, unlike class II signs. Haugen (1950) identified a process he called *hybrid creation,* which is defined as loan morphemes substituted into native models. Haugen cites the Yaqui word *liosnooka* (God-to speak, which means *to pray),* which contains the Spanish word *dios,* a borrowed form. There was no imitation of a Spanish model but only a borrowed morpheme inserted in a Yaqui model (accompanied by phonological integration). Haugen does not think of this as borrowing but as a creation drawing on two distinct languages. This type of lexical creation corresponds quite well to class II signs, which use an element of the oral language to create a sign using means of lexical creation native to the sign language. In effect, established and nonestablished signs of class II all respect models of the sign language, using a base sign as model or using the different means of lexical creation of the sign language.

This analysis explains, in a more efficient way, the structural difference we find between class I and II signs. We are examining two different processes, in one case code-switching and borrowing (class I signs) and in the other, lexical creation of the sign language, but using an element of the oral language (class II signs). This analysis can also explain the presence of class I established signs.

CONCLUSION

Our observations have made it clear that Deaf people use initialization as a means of lexical creation. It is one outcome of contact between French and LSQ. I hypothesized that the status of initialized signs would be either code-switches, borrowings, or hybrid creations. However, what appears to be most important to us is to consider the initialization process as an outcome of language contact, which could eventually contribute to the study of these phenomena.

Editor's note. Numerous examples of what can be termed *loan translations* exist in American Sign Language. These consist of spoken English compounds that have been translated into ASL compounds (e.g., HOMEWORK, BOYFRIEND, HOMESICK). In addition, there are some cases where parts of ASL signs have been lexicalized as English words. For example, the mouth configuration meaning "large" is often glossed as CHA and is sometimes used by bilinguals as an English word, as in "I have cha homework." The ASL sign PAH, glossed as *at last!* or *finally!* has been seen in print as an English work—"PAHED", presumably meaning "finally done."

REFERENCES

Battison, R. 1978. *Lexical borrowing in American Sign Language.* Silver Spring, Md.: Linstok Press.
Bellugi, U., and D. Newkirk. 1981. Formal devices for creating new signs in American Sign Language. *Sign Language Studies* 30:1–35.

Bourcier, P., and J.E. Roy. 1985. *La langue des signes [LSQ]*. Montréal: Publication Bourcier et Roy, enregistré.

Davis, J. 1989. Distinguishing language contact phenomena in ASL interpretation. In *The sociolinguistics of the Deaf community*, ed. C. Lucas, 85–102. San Diego: Academic Press.

Desouvrey, L., C. Dubuisson, and A. Vercaingne-Ménard. 1992. L'épellation en langue des signes québécoise. *Actes du congrès annuel de l'Association canadienne de linguistique*, 63–78.

Hansen, B. 1990. Trends in the progress toward bilingual education for Deaf children in Denmark. In *Sign Language Research amd Application*, ed. S. Prillwitz and T. Vollhaber, 51–62. Hamburg: Signum Press.

Haugen, E. 1950. The analysis of linguistic borrowing. *Language* 26:210–231.

Johnston, T. 1989. *Auslan dictionary: A dictionary of the sign language of the Australian Deaf community*. Sydney: Deafness Resources Australia Ltd.

Kyle, J.G., and B. Woll. 1985. *Sign language: The study of Deaf people and their language*. Cambridge: Cambridge University Press.

Lacerte, L. 1991. Bilinguisme et diglossie chez les sourds. *Revue québécoise de linguistique théorique et appliquée* 10(1):141–155.

Lambert, Abbé. 1865. *Le langage de la physionomie et du geste*, ed. J. Lecoffre. Paris: Np.

Lucas, C., and C. Valli. 1989. Language contact in the American Deaf community. In *The sociolinguistics of the Deaf community*, ed. C. Lucas. San Diego: Academic Press. 11–40.

———. 1992. *Language contact in the American Deaf community*. San Diego: Academic Press.

Myers-Scotton, C. 1992. Comparing codeswitching and borrowing. *Journal of Multilingual and Multicultural Development* 13(1 & 2):19–39.

Poplack, S., D. Sankoff, and C. Miller. 1988. The social correlates and linguistic processes of lexical borrowing and assimilation. *Linguistics* 26:47–104.

Sankoff, D., S. Poplack, and S. Vanniarajan. 1990. The case of the nonce loan in Tamil. *Language Variation and Change* 2:71–101.

Sternberg, M. 1981. *American Sign Language: A comprehensive dictionary*. New York: Harper and Row.

Stokoe, W. C. 1970. Sign language diglossia. *Studies in Linguistics* 21:27–41.

Stokoe, W. C., D. Casterline, and C. Croneberg. 1976. *A dictionary of American Sign Language on linguistic principles*. Silver Spring, Md.: Linstok Press.

Supalla, S. J. 1990. The arbitrary name sign system in American Sign Language. *Sign Language Studies* 67:99–126.

Swisher, M. V., and D. McKee. 1989. The sociolinguistic situation of natural sign language. *Applied Linguistics* 10(3):294–312.

Woodward, J. 1979. Quelques aspects sociolinguistiques des langues des signes américaine et française. *Langages* 56:78–91.

The Manual Alphabet of LSQ

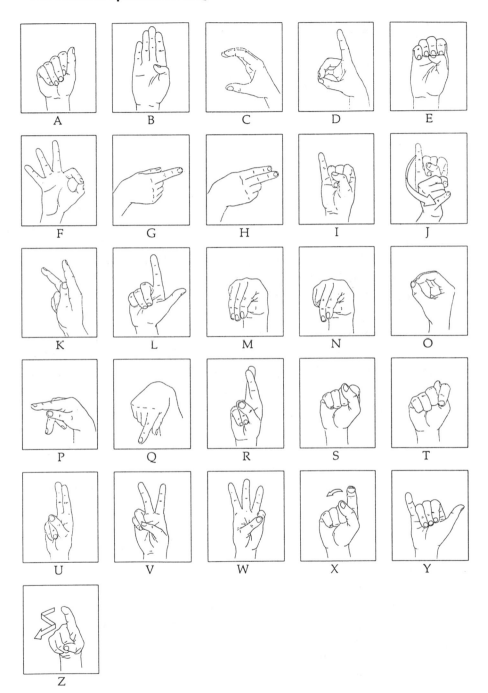

Fingerspelling Interaction:

A Set of Deaf Parents and

their Deaf Daughter

Arlene Blumenthal-Kelly

INTRODUCTION

Since 1985, the Culture and Communication Studies Program (CCSP), a unit within the Gallaudet Research Institute, has collected ethnographic data on Deaf children of Deaf parents by videotaping these families at home and appending fieldnotes. Spontaneous interaction between children and their parents and other relatives is taped, capturing household activities such as storyreading, play, mealtimes, bedtime routines, and even a parent's birthday. Because of my personal interest in fingerspelling itself, I began by looking at receptive and expressive fingerspelling skills in a young Deaf child. I was curious about how these skills were developed.

I present here some preliminary findings of this work-in-progress. Therefore, what I present here is not conclusive; it is intended to show what has already been observed in one young Deaf child from infancy to toddlerhood.

I wish to thank the members of my team, Dr. Carol J. Erting, Ms. Carlene Thumann-Prezioso, Dr. Sue Mather, and Mr. Charles Reilly, for their support and belief in my work. I also thank the members of the family that is the subject of this study, especially Debbie, who graciously opened their hearts and hearth to my team for the purposes of this research. And many thanks to Bruce D. Snider for editorial assistance.

Deaf with a *D* is used in this chapter to indicate those who consider themselves both culturally Deaf and members of the Deaf community.

Fingerspelling is one outcome of the contact between ASL and English. For every letter of the English alphabet there is a corresponding ASL sign. As if writing in the air, a person can manually reproduce any English word (only two signs are actually "written" in the air: J and Z) (Schein 1984). An earlier analysis of the full fingerspelled form by Battison (1978) showed that for all signs except G, H, J, P, and Q, the hand was placed in the high-chest space with the orientation of the volar surface (palm) outward and the metacarpal (knuckles) facing upward.

Some examples of full fingerspelling, as seen in this videotaped data, in which English words were spelled sign-by-sign with the manual alphabet, were J-O-B, B-A-C-K, E-A-R-L-Y, P-O-L-L-E-N, D-R-A-G-O-N-F-L-Y, and C-E-R-E-A-L. (Full fingerspelling is represented by individual capital letters separated by hyphens [Battison 1978].)

Fingerspelling, in general, is often used to represent proper nouns and English terms that do not have ASL lexical equivalents (Davis 1989), but it is often used when a sign already exists for a given concept (e.g., BED, BUSY) and also seems to have broader discourse functions (Kelly 1991, 1992).

Battison also discussed another class of fingerspelling. His restructuring profile theory described phonological changes: shifts in location, orientation, and handshapes of fingerspelled words that result in lexicalized signs (also known by Battison as "loan signs"), fingerspelled words that are incorporated into the ASL lexicon. Some of his lexicalized examples are #JOB,[1] #BACK, #EARLY, #MILK, #NO, #CAR, and #DO.

There has been very little research done on fingerspelling in Deaf children. The present work builds on the work of Padden and LeMaster (1985), whose study found that Deaf children learned to fingerspell before mastering reading and writing skills and before becoming aware of the correspondence between fingerspelling and print (p. 161). They also noted that, whereas many parents exposed their children to fingerspelling from birth, it usually was not until around the second birthday that children produced fingerspelled items independently (p. 167). These early attempts were not identical to Deaf adults' complex hand configurations

1. Lexicalized fingerspelling is represented by a crosshatch preceding the capital letters (Battison 1978).

because the child had to master three things in order to produce well-formed fingerspelling: production of all twenty-six signs for English orthographic symbols; comprehension of sequentiality; and finally, the smooth execution of movements from one sign to another (p. 168).

Mayberry and Waters (1991) suggested that because speakers use a phonological code in learning spoken words, signers likewise use such a code to learn fingerspelling. They found that errors in the production of fingerspelled terms tended to be phonological or according to formational parameters: for example, missing a handshape or two or executing bumpy movements. They also noted that children were able to remember words expressed in purely fingerspelled form without the support of the sign (p. 227).

A SINGLE SUBJECT STUDY

The subject of this study is Debbie (not her real name), a Deaf daughter of Deaf parents. Debbie is (as of October 1993) 4.4 years old and lives in the eastern part of the United States with her parents, who are white and college-educated. All of Debbie's grandparents, maternal and paternal, are Deaf. One set of great-grandparents was Deaf, too, making this child fourth-generation Deaf. Debbie also has a younger sister who is Deaf.

Methodology

CCSP videotaped Debbie and her family monthly starting when Debbie was five weeks old, collecting (as of September, 1993) forty-two tapes containing a total of thirty-one hours of interaction. The average video-taped session ran approximately forty to forty-five minutes.

Analysis of the videotapes included several steps. In the first round, I watched the forty-two videotapes and transcribed all the fingerspelled items that the parents and other adult relatives produced. I also subsequently transcribed fingerspelled items that Debbie herself produced.

In the second round of analysis, I eliminated fingerspelled items that Debbie might not have seen. For example, there were many instances in which one or both parents produced fingerspelling directed only to each other or to the person operating the videocamera. Although these fingerspelled items might have fallen within Debbie's peripheral field of vision, we could not be certain that she actually saw them. The focus of this analysis, then, was on items that the parents and other adults intentionally fingerspelled to Debbie. Also included were instances when either parent fingerspelled to the camera-person or to the other parent with Debbie earnestly watching the discourse.

The third round of analysis was focused on the linguistic context of each fingerspelled item: was fingerspelling produced in isolation or as part of a phrase or sentence? In addition, I categorized each fingerspelled item according to which part(s) of speech it represented. The traditional definition of parts of speech includes categories such as nouns, verbs, adverbs, adjectives, and prepositions (Akmajian et al. 1988, 60). In ASL, fingerspelled items such as #OK also frequently appear as *tag questions*— questions occurring at the end of a sentence. English examples of tag questions are "John is not running, is he?" and "Jane bought a coat, didn't she?" (Akmajian et al. 173).

Mixed, or *sandwiched*, ASL phrases (Kelly 1991, 1992) were also identified. Such a phrase is one in which initial and final items of one variety (i.e., either signed or fingerspelled items) occur immediately before and immediately after a medial item of another variety. In my earlier work, I noticed such patterns in which my subjects would combine signs and fingerspelling of the same or similar meanings. For example, my findings yielded the following: NUN #NUN NUN; LOST M-I-S-C-A-R-R-I-A-G-E; and WRITE D-O-W-N WHAT. These mixed items can be further categorized as *full sandwich* or *half sandwich*. The first variant is an ASL phrase or sentence in which the initial word is fingerspelled, the second word is signed, and the final word is fingerspelled (or vice versa) using either exactly the same English word or its approximation. Examples of full sandwiches in this videotaped data are #DO TODAY #DO and BEFORE #SUN RISE BEFORE. The half-sandwich variant is an ASL phrase or sentence in which the initial word is fingerspelled, and the next word is signed (or vice versa), again using either exactly the same English word or its approximation. Examples of half sandwiches in this work are BATH #TUB and PONYTAIL #PONYTAIL.

FINDINGS

Age One Month to Six Months

The earliest CCSP videotape was made when Debbie was five weeks old, and on this tape the parents did not fingerspell to Debbie. However, at eight weeks Debbie's mother fingerspelled the following two full sentences and one question: LOOK #AT ME; YOU SHOULD SMILE FOR #THE #CAMERA; and SHOW SMILE #OK-q. At fourteen weeks, we had the mother asking Debbie, LAUGH #AT ME-q. At seventeen weeks, Debbie's mother made the following three utterances: LOOK #AT YOURSELF IN #THE MIRROR; WHAT WANT (2h)[2] #DO NOW-q (outstretched palms); and #RICE C-E-R-E-A-L. At twenty-one weeks, Debbie's father made the following five utterances: "relax"[3] #RELAX; WANT YOUR WAY-q #OK!; WANT YOUR WAY-q #OK!; #OK: and FINISH-q #OK.

Age Seven to Twelve Months

During this second half of the first year, eighteen parental utterances contained fingerspelling. There was a marked increase in the use of #DO-q and #OK, either in isolation, in sentences, or (in the case of . . . #OK-q) as a tag question. A few instances of labelling objects occurred in this period, for example, #QUACK, C-E-I-L-I-N-G, and #SOAP.

Age Thirteen to Eighteen Months

This period saw a great increase in the parents' use of #NO in isolation. Although #OK was still prominent, as in the previous period, it tended to be half-sandwiched with FINISH-q. Up to this point, Debbie had not produced any fingerspelled items.

Age Nineteen to Twenty-four Months

Debbie's parents promoted the learning of fingerspelling by identifying individual letters on blocks. In one instance, both parents were on

2. (2h): This symbol for "two hands" is written before a gloss and indicates that the sign is made with both hands (Baker and Cokely, 1980).
3. Double quotes around a gloss indicate a gesture (Baker and Cokely, 1980).

the floor with Debbie, playing with blocks. Together they identified the first letter of each family member's name—M for Mommy, D for Daddy, N for Nana, etc.—by simultaneously pointing out the corresponding block and producing the appropriate hand configuration.

At twenty-two months, the family was playing with blocks again. This time, Debbie identified the letters more readily and was able to point out which letter corresponded to which family member, including her infant sister.

When Debbie was twenty-four months old, her father asked if she wanted some POTATO #CHIPS, and Debbie imitated him by signing, POTATO #CHP #CHP #CHP POTATO, mainly to herself.

Age Twenty-four to Thirty-six Months

This period showed an increase in the use of #OR in parental utterances. Also, because Debbie was now going to school, we saw some sophistication in her use of lexicalized terms such as #BUS, #NAP, #TV, #JOKE, #NO, and #OK. #DO-q continued to be used frequently by both Debbie and her parents.

Interestingly, it was during Debbie's thirtieth month that she invented a name for her new doll: #SILA. Although we were not familiar with this name, it is phonologically correct in English. Debbie also engaged in a discourse with her Deaf aunt about her uncle's job at #IBM.

Age Thirty-six to Forty-eight Months

At forty-one months, Debbie's mother devised a game in which she wrote nouns and proper names of immediate family members in capital letters on index cards. The mother flashed the cards to Debbie, encouraging her to imitate the letters. Debbie clearly delighted in this game, asking if there was a prize for winning. Her mother replied that there were no winners or losers here. Data seen here showed that when Debbie imitated each letter of a word, she struggled to understand the whole word. However, when her mother repeated the word with a lexicalized sign, Debbie caught on to the meaning of the word. For example, when Debbie did not understand R-I-C-E and S-E-E-D, her mother provided the lexicalized signs #RICE and #SEED. Debbie demonstrated her comprehension by responding with these same lexicalized signs. At 47.5 months, Debbie, while playing by herself, recited the whole manual alphabet, albeit haltingly. At 50 months, Debbie fingerspelled the whole manual alphabet again with only one error: she fingerspelled . . . N-O-Q- . . . , suddenly caught herself, and repeated, . . . P-Q-R . . . , until she reached z.

FINGERSPELLING AS PART OF A PHRASE OR SENTENCE

Most of Debbie's parents' utterances that included fingerspelled items were in sentence form. One fingerspelled item that appeared both in tag questions and in isolation was #OK.

As discussed earlier, the first three videotaped sentences produced by Debbie's parents that contained fingerspelling appeared at eight weeks. The fingerspelled terms included a preposition, #AT; a noun phrase, #THE #CAMERA; and a tag question, #OK-q.

In a few instances, sentences were inverted, or reversed. For example, at thirty-two months, Debbie's father read her a story. He signed, WHERE #MILK TRUCK "drive." Then, after allowing Debbie to look at the pictures in the book, he inverted the sentence: MILK WHERE #TRUCK.

PARTS OF SPEECH

The earliest fingerspelled noun Debbie produced in front of the videocamera occurred at 24 months, that being POTATO #CHP #CHP #CHP POTATO. Debbie's earliest fingerspelled proper name captured on videotape occurred at 25 months, when she mentioned the name of a friend. The earliest videotaped verb, #DO-q, occurred at 43 months: it is possible that this particular utterance was produced much earlier but not captured on tape until this point. Debbie's earliest fingerspelled adjective, #LO and #LOOLO (for #LOOSE) came at 49.5 months.

SANDWICHES

At twenty-one weeks, we found Debbie eating too quickly. Her father told her to "relax" #RELAX, thus making a half-sandwich utterance.

At 9.5 months, Debbie pointed at the ceiling. Her mother looked up and pointed at the ceiling too, saying, WHITE C-E-I-L-I-N-G, and closed by pointing to the ceiling again, thus making a full sandwich. Also at this age, Debbie pulled on an object that was obscured from the videocamera. Her father sandwiched his utterance: PULL #NO PULL.

At eleven months, Debbie fake-coughed for attention and her mother told her, FAKE #FAKE YOU. At twenty months, Debbie's grandmother searched for a fork, sandwich-signing, WHERE YOUR FORK #FORK-q twice.

SANDWICHING FOR LABELLING

At thirty-four weeks, Debbie's father introduced a toy duck to her by signing, DUCK DUCK Q-U-A-C-K. At sixteen months, her mother signed, WHITE #CAR CAR. At twenty-six months, after pointing at each of a group of toys, her mother sandwiched her labels with fingerspelling: T-O-O-L-S T-O-O-L-S HAMMER; B-A-R-B-I-E; and K-E-N. During a very detailed conversation at forty-one months, her father signed the following: WANT PONYTAIL #PONY-TAIL; #LAKE (2h)L-cl⁴ COLD; "sh sh" #OK "sh sh"; and LIPSTICK C-H-A-P-S-T-I-C-K LIPSTICK. At forty-two months, Debbie saw her mother introduce DEER L-L-A-M-A.

SANDWICHING WHILE READING A STORY

At thirty-three months, we found Debbie's father saying the following: "open" #REF "open" COLD "open"; "open" #CUPBOARD SHELF; and #PO LETTER. At forty months, her mother read a story about cats taking a bath: NOT LIKE IN BATH #TUB. At fifty months, her father used the following fingerspelled terms: BEFORE #SUN RISE BEFORE; SQUEEZE DRY #UP SQUEEZE; BEAR DON'T-WANT #HONEY DON'T-WANT; and WANT #TAIL WANT.

Debbie herself used sandwiches, starting at thirty-seven months by asking her younger sister, #OK-q #OK-q. At thirty-eight months, Debbie answered an off-camera question, #NO #NO. At forty months, we found Debbie informing her younger sister that they had visitors in the house: A-namesign #JIM A-namesign. Debbie's most frequent question was #DO-q TODAY #DO-q or #DO-q NOW #DO-q. At forty-four months, during dis-

4. The symbol -cl is written after the handshape symbol to denote that the handshape is used as a classifier in a classifier predicate. (Baker and Cokely 1980; Valli and Lucas 1992).

course with her mother, Debbie signed, SLEEP #NAP. And at forty-nine months, while playing with dolls with her younger sister, Debbie signed, #NO ZERO and NOT HIT #NO+++.

DISCUSSION

Debbie's parents exposed her to fingerspelling immediately after her birth. We have on record such evidence from when she was eight weeks of age. Her fingerspelling of individual letters, as shown in her play with blocks at nineteen and twenty-two months, exhibited clear hand configurations. Debbie fingerspelled to herself for the first time at her own second birthday party. This time frame matched that described by Padden and LeMaster (1985), who noted that it usually was not until around the second birthday that children produced fingerspelled items independently (p. 167).

In the same vein, Padden and LeMaster suggested that a child's production of fingerspelling is not identical to an adult's production. Debbie's first idiosyncratic fingerspelling, POTATO #CHP #CHP #CHP #CHP POTATO, was missing the medial letter(s), and her execution was not smooth, bouncing between H and P. When Debbie, at thirty months, signed #IBM, the B jumped out of the high-chest space, and then the hand moved far down for the M, producing a jumpy execution.

Sequentiality, as suggested by Padden and LeMaster, remained ambiguous to Debbie even at thirty months, when she attempted to fingerspell her own name; she reversed two medial handshapes and added a new handshape. It was not until approximately thirty-four months that she mastered sequentiality with her #OFF. At thirty-six months, she fingerspelled her name in the correct sequence. At forty-seven months, Debbie showed that she had conquered sequentiality almost completely by reciting the entire manual alphabet with no assistance. Moreover, there was no bouncing or jumping; she glided smoothly from one hand configuration to the next. Also at this age, Debbie fingerspelled the names of family members smoothly. However, when she fingerspelled the names of some friends, the sequence was slightly mixed up, and the execution was bouncy.

Mayberry and Waters (1991) suggested that children were able to remember words expressed in purely fingerspelled form without the support of sign. We found this to be true of Debbie, as evidenced by her participation in the index card game at forty-one months. At this age, Debbie was not able to comprehend words that were fingerspelled in full form. However, when her mother repeated these words in lexicalized form without the support of other signs, Debbie responded with either the signed version or the lexicalized form itself.

Sandwiching, either half or full, appeared useful in labelling objects— introducing the orthographic form as well as the ASL form—and occurred frequently in the signing of Debbie's parents. They tended to point at an object, then fingerspell, and finally sign. This behavior also occurred in reverse order: signing, fingerspelling, then pointing. Sandwiching also appeared frequently in reading stories and included, in this context, pointing at the graphics in the books. It became apparent that sandwiching, in addition to pointing, is used frequently by Deaf parents in the early education of their young Deaf children.

In closing, I would like to relate an anecdote involving Debbie and a visiting six-year-old friend. Debbie showed me a burn on her arm, fingerspelling B-U-N. Her friend chided her, saying that it was a #BURN. (In this lexicalized form, the palm orientation of the B faces skyward, and the execution requires a quick twist of the wrist that leaves the palm facing downward at the end.) Debbie looked at me with puzzlement. I explained that we could say either B-U-R-N or #BURN, and that it was her choice. Debbie, looking at her friend, chose #BURN. This anecdote implies that Deaf children enjoy and understand lexicalized forms of fingerspelling rather than full forms: recall the index card game between Debbie's mother and Debbie at forty-one months old in which Debbie understood #RICE rather than R-I-C-E.

FUTURE RESEARCH QUESTIONS

Many people have asked when and how often Deaf parents should expose their Deaf or hearing children to fingerspelling. Evidence from Padden and LeMaster (1985) and Mayberry and Waters (1991) have shown that children acquiring ASL also acquire the ability to produce and understand fingerspelling at a very early age (Johnson 1994). This current study also suggests this notion, and I advocate that parents incorporate fingerspelling in their daily discourse with their Deaf infants as early as possible.

The role and essence of sandwiching fingerspelled items needs to be explored further. Do parents or caretakers use it for instructional purposes, or is it a natural part of ASL discourse, as seen in the study of Baltimore's Deaf senior citizens by Kelly?

In terms of execution, are the most frequently fingerspelled items more likely to become smoother than those less frequently spelled? We saw that Debbie fingerspelled the names of immediate family members smoothly but bounced with the names of friends. Does this indicate that familiarity produces smoothness? The same holds true in Debbie's recitals of her own name: bouncy at thirty months, but smooth at forty-seven months.

Another interesting research question would be to explore when the child herself asked specifically for fingerspelling and at what age. This would suggest the child's general understanding of the connection between fingerspelling and the printed word.

REFERENCES

Akmajian, A., R.A. Demers, and R.M. Harnish. 1988. Linguistics: *An Introduction to language and communication*. Cambridge, Mass.: MIT Press.

Baker, C., and D. Cokely. 1980. *American Sign Language: A teacher's resource text on grammar and culture*. Silver Spring. Md.: TJ Publishers.

Battison, R. 1978. *Lexical borrowing in American Sign Language*. Silver Spring, Md.: Linstok Press.

Davis, J. 1989. Distinguishing language contact phenomena in ASL interpretation. In *The sociolinguistics of the Deaf community*, ed. C. Lucas, 85–102. San Diego: Academic Press.

Johnson, Robert E. In press. Possible influences on bilingualism in early ASL acquisition. In *Teaching English to deaf and second-language students*.

Kelly, A.B. 1991. Fingerspelling use among the deaf senior citizens of Baltimore. School of communication student forum, ed. E.A. Winston, 1:90–98. Washington, D.C.: Gallaudet University School of Communication.

Kelly, A.B. 1992. Fingerspelling analysis: Baltimore's deaf senior citizens. Poster session presented at the International Theoretical Issues in Sign Language Research Conference, August 1992. San Diego.

Mayberry, R.I., and G.S. Waters. 1991. Children's memory for sign and fingerspelling in relation to production rate and sign language input. In

Theoretical issues in sign language research: Vol. 2. psychology, ed. P. Siple
and S.D. Fischer. Chicago: University of Chicago Press.

Padden, C. A. 1991. The acquisition of fingerspelling by deaf children. In
Theoretical issues in sign language research: Vol. 2. psychology, ed. P. Siple
and S. D. Fischer, Chicago: University of Chicago Press.

Padden, C.A., and B. LeMaster. 1985. An alphabet on hand: The acquisition of
fingerspelling in deaf children. *Sign Language Studies* 47:161–72.

Petitto, L.A., and P.F. Marentette. 1991. Babbling in the manual mode: Evidence
for the ontogeny of language. *Science* 251:1493–1496

Schein, J. 1984. *Speaking the language of signs: The art and science of sign
language.* New York: Doubleday.

Valli, C., and C. Lucas. 1992. *Linguistics of ASL: A resource text for ASL users.*
Washington, D.C.: Gallaudet University Press.

Part 3 **Multilingualism**

A Sociolinguistic Description of Sign

Language Use in a Navajo Family

Jeffrey Davis and Samuel Supalla

In what is perhaps the most well known quote in the field of sign language studies, George Veditz (1913) stated that "as long as we have deaf people we will have sign language." The fact that deaf people have a strong inclination for developing and acquiring sign language can be traced through history and is common throughout the world. Sign use in deaf communities ranges from the development of "home" sign systems developed within single families and used within one generation to conventional sign languages that are full-fledged linguistic systems used across generations of signers. The existence and acquisition of sign language, however, are not necessarily based on the single condition of hearing loss. A substantial body of literature supports the statement that sign language has also been developed and acquired cross-generationally among some indigenous populations, such as North American Indians and Australian Aborigines (cf. West 1960 and Kendon 1988). The literature suggests that, even in the absence of community members who are deaf or in cases in which only a small percentage of the population is deaf, there is nonetheless widespread use of sign. However, there has been no research to date to determine the outcome of sign language

Many individuals have participated with us on this project. We have benefitted greatly from their support, comments, and insights. In particular, we would like to thank Ted Supalla, Jeannette Maré, SueAnne Hammond-McCreery, Lin Marksbury, Monty Jim, Melanie Cody, and the members of the Navajo family in this study. We also want to thank Lidia Batylda for her expert assistance in the preparation of the manuscript. All interpretations, as the saying goes, are the responsibility of the authors. Finally, we would like to acknowledge the support provided for the project by the Office of the Vice President for Research at The University of Arizona, the National Science Foundation, and the Laurent Clerc Cultural Fund from The Gallaudet University Alumni Association.

acquisition if a deaf child is born into a linguisitic community in which there is an alternate sign language used by hearing members of the community. Prior to this study, there was no published research concerning the use of sign between deaf and hearing North American Indians.[1] The primary focus of the present study is a Navajo family in which six out of eleven siblings are deaf or hard of hearing and who have naturally acquired sign means of communication. The nature of linguistic interaction (e.g., language functions and domains of use) between the deaf and hearing participants in this rarified situation will be described.

First, however, a review of the literature on alternate sign systems (i.e., sign communication developed and used by individuals already competent in a spoken language) is presented. In these cases, depending on the setting, participants, and topic, hearing members of the community will: "turn-off" the oral channel in favor of using the manual channel, even when there are no deaf people present. In some communities, in which there is a high incidence of genetic deafness, there is widespread use of sign language by both deaf and hearing people (Washabaugh 1986; Groce 1985; Johnson 1989). The cross-generational use of alternate sign systems and their role in the development of primary sign language, however, has not received adequate attention in the literature. Specifically, when there is a high incidence of deafness within a community in which the alternative use of a sign system is already well established, what effect does this have in the development of its use as a primary language among the deaf members of the community? Further research is needed to determine how these so-called alternate sign systems have evolved and to determine the similarities and differences between these systems and the sign languages used in deaf communities around the world.

Based on numerous accounts (as early as Socrates in ancient Greece), signed languages, like spoken languages, have existed throughout human history. Yet, because they are "generally omitted from surveys of the world's languages, sign languages are ubiquitous. No one really knows

1. Many terms are commonly used to label the descendants of the first Americans—Indian, American Indian, Alaska Native, and Native American—but the first two are preferred by most members of these cultural groups (Dillard 1983). In this article, the term *Indian* is generally used. *North American Indians* is also used to distinguish this group from Central and South American Indians, for example.

how many there are, for their boundaries do not coincide with those of oral languages and there is simply no information about the number of sign languages in use in vast areas of the world" (Perlmutter 1986, 515). Further, the propensity for indigenous peoples to develop a highly elaborated system for sign communication is well documented in the literature and is the focus of the present study.

ALTERNATE VS. PRIMARY SIGN SYSTEMS

Kendon (1988) has conducted extensive ethnographic fieldwork and linguistic analysis that demonstrate that the sign systems used among aboriginal populations have developed as highly elaborated alternatives to spoken language. These sign systems have evolved from use in cross-linguistic situations or from circumstances where the use of speech is difficult or taboo. Both the origin and use of these sign systems differ considerably, however, from sign languages that are used in deaf communities. To help clarify the distinction, Kendon (1988) proposed that the sign language of deaf communities be called "primary sign language" and the sign language of people already competent in spoken language be called "alternate sign language."

Alternate Use of Sign Language Among Indigenous Populations

According to both historical and modern accounts, sign use among the aboriginal peoples of Central Australia and among populations of the Americas (South America, Central America, Mexico, the Caribbean, the U.S., and Canada) is evident. In North America, for example, sign language appears to have developed as a lingua franca for intertribal communication in circumstances in which Indians speaking different languages came into brief but repeated contact with one another. By historical accounts, sign use was by no means restricted to communication between tribes speaking different native languages. It was also used within tribes in oratory, ceremonial performance, and storytelling, and for communicating in situations where the use of speech was difficult or taboo (West 1960).

The historical evidence suggests that the use of a signed lingua franca became widespread among Indian populations throughout North America. This was particularly true for the Plains Indian tribes (e.g., the Cheyenne, Crow, Sioux, Assiniboin, Gros Ventre, Piegan, Flathead, Nez Perce, Arapaho, and Ute). The Plains Indian culture covered a geographic area ranging from Canada to southern Texas and northern Mexico.

This area is (or was) an area of extreme linguistic diversity. The earliest accounts of the use of signs in this area were made by Coronado in 1541, and there were subsequent accounts in the eighteenth century (e.g., Santa Ana in 1740). The use of sign among the Plains tribes continued well into the twentieth century and is preserved in the motion pictures, dictionaries, and books produced by scholars such as Clark (1882), Scott (1931), Seton (1918), Tomkins (1926), Voegelin (1958), Weil (1931), and West (1960). These researchers focused on the "Plains Indian Sign Language" and described the nature and structure of the system and argued that it had a linguistic structure of its own independent of the respective tribe's spoken language. In addition to the structural properties and production of sign, these early linguists and anthropologists carefully examined the lexicon, semantics, and possible origins of the system. Voegelin (1958) and West (1960) also developed an elaborate transcription system and phonemic-like inventory for Plains Indian Sign Language.

Apparently, the widespread use of signed language as an alternate to spoken language or as a lingua franca declined as aboriginal groups learned English as a second language. That is, given the establishment of Indian schools across the West and Southwest in the late nineteenth and early twentieth centuries, young Indian children and adolescents were systematically taken from their families and institutionalized. The policy at that time was for the "cultural and linguistic assimilation" of aboriginal children. This translated into loss of native language and culture for many Indian children. Specifically, the native children were taught English only and in most cases were forbidden to follow or practice their cultural traditions (e.g., Prucha 1986). Along with the decline of the children's native language and culture, in most cases, was no doubt also the loss of sign language as an alternate means of communication. This is evidenced in the early ethnographic work and motion pictures produced by Hugh Lennox Scott (1931), which are well preserved in the National Archives in Washington, D.C. In the introduction to the film showing chieftains and elders from thirteen different tribes using sign language, Scott tells the chieftains that "it is important to preserve your signing through film because your sons are not learning the sign language."

Although most of the early research focused on the Plains Indian Sign Language, there are also several references in the literature to the use of sign among Southwestern tribes such as the Navajo, Hopi, Apache, and Comanche (West 1960). Fortunately, there is evidence to suggest that sign language is still in use among some American Indian groups. In the preliminary stages of the present research project, for example, some Navajo consultants have reported and demonstrated that sign communication is still in use in some situations (e.g., for ceremonial purposes and during male intergroup activities). Since West's (1960) work, which remains only as a doctoral dissertation and collection of films at the University of Indiana in Bloomington, no original work has been done in the area of North American indigenous sign language use. Furthermore, there has been no research to determine the role of sign among both deaf and hearing American Indians and the extent to which it is in use today.

Besides its use among the Indians of North America, other aboriginal groups have also made extensive use of sign language. Kendon (1988), in his comprehensive work on sign language as an alternate communication system, documents the widespread use of sign language among Australian aborigines. The studies of alternate sign systems, however, make only passing reference to what happens when a deaf child is born into a community in which the hearing members make use of alternate sign communication. Kendon, however, did not study deaf aborigines. Based on unpublished accounts by others, he claims that "deaf Aborigines do not, apparently, become highly fluent in the prevailing Aboriginal sign language. Like isolated deaf elsewhere, they rely upon a sign system improvised within their immediate family." On this point, Kendon concludes that "it looks as if deaf persons, in a community where an alternate sign language is in use, do not themselves use this sign language, but develop one of their own" (1988, 406).

Likewise, La Mont West did not focus on sign use by deaf American Indians. In his extensive study of the sign languages of the Plains Indians of North America, West only mentions that "Indian deaf mutes often develop a home made sign language within the family or neighborhood circle, rather than learning the fuller Plains Indian sign language" (1960, 64). Further research is needed to determine the linguistic outcome of a deaf child's being born into a community in which the hearing members use alternate sign language.

Again, it should be emphasized that both Kendon and West did not focus on the signing of the deaf members of the native communities in their studies. These researchers were interested in the alternate use of sign by the hearing members of the community irrespective of the presence of deaf community members. What West and Kendon may be overlooking is that the deaf community members in these situations may be expanding upon the input received from the use of alternate signing by hearing community members. That is, the alternate sign system used by the hearing community members may be the resource from which the deaf community members expand their language. This raises the question: what happens when an alternate sign system becomes a primary system?

Communities in Which Both Deaf and Hearing Members Use Sign

Also relevant to the present study are communities in which both deaf and hearing members use sign. For example, Robert E. Johnson (1989) describes a situation in Chican, a traditional Yucatec Maya village in the state of Yucatan in Mexico. In this village of about four hundred inhabitants, there are thirteen deaf people (a very high proportion of the population, due to marriage patterns). According to Johnson, both deaf and hearing people in the village acquire sign language naturally. Cases of widespread indigenous sign use have also been reported on Providence Island (Washabaugh 1986) about 150 miles east of Nicaragua and among the Urubú, a community along the Gurupí River in the state of Maranhao in the Amazonian jungle (Kakumasu, as cited in Perlmutter 1986). Sebeok and Umiker-Sebeok (1978) provide a more detailed and exhaustive account of aboriginal sign language use in the Americas and Australia.

Finally, in what is perhaps the most well documented historical account of sign use by both deaf and hearing members of a community, Nora Groce (1985) reports that "English-Sign bilingualism" was prevalent on Martha's Vineyard (Massachusetts) for more than 250 years. Based on genealogical records prepared by Alexander Graham Bell in the 1890s, on the island as a whole, one child out of 155 was born deaf (much higher than in the general population, in which one child out of one thousand is born deaf). Further data-driven and comparative research of the development and use of sign language between deaf and hearing individuals in native populations is needed.

Taxonomy of Sign Communication Systems

In order to clarify some of the terms used in the literature to describe the differences between the sign communication systems (Johnson 1978; Frishberg 1987; Sebeok and Umiker-Sebeok 1978; and Kendon 1988), we have developed table 1. The taxonomy shown in figure 1 graphically illustrates the four major categories of sign communication systems relevant to the present study.

The major distinction between primary and alternate sign systems is that the former are developed, transmitted, and used by deaf people as their first language, whereas the latter are developed, transmitted, and used by hearing individuals already competent in a spoken language, irrespective of the presence of deaf people. Alternate systems may be used cross-linguistically or within a community whose members share the same native language. When used cross-linguistically, alternate signing tends not to co-occur with speech. And when used by community members who share the same spoken language alternate, signing may either substitute for speech or be used as an accompaniment to speech. Furthermore, in contrast to primary sign systems that are used across a wide range of functions and domains, alternate sign systems have more restricted functions and limited domains of use, for example, storytelling, monastic, and specific occupational settings. Despite these differences, both primary and alternate systems do nonetheless share some important linguistic properties; for example, both systems are rule-governed and conventionalized (Voegelin 1958; West 1960). And unlike home-sign systems, both primary and alternate systems are transmitted and acquired cross-generationally.

THE PRESENT STUDY

The primary purpose of the present research project is to study the sign system[2] that is being used extensively in a Navajo family in northern

2. At this time, the authors refer to *sign system* until further research is conducted in order to determine the nature and structure of this sign system as a

TABLE 1. *Signed Communication Systems*

I. *Primary Sign Systems* are rule-governed, conventional signed languages that are full-fledged autonomous linguistic systems that have evolved within specific historical, social, and cultural contexts and that have been used across generations of signers (e.g., ASL, French Sign Language, Danish Sign Language, etc.).

II. *Alternate Sign Systems* are highly elaborated systems of signed communication developed and used by individuals who are already competent in spoken language. The signs used in these alternate systems are codified, that is, they are standardized and are commonly used as alternatives to spoken expressions. Alternate signing is distinct from other forms of communicative kinesis (e.g., spacing, orientation, movement style, facial expression, etc.) and is also distinct from gesticulation that co-occurs with spoken language (cf. Kendon 1988). There are several different categories of alternate sign use:

    A. *Cross Linguistic* use of sign between groups of hearing individuals who do not share the same native language (e.g., the complex sign system used by the Plains Indians of North America).

    B. *Shared Spoken Language* use of sign within a linguistic group who share the same native spoken language but who use sign as a substitute or as an accompaniment to speech. There are also several subcategories here:

        1. *Aboriginal Sign Communication* developed by the native peoples of the North Central Desert of Australia as an alternative to the native spoken language when the use of speech is taboo, such as periods of mourning or during male initiation rites (Kendon 1988).

        2. *Monastic Sign Communication* developed for use in Cistercian, Cluniac, and Trappist monasteries following a rule of silence ordered by St. Benedict in the sixth century. Though the use of spoken language was forbidden, sign systems of varying levels of complexity were developed by the hearing monks to meet communication needs (Sebeok and Umiker-Sebeok 1978).

        3. *Occupational Sign Communication* developed for use in work settings where the use of spoken language is not permitted or is not possible. For example, limited use of manual means of communication has been reported by auctioneers, scuba divers, broadcast engineers, etc. More complex sign

TABLE 1. *Signed Communication Systems (continued)*

systems, however, have been reported in other occupational settings, such as those developed by workers in the sawmills of North America (Johnson, 1978).

III. *Home-Sign Systems* refers to the gestural communication systems developed when deaf individuals are isolated from other deaf people and need to communicate with the hearing people around them. In many cases so called home-sign is the first communication system used by young deaf children and their hearing families who do not know the standardized signed language of the larger adult deaf community (Frishberg 1987).

Arizona in which there is a high incidence of genetic deafness. This Navajo family represents a multilingual community in which several autonomous languages are used (e.g., spoken Navajo, spoken English, and American Sign Language) in addition to the sign communication system shared by both deaf and hearing family members. The present study involves systematic ethnographic and sociolinguistic research to answer several important questions: What is the role and function of the Navajo sign system? To what extent and in which domains do Navajo who are deaf and hearing use sign? To what degree is the system used outside the Navajo family in this study? What is the etymology of the system, and how is the system transmitted and acquired? Is there evidence of lexical borrowing or code-switching among the languages in contact? How does this linguistic situation reflect the processes of pidginization and creolization?

The Navajo family involved in this study is unique because out of eleven children, six are deaf or hard of hearing, apparently due to genetic causes.[3] The older siblings—two deaf sisters and a hard of hearing

------

full-fledged language. In this case, however, the so-called sign system appears much more complex than either "home-signs" or "gestures" that accompany spoken languages. Sign is considered to be a form of communication analogous to speech, whereas gesture is more rudimentary and not language based (see Discussion beginning on p. 97).

3. In order to protect the anonymity of the family involved in this study, throughout this article the group will be referred to as "the Navajo family." Other family members will be referred to according to English language kinship terms,

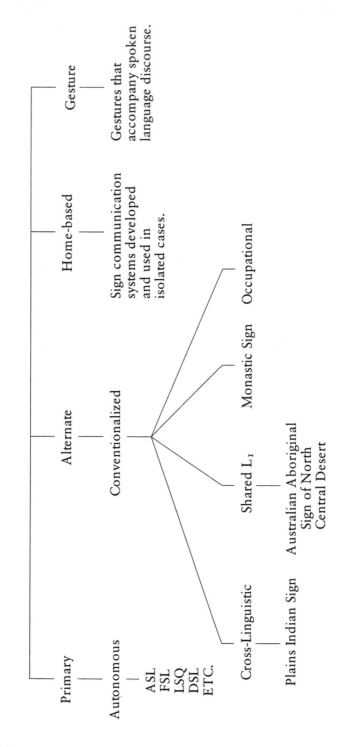

FIGURE 1. *Taxonomy of Sign Communication Systems.*

brother in their mid- to late forties—have never been to school. The older deaf siblings, having lived very traditional lives in the remote plateau country of northeastern Arizona with minimal contact with outsiders, have used an elaborate sign-based communication system that is distinct from American Sign Language (ASL). In contrast, the three younger sisters (two are deaf and one is hard of hearing) and a male cousin who is also deaf, having been educated at the Arizona State School for the Deaf and Blind (ASDB) in Tucson, have mastered ASL as a second language. They, however, use the family sign system when interacting with family members. There is an approximate thirty-year age span between the oldest deaf sibling, who is fifty years old, and the youngest deaf sibling, who is in her early twenties.

Although the younger deaf siblings and cousin are fluent in ASL, they continue to use the family sign system when they visit their deaf and hearing relatives on the reservation. The three older deaf siblings have apparently never learned ASL. During this ethnographic study, they were observed using only a few ASL signs and fingerspelling in what was otherwise the context of their own family way of signing. Out of twenty-three family members, including the parents, the siblings, and their children, twelve family members still live within easy walking distance of one another, and this core group is the focus of the present study.

Ethnographic Fieldwork and Analytic Procedures

The authors first visited the Navajo family on their land in northeast Arizona on June 21, 1990. At the time of the first visit, the family lived in the remote plateau country, an eight-hour drive from Tucson. The family outfit[4] comprised two traditional hoghans and a four-walled house

---

such as sister, brother, cousin, etc. It should be noted, however, that in the Navajo language there are elaborate and complex terms to express kinship and social relationships (Witherspoon 1975).

4. Witherspoon (1975) defines the Navajo outfit as a set of subsistence residential units that are subdivisions of an earlier and larger unit. All personnel of the outfit can trace their relationship back to the head mother of the original unit. The intensity of the bond between two subsistence residential units is, to a great extent, proportionate to the generational distance between the current head mothers of each and the original head mother. Traditionally, then, the Navajo maintain a matrilineal society.

without electricity or running water. The authors were first introduced to the family by SueAnne Hammond-McCreery, a social worker from the Community Outreach Program for the Deaf in Flagstaff, who had been working with the deaf members of the family for two years prior to the initial research visit. Navajo scholars inform us that the access we received to this traditional Navajo family is extremely rare. The willingness of this family to share their experiences with the authors is perhaps attributable to the rapport established by Hammond-McCreery during her prior social work with the family and perhaps to the family members identifying with Samuel Supalla as also being deaf. The primary consultant, the male Navajo cousin who is deaf, also played a major role in the rapport building process. The male cousin is fluent in ASL, written English, and in the Navajo sign system used by his deaf cousins and their family. In addition, he is a self-reported fluent user of the sign system used by the larger hearing Navajo community.

One month following the first visit, a second visit was made on July 11, 1990. During the first two site visits, approximately six hours of videotaped data were obtained. Since the time of the first and second site visits, the family has relocated to the "new lands" that are a part of the Navajo Nation. The family relocated as a result of the Hopi-Navajo land dispute. In contrast to the hoghans in which they lived just two years ago, eleven family members (the deaf siblings' father passed away soon after the relocation) now live in six separate houses with electricity and modern conveniences, including VCRs and microwave ovens. The six houses in which the family lives are within a short walking distance of one another. During our field work, we were informed that the older deaf siblings, the hearing daughter of the eldest deaf sister, the hearing sisters, and nieces and nephews are in daily contact with one another. The younger siblings and cousin, who are deaf and frequent users of ASL, only occasionally visit the family at their new location on the reservation.

Since the relocation, there have been two additional site visits to the family in their new homes (August 13–14, 1991, and May 22–23, 1992). The primary consultant (the male cousin who is deaf) accompanied Supalla and Davis during each site visit to participate in pre- and postsessions with the researchers and has made follow-up visits to the University of Arizona in Tucson. All visits to the Navajo family and sessions with the primary consultant have been filmed using Super VHS videoequipment. To date, approximately twenty hours of videotaped data have been collected.

There are two phases to the Navajo sign research project. Phase one involves systematic sociolinguistic and ethnographic research and is the focus of this article. Phase two, currently under way in the Sign Language Research Lab at the University of Arizona, involves linguistic structural analysis and consideration of psycholinguistic dimensions of the Navajo sign system and the acquisition of the system by its users. Jeannette Maré, a research assistant, has worked approximately six hundred hours assisting the authors in the transcription, verification, and analysis of the data. Currently, the authors are in the process of finalizing a formal structural analysis of the family's sign system.

In sum, each of the four site visits involved extensive ethnographic interviews and observations, interaction with the deaf and hearing Navajo participants, and pre- and postworking sessions with the male deaf cousin acting as the primary consultant for the study. Two day-long work sessions were also conducted in the research lab with the primary consultant. During these sessions additional ethnographic interviews were conducted, and the primary consultant assisted the researchers in the review, verification, and analysis of the field data. In addition to the interviews with the family members, input was received from two deaf Navajos and two hearing Navajos unrelated to the family and from two researchers of language and culture who are Navajo. The results of these ethnographic interviews and observations are presented below.

RESULTS OF THE ETHNOGRAPHIC STUDY

As mentioned above, the present article reports the results of Phase one of the Navajo sign project, which is an ethnographic analysis and description of the videodata and field notes collected during the research process previously described. The first area to be reported involves the use of sign by both deaf and hearing family members followed by the use of sign by hearing Navajos outside the family. During the site visits it was documented that, in addition to the three oldest deaf siblings, there were ten hearing family members living in the family outfit (see footnote 2).

Also, as we have pointed out, the older siblings—the two deaf sisters, and a hard of hearing brother in their mid- to late forties—have never been to school. In contrast, the younger siblings, three sisters (two deaf and one hard of hearing) in their late twenties and early thirties, attended the residential school for the deaf in Tucson. These three younger sisters are reportedly fluent in ASL. The younger deaf and hard of hearing sisters were never present during the site visits, as they live in the city and not on the reservation. The researchers, therefore, were unable to make any observations of the signing used by the younger deaf siblings. Comments, however, made to the researchers by the other family members about the younger deaf siblings' use of signs are reported here. The primary consultant (i.e., deaf male cousin) for the study also attended the residential school for the deaf and is fluent in ASL and the family sign system. Specifically, this study includes observations of the three deaf and ten hearing family members living together on the reservation.

Figure 2 shows the Navajo family tree. This family tree was based on descriptions provided by the family members. The hearing status and ages of family members are indicated, beginning with the oldest sibling, who is fifty years old. In this study the oldest sibling is considered facilitator of the family sign system. Being the eldest deaf child, her hearing parents reportedly began using sign. Her role as the facilitator is supported by the fact that she reportedly introduced the sign system to her younger deaf and hearing siblings and to the male deaf cousin. Thus, being the eldest child, she helped ensure the widespread and frequent use of sign in the family. The Navajo family tree illustrated in figure 2 does not include the offspring of the siblings, that is, the hearing daughter and nine nieces and nephews of the oldest deaf sibling (i.e., the facilitator). Her daughter and five of her nieces and nephews are in daily contact with her on the reservation.

Sign Use Among Deaf and Hearing Family Members

Based on ethnographic observations and interviews with the primary consultant, the older deaf siblings, and the hearing family members, the researchers obtained information about sign use among the deaf and hearing family members. It was reported by the consultants, but not observed by the researchers, that the hearing parents could sign. It was not possible to obtain videotaped data of their use of sign since the father passed away following the second site visit and the mother was hospitalized during subsequent site visits.

Fortunately, extensive videotaped data of the other hearing family

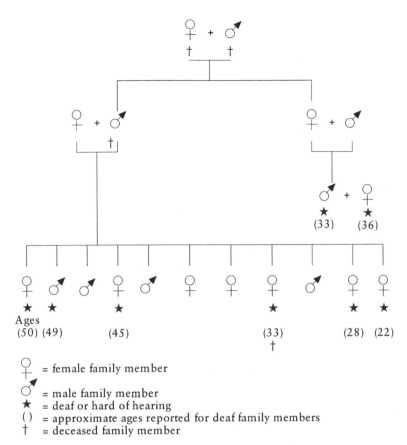

= female family member

= male family member

★ = deaf or hard of hearing

( ) = approximate ages reported for deaf family members

† = deceased family member

FIGURE 2. *The Navajo family tree.*

members' signing was obtained. It should be pointed out that, although one of the hearing sisters and the hearing daughter of the oldest sibling learned some ASL signs from the younger deaf siblings who attended the residential school for the deaf (ASDB), they were never observed signing ASL during our visits. The eldest brother, who is hard of hearing, and the second oldest deaf sister have never been married and do not have children. The other hearing sister and the four hearing children of both hearing sisters also use only the sign system of the family. During the third and fourth site visits, the son of one of the younger deaf sisters was living with the family. Since the younger deaf sisters are fluent users of both ASL and the family sign system, it may be that her hearing son also knows both systems or will eventually learn both. During our visits, however, the hearing nieces and nephews were only observed using either spoken Navajo or the family sign system. Specifically, no hearing family member was ever observed using ASL, even though ASL was the only sign language used by the researchers and ASL is also the reported dominant language of our consultant, the male deaf cousin. Some lexical borrowing from ASL was observed (see Summary and Conclusions, pp. 102–104).

Interestingly, the family sign system appears to be just as capable of functioning as a language as ASL. For example, we have documented on film both the deaf and hearing family members participating in sign conversations covering a wide range of topics other than just their daily routines (e.g., rug making and sheep herding). The family uses their sign system to refer to childhood days, discuss the mechanics of a newly acquired vacuum cleaner, and retell a serious and distressing break-in that occurred the evening before one of our visits.

The deaf family members report that out of all of the hearing family members, the hearing sisters and the hearing daughter of the eldest deaf sister are the most fluent users of the family sign system. They were observed to be fluent users of the family sign system and in many situations would comfortably interpret from spoken Navajo or English into the family sign or vice versa. As one of the hearing sisters put it, "that's the way to make them [the older deaf siblings] really understand; we have to really put an expression on our face and then tell them the way we want them to understand; we never leave anything out." In fact, during Hopi-Navajo relocation meetings, the older deaf siblings were full participants. This meeting was officiated by an official representative of the Navajo nation, and the inclusion of the older deaf siblings was facilitated by the hearing sisters' interpreting spoken Navajo into the family sign system. Fortunately, we were able to document this relocation meeting on film.

Sign Use by Hearing Navajo Outside the Family

The participants in this study also tell us that in addition to these ten hearing family members living together on the reservation, extended family members who are hearing, such as aunts and cousins, and others in the surrounding Navajo community also use sign communication. For example, one hearing aunt was able to sign and participate in one of our visits. Furthermore, several other deaf and hearing Navajo consultants unrelated to the family reported the use of sign among hearing Navajos even when deaf people were not present. The participants in this study described differences between the family sign system and the sign used by hearing Navajo outside the family, both of which they report as being distinct from ASL.

In fact, we filmed the primary consultant retelling a story according to each sign system: first, in the hearing Navajo sign system, then in the family sign system. A formal structural analysis of the two different Navajo ways of signing is currently under way, made possible by the two renditions of the signed narrative performed by the primary consultant. According to the primary consultant, one rendition is more appropriate when signing to family members, and the other version is for hearing Navajos in general.

Both the deaf and hearing Navajo participants described the hearing Navajo way of signing as distinct, albeit related to the family's way of signing. Specifically, there is frequent reference in the ethnographic field notes to "signing the Navajo way" and "the family sign." As the primary consultant puts it:

> I grew up signing the Navajo way and then when I was eleven, I was sent to school where I learned ASL and English. When I would come home, my parents would still use Navajo sign with me. The people in my family would use their own signs, kind of like home signs. There was a lot of communicating going on.

The differences between these ways of signing as described by the deaf and hearing Navajos in this study are presented below.

Analysis of the context in which the deaf and hearing consultants refer to the "Navajo way" of signing indicates that at least a segment of the hearing Navajo population signs when interacting with deaf Navajos. One deaf Navajo consultant who is not related to the Navajo family in this study told the researchers that "some hearing Navajos just talk, but some know how to sign. I'm lucky that I can sign Navajo. I must have learned it way back, but I don't know how."

The so-called Navajo way of signing is reportedly distinct from spoken Navajo and the family's sign system, although it shares some of the same lexical forms as the family's sign. The consultants told us that the family's sign is distinct from the Navajo way of signing, primarily in that the two systems do not share all of the same vocabulary.

When the researchers asked the primary consultant about the nature of his sign use when interacting with hearing Navajos, he told us that "I just indicate that I'm deaf and I sign. Sometimes it's difficult because we have different signs." The primary consultant and the two deaf Navajos unrelated to the family reported that hearing Navajos frequently make use of signing when interacting with deaf Navajos. They claimed that the signing used by hearing Navajos is much more elaborate than the gesturing used by hearing Anglos.

For example, one of the deaf Navajos unrelated to the family told us that "about half of the hearing Navajos know Navajo sign. Definitely not all. But maybe about half. With some people I have to write notes to, some I can sign with. It varies." When asked why some Navajos do not sign, this informant responded, "I don't know. Some hearing Navajos just don't know sign and have to write notes instead."

Apparently, based on these reports, hearing Navajos who are English literate may simply choose to write English to the deaf Navajos who have been educated at the deaf school and who are also English literate. Other hearing Navajos, therefore, never having learned to write English, are more likely to sign with deaf Navajos.

The primary consultant reported that all of his hearing siblings are proficient communicators in their so-called family sign system. Some hearing Navajos, however, who do not have contact with deaf Navajos or with this Navajo family, told us that they have never seen sign used among the Navajos. Further interviews with both deaf and hearing Navajos outside the family are needed to determine the extent to which sign may or may not be used within other Navajo communities.

Two of the hearing Navajos we interviewed from outside the family did report that there are special situations in which sign is still used as an alternate to spoken Navajo. For example, one of these consultants works on the railroad and reported that the Navajo men in this context sign extensively with each other on a daily basis. The other consultant described her grandfather's, father's, and husband's use of sign as an alternate to spoken Navajo. According to this consultant's detailed historical account, when hearing Navajo men came into contact with speakers of other languages (e.g., speakers of Hopi or Spanish), sign was used. Both of these consultants described the use of sign as being predominantly used by male Navajos, although it was reported that the female Navajos could understand the males' signing. Again, further interviews with additional hearing Navajos are needed to corroborate these claims. Interestingly, the grandfather, father, and eldest brother from the Navajo family that is the focus of this study also worked on the railroad.

Etymology of the Family Sign System

In this section we report what the family members have told us about what they believe to be the origins of their sign system. According to the hearing sisters, their paternal grandmother had a premonition about the birth of her four deaf granddaughters. The dream as retold by one of the hearing sisters is as follows:

> When my dad was fifteen years old, my grandmother had a dream. In her dream, she and her husband were working in a cornfield when she looked to the east and saw a basket with a girl standing in it. She looked to the west and saw another basket with another girl standing in it. She looked to the north and to the south and saw two more baskets with two more girls. The four girls weren't talking, but they were all doing something with their hands. She didn't think much of the dream until later when my sisters were born, and they were deaf.

The Navajos refer to deaf individuals as "Diné doo da'diits' a'ígíí dóó doo yadaaltí'ígíí," which translates as "Navajo people who do not hear or speak." It has been reported (for example, Marksbury 1990) that, according to traditional Navajo cultural beliefs, the condition of deafness is not considered to be a major handicapping disability, as it is within Anglo-American society. A more extensive treatment of the psychosocial aspects of the deaf experience within traditional Navajo culture has been the focus of other studies (Eldredge and Hammond 1992).

When asked when and how the parents learned to sign, the primary consultant said that "they just invented it; I think they just learned it themselves." Further, he explained that hearing Navajos "invent" it, "I indicate that I'm deaf, I just follow their way." On the other hand, the family members also stated that the family sign system was "invented" by the eldest deaf sister (the facilitator), who then taught the system to the other deaf and hearing siblings. The notion that "they just made it up as they went along" is expressed by both the deaf cousin and hearing daughter of the facilitator. When asked how her grandmother learned to sign, for example, the hearing daughter of the facilitator responded that, "I think she just made it up, that's what I think, because my mom and these ladies here . . . if they see someone new, they'll have a sign identifying that person." The hearing daughter then went on to show the name sign they have for each family member.

The participants and primary consultant made several other important distinctions in referring to the sign communication systems they use. ASL is variably referred to as "Anglo signing," "the Anglo way," and "English sign language." The family sign system is called "our signs," or "family sign." In some instances the primary consultant labelled it with the name of the facilitator. The hearing Navajo way of signing is referred to as "the Navajo way," "Navajo sign," and "Indian sign."

Acquisition of the Family Sign System

The parents of the facilitator are given credit for creating signs and the facilitator for subsequently teaching the signs to her younger deaf and hearing siblings, hearing daughter, hearing nieces and nephews, and deaf cousin. In response to the question about how she learned to sign, one of the hearing sisters said, "When we were kids, they were deaf, and we already knew our signs." According to the male cousin,

Mostly I grew up with [the eldest deaf sister]. She took care of me. My father would go away, and my mother had all of these boys to take care of, so she got [the eldest deaf sister] to take care of me since the two of us could communicate. We signed Indian sign together. She helped out a lot. I grew up signing with her when she was 20, 21, 22 years old; I was 4, 5, and 6, and it went on always signing. Then I was sent to school.

Even though the deaf cousin and younger deaf sisters attended the Arizona State School for the Deaf and Blind, they reportedly use the family sign system only when interacting with the family members on the reservation. During all our visits, we observed only a few ASL signs and minimal use of fingerspelling in what was otherwise the family way of signing.

When asked whether or not he teaches the older deaf family members ASL, the primary consultant said that he signs the same (i.e., in the family sign) and does not "change" for them. Further, in response to the same question, he tells us,

No, I stay the same. I like the way they sign, so I sign the same way with them. I mean, why teach them [the older deaf sisters] ASL or the

96 : JEFFREY DAVIS AND SAMUEL SUPALLA

English sign? That would just confuse them. I can communicate with them anyway, you know. I just leave it alone. They're used to the way they grew up signing, and I just prefer to sign it that way. I don't want to mess things up. It is hard for the parents to read and write, read English, so I don't change for them."

Interestingly, even though the primary consultant did not enter the school for the deaf until he was eleven years old, he graduated with his own age group and was accepted into the National Technical Institute for the Deaf (NTID). He told us that he was the first deaf Indian to have graduated from NTID. Certainly, in most cases of such delayed educational placement, one would also expect severe delays in matriculation through the educational system. Such delays are well documented in the deaf education literature, even in cases where home-sign is used prior to educational placement. Either the primary consultant is an exceptional deaf individual, having overcome delayed educational placement, or arguably, the family sign system and the facilitator played an important role in his social, linguistic, and cognitive development.

DISCUSSION

One of the central theoretical questions in the field of linguistics concerns language innateness—that is, the biological origins and human capacity for language. Obviously, to isolate newborns from all language contact to determine what the language outcome will be is not an ethical option. In fact, however, many deaf children are born into such situations—completely isolated from a language that they can access freely. This, of course, is due to the inability to hear the spoken language of the parents and the lack of exposure to a sign language. These children are in essence without language models. Therefore, what is the linguistic outcome? According to Goldin-Meadow and Mylander (1984, 165), "a child exposed to no language model or to an impoverished model will develop certain linguistic properties but not others." The fact that children will create a linguistic system without the benefit of a language model supports the theory that language is innate to some degree. Other studies, for example, Singleton and Newport (in process) and Newport and Meier (1985) have dealt extensively with the topic of deaf children surpassing the language models presented by their caregivers.

A Home-Based Sign System?

In this section, we will discuss the fact that the family's sign system, having been used cross-generationally for at least fifty years, appears much more complex than simply a home-based sign system. According to the participants and primary consultant in this study, the hearing Navajo way of signing is viewed as being related, but distinct. When asked what makes it different, the Navajo sources involved in this study report that the family sign is less transparent and environmentally dependent and is signed much faster than the hearing Navajo way of signing.

The Navajo family members in this study have reported that their family sign system was invented by their parents and by the eldest deaf sister. Arguably, this family sign system developed out of a need to communicate with the deaf members of the family. As we know, it is not at all uncommon for deaf children and their families to develop a home-based sign system for this purpose. The situation in this Navajo family, however, is unique in several important ways. We will discuss how the Navajo family sign system does not fit the framework for home-based sign systems set forth by other researchers (for example, Goldin-Meadow and Mylander 1984, and Frishberg 1987). First, however, in order to understand how the family sign system is different, it is necessary to briefly discuss the literature on home-sign.

Frishberg (1987, 128) defines home-sign as "the generic term for the idiosyncratic sign languages or gestural behavior that is developed when deaf individuals are isolated from other deaf people and need to communicate with the hearing people around them." The Navajo children in this family, or course, were not isolated from deaf people, as there were many in their own family. They were, however, isolated from a primary sign language and therefore needed to create their own. The question is: to what extent did their hearing Navajo parents and relatives contribute to this process?

Frishberg (1987) discusses that all true languages are conventional (have a consistent meaning-symbol relationship), are traditional (passed on from generation to generation), are shared by a large group, and are standard (considered the same over a community of users). Home-sign systems tend not to have these features. The Navajo family sign system appears more conventional than what is typically described for home-sign. For example, the meaning-symbol relationship is consistent for cultural concepts such as herding sheep, weaving, Indian dancing, and so forth. The family sign system has also been passed on from the eldest deaf daughter to her deaf and hearing siblings, her hearing daughter, her deaf cousin, and her hearing nieces and nephews. The system also appears standard insofar as it is signed the same way within the bounds of the family. Many of its signs, however, are reportedly different from the signs used by hearing Navajos in the outside community.

In the case of home-sign, the responsibility for the development of the system is usually left to the deaf child. Sometimes the parents may become involved in the creation of the system, but others may stay completely out of it. Again, in the case of this Navajo family, it seems that responsibility for the development of the system was primarily with the eldest deaf daughter. Because of the high incidence of deafness in the family, it is likely that all of the siblings (both deaf and hearing) contributed to the development of the system and all are maintaining it as well.

Although Frishberg (1987) reports that home-sign systems do share some features with natural languages (e.g., individual signs are segmentable, and can be assigned to semantic categories, etc.), they also have specific characteristics that distinguish them from conventional sign languages. For example, signing space for home-sign is larger, signs and sign sequences tend to be repeated, the number of distinct handshapes are fewer, eye gaze functions differently, the systems are more environmentally dependent, and signs are produced more slowly, awkwardly, and less fluently. Some of these characteristics are evident in the signing of the Navajo family members, whereas others are less so, and some are seen more with certain users than with others. A more proficient user is less likely to exhibit typical home-sign characteristics in signing. In some cases, for example, the sign system may appear environmentally dependent, such as when a signer points to a color in the environment instead of signing the color. The more fluent signers (such as the eldest deaf sister) appear to rely less on environment and tend to sign in a smaller signing space than those family members who are less fluent. This indicates that the family signing is expanding from a transparent and iconic system to an arbitrary and conventionalized system.

Washabaugh (1986) has also discussed the relationship between home-signs and hearing gestures; he concludes that hearing gestures may be a resource from which parts of some sign languages may grow. According to the Navajo family, their sign system is distinct from the system used by hearing Navajos, although there are similarities between the two. Evidently, the development of the family sign system was influenced and enriched by the hearing gestures used in the community but has evolved into a distinct system.

The situation in this Navajo family, then, is unique in several important ways. First of all, the eldest daughter was born into a culture in which the alternate use of sign communication can be historically traced. Unlike the majority of situations in which deaf children are born (at least in Western societies), the Navajo parents in this study signed to their eldest daughter, who was born deaf. Further research is needed to determine the etymology of the Navajo sign system.

We have already related that one of our hearing Navajo sources provided an elaborate historical account of how her father and grandfather, who worked on the railroad, used signed means of communication. According to her account, this was needed in order for the Navajo men to communicate with the Hopi and Zuni with whom they came into contact and whose native spoken languages were not mutually intelligible. We also interviewed her Navajo husband, who still works on the railroad. He reported that sign is still used a great deal by the Navajo men working with him. According to him, sign is needed because of the noisy working conditions on the railroad. This is parallel to other cases of occupational sign language that are documented in the literature (Johnson 1978).

What is different in this case, however, is that the grandfather, father, and eldest brother from the Navajo family that is the focus of this study, all worked on the railroad. Perhaps the alternate sign system used by Navajo men in the occupational setting of the railroad was the source for the sign used by the Navajo father with his eldest deaf daughter.

Perhaps the most important dimension that sets the Navajo family sign system apart from other so-called home-based systems is that the former has been used for at least fifty years. As we know, this is not at all characteristic of home-sign systems, as they are most often replaced by standard sign language when deaf children are exposed to them. Clearly this is not the case in this Navajo family. The sign system is still very much in use today and by way of the facilitator (the eldest deaf daughter) is still being acquired natively by the children of the family. Given the fact that the family sign is being used intergenerationally—that is, between both first and second generations of the family—we would expect to see the emergence of creolization patterns.

Pidginization and Creolization

Theories of pidginization and creolization may also contribute significantly to the discussion of this linguistic situation. According to DeCamp (in Appel and Muysken 1987, 175), a pidgin is "generally defined as a strongly reduced linguistic system used for incidental contacts between speakers of different languages, and that is the native language of nobody." A creole emerges when a pidgin acquires native speakers. According to this definition, then, it would not be accurate to describe the Navajo sign system as a pidgin. The system was not used for incidental contact between users of different languages but instead developed out of the innate need to communicate with other human beings.

Whereas some scholars believe that there must be a link between pidgins and creoles, others argue that it is possible to identify creole features without a pidgin stage. Romaine (1988, 2), for example, points out that "pidginization involves reduction of linguistic resources and restriction of use, while creolization involves expansion along both these dimensions." Characteristic of creoles, the development of the Navajo family sign system involves expansion, not reduction. If reduced linguistic systems called pidgins may be creolized through time to become full languages, perhaps simplistic linguistic systems such as home-sign may be creolized to become full-fledged languages by the same principles. This expansion and development is dependent on consistent (cross-generational) use by a linguistic community, a situation that is typically not found in home-based sign systems. In the case of this Navajo family, however, following several decades of use, expansion seems to have taken place (and is still taking place) in response to the communicative needs of its users. Further research is needed in this area.

Alternate or Primary Sign System?

Alternate sign systems develop as alternatives to spoken language when the use of speech is difficult or taboo. The Navajo family sign system also appears more complex than what has been described for alternate signed systems. According to Kendon (1988, 437), in contrast to primary sign systems, in alternate systems "space is little exploited for the expression of grammatical relations, the 'layered' inflectional system is little developed, and the use of so-called 'classifier' forms is not found. Head and face action is scarcely used for the production of lexical signs, and not at all as a means of bracketing segments of discourse to display their grammatical status." Kendon (1988) concludes that these features, so widely found in primary sign languages, demonstrate how the visual-gestural modality may be exploited in shaping language. Further formal structural analysis and description of the Navajo family sign system is needed. Preliminary analysis of the sign system, however, has revealed a rich use of head and face action in the production of lexical signs and classifiers.

In Table 1 we described three major classes of sign communication. The Navajo family sign system that has been the focus of his study shares characteristics of all three types: primary, alternate, and home-based. The system has emerged from specific historical, social, and cultural contexts. Furthermore, in this case, it appears to have evolved from a home-based system into a more enriched linguistic system that is being used across generations of signers. At this point, as on Martha's Vineyard for more than two hundred years, both deaf and hearing members of the community use sign language. Only time will tell, as on Martha's Vineyard, upon the passing of the last deaf person in the community, whether the Navajo sign system will be maintained.

SUMMARY AND CONCLUSIONS

The Navajo family that is the focus of the present study represents a rarified linguistic community within the larger hearing Navajo community. We have described the specific historical, social, and cultural contexts in which the Navajo family sign system has evolved. The family's use of the sign has emerged as more complex than simply a home-based or alternate sign system. Specifically, the family sign system has been used for at least fifty years and has evolved across two generations of users. The eldest deaf daughter, whom we refer to as the facilitator of the system, is fifty years old, and there is approximately a thirty-year age difference between the oldest and youngest sibling. The facilitator has a hearing daughter and has been the primary caregiver for her younger deaf and hearing siblings, her deaf cousin, and hearing nieces and nephews. As a result, both deaf and hearing family members have natively acquired the family sign system from the facilitator.

Based on our ethnographic interviews, observations, and analysis of the videotaped data, it is evident that the sign system being used by the deaf and hearing members of the Navajo family is not based on ASL. For example, although there has been subsequent contact between the family sign system and ASL, our analysis of the data has revealed only minimal lexical borrowing from ASL and some use of fingerspelling. The signs borrowed from ASL are predominantly terms for family relations, food signs, and color terms. Some fingerspelling is used to express proper nouns. It should be pointed out that during our visits, the hearing family members were only observed using either spoken Navajo or the family sign system. Specifically, no hearing family member was ever observed using ASL, even though ASL was the only sign language used by the researchers and is also used by the male deaf cousin who was our primary consultant. During our interviews with the hearing Navajo family members, they alternately refer to ASL as either the "English sign" or "the Anglo way of signing."

The widespread use of sign language as an alternate to spoken Navajo throughout the general Navajo population is neither clear nor conclusive. Only isolated cases have been reported. Deaf Navajos report that although many hearing Navajos do use sign communication with them, many other hearing Navajos reportedly do not. Further research is needed to determine whether hearing Navajo individuals throughout the community use sign as an alternative to their native spoken language, as is documented in the literature for other Native American communities. We also need to study other Navajo families in which there are deaf family members in order to determine whether these families demonstrate similar linguistic development.

In sum, the situation that is the focus of this study is of particular interest because it offers the opportunity to observe a sign system that has been developing over several decades among a community of users. The level of complexity that this system has reached lends support to the theory of language innateness and to the creolization process. Prior to this study, there was no published research concerning the interaction of deafness and sign language use in North American Indian communities. The preliminary research has shown that the Navajo family sign system is an autonomous linguistic system from ASL, spoken Navajo, and spoken English.

At this point, additional research is needed to describe the structure of the Navajo sign system. A comparative study of indigenous signed languages and ASL is needed in order to determine what sign language universals may exist. In this article, we have described a rare and complex linguistic community that contributes to our understanding of the biological origins and human capacity for language. This study has important theoretical and practical applications to the fields of linguistics, anthropological linguistics, and sociolinguistics.

REFERENCES

Appel, R., and P. Muysken. 1987. *Language contact and bilingualism.* Baltimore: Edward Arnold Ltd.

Clark, 1882. *The Indian sign language.* Lincoln, Neb.: University of Nebraska Press.

Dillard, J.M. 1983. *Multicultural counseling.* Chicago: Nelson-Mall.

Eldredge, N. 1993. Culturally affirmative counseling with American Indians who are deaf. *Journal of the American Deafness and Rehabilitation Association* 26(4):1–18.

Eldredge, N.M., and J. Carrigan. 1992. Where do my kindred dwell? Using art and storytelling to understand the transition of young Indian men who are deaf. *The Arts in Psychotherapy* 19:29–38.

Eldredge, N., and S. Hammond. 1992. Distant visions: Two studies of deafness and Navajo traditional life. *Hearing Health:* 10–13.

Frishberg, N. 1987. "Home Sign." In *Gallaudet encyclopedia of deaf people and deafness,* ed. J.V. Van Cleve, New York: McGraw Hill. 3:128–131.

Goldin-Meadow, S., and C. Mylander. 1984. The development of morphology without a conventional language model. *Chicago Linguistic Society* 20:165–177.

Groce, N. E. 1985. *Everyone here spoke sign language: Hereditary deafness on Martha's Vineyard.* Cambridge, Mass.: Harvard University Press.

Hammond, S., and L.H. Meiners. 1993. American Indian deaf children and youth. In *Multicultural issues in deafness,* ed. K.M. Christensen and G. Delgado, 143–166. White Plains, N.Y.: Longman.

Johnson, R. 1978. A comparison of the phonological structures of two Northwest sawmill sign languages. *Communication and Cognition* 11:105–132.

Johnson, R.E. 1994. Sign language and the concept of deafness in a traditional Yucatec Mayan village. In *The Deaf Way: Perspectives from the international conference on Deaf culture,* ed. C. Erting, R. Johnson, D. Smith, and B. Snider, 102–109. Washington, D.C.: Gallaudet University Press.

Kakumasu, J. 1968. Urubú Sign Language. *International Journal of American Linguistics* 34:275–281.

Kendon, A. 1988. *Sign languages of Aboriginal Australia: Cultural, semiotic, and communication perspectives.* Cambridge: Cambridge University Press.

Kwek, J. 1991. Occasions for sign use in an Australian aboriginal community. *Sign Language Studies* (summer):143.

Lane, H. 1984. *When the mind hears: A history of the deaf.* New York: Random House.

Ljung, M. 1965. Principles of a stratificational analysis of the Plains Indian sign language. *International Journal of American Linguistics* 31: 119–127.

Lucas, C. ed. 1989. *The sociolinguistics of the Deaf community.* San Diego: Academic Press.

Mallery, G. 1972. *Sign language among North American Indians compared with that among other peoples and deaf-mutes.* Paris: Mouton.

Marksbury, L. 1990. Diné: People of the earth's surface and "Those who do not hear or speak." Unpublished manuscript, Tucson: The University of Arizona.

Newport, E. L., and R. P. Meier. 1985. The acquisition of American Sign Language. In *The crosslinguistic study of language acquisition,* vol. 1, ed. D.I. Slobin. Hillsdale, N.J.: Lawrence Erlbaum Associates.

Perlmutter, D. 1986. Topic . . . comment: No nearer to the soul. *Natural Language and Linguistic Theory* 4:515–523.

Prucha, F. P. 1986. *The great father.* Lincoln, Neb.: University of Nebraska Press.

Romaine, S. 1988. *Pidgin and creole languages.* New York: Longman.

Sacks, O. 1989. *Seeing voices: A journey into the world of the deaf.* Berkeley: University of California Press.

Scott, H. L. 1931. *Film dictionary of the North American Indian sign language.* National Archives, Washington, D.C.

Sebeok, T. A., and J. Umiker-Sebeok, eds. 1978. *Aboriginal sign languages of the Americas and Australia.* Vol. I-II. New York: Plenum Press.

Seton, E.T. 1918. *Sign talk.* Doubleday, Page, and Company.

Singleton, J., and E. Newport. N.d. When learners surpass their models: The acquisition of American Sign Language from impoverished input. Unpublished manuscript, The University of Illinois, Department of Psychology.

Taylor, A. R. 1975. Non-verbal communication systems in native North America. *Semiotica* 13:329–374.

Taylor, A. R. 1978. Nonverbal communication in aboriginal North America: The Plains Indian sign language. In *Aboriginal sign languages of the Americas and Australia,* ed. T. Sebeok and J. Umiker-Sebeok. Vol. I–II. New York: Plenum Press. 223–244.

Tomkins, W. 1926. *Universal Indian sign language of the Plains Indians of North America.* San Diego: William Tomkins.

Trimble, S. 1986. *Our voices, our land*. Flagstaff, Ariz.: Northland Press.

Veditz, G. 1913. *Preservation of the sign language*. Silver Spring, Md: National Association of the Deaf. Film.

Voegelin, C.F. 1958. Sign language analysis, on one level or two? *International Journal of American Linguistics* 24:71–77.

Washabaugh, W. 1986. *Five fingers for survival*. Ann Arbor, MI: Karoma.

Weil, E. 1931. Preserving the Indian sign language. *New York Times magazine*, 5 July, 8.

Weinreich, U. 1953. *Languages in contact*. The Hague: Mouton.

West, L. 1960. The sign language: An analysis. Vol. I-II. Ph.D. diss., Indiana University, Bloomington.

———. 1961–1965. Sign language films, A20–7–1 to A20–7–6. Australian Institute of Aboriginal Studies Library. Canberra, Australia.

Witherspoon, G. 1975. *Navajo kinship and marriage*. Chicago: The University of Chicago Press.

Part 4 **Language Policy and Planning**

Politics and Language: American Sign

Language and English in Deaf Education

Stephen M. Nover

INTRODUCTION

Language and power are essential ingredients of the politics of every-day life. This paper examines the role of American Sign Language (ASL), pedagogical practices, and bureaucratic institutions in the education of deaf children and young adults within the framework of "language planning" (Eastman 1983; Nover and Ruiz 1992; Ruiz 1994; Tollefson 1991). Language planning refers to "the activity performed by people who make language choices and policies. Language plans are carried out by means of policies that are formulated, codified, elaborated, and implemented once the target language or languages are chosen" (Eastman 1983, 25; Nover and Ruiz 1992).

This paper looks at how American Sign Language and English are deliberately manipulated to achieve social and political goals within deaf education. Historically, language policies within deaf education have been founded on auditory-based assumptions about ASL and English. Thus, traditional researchers and educators have translated the distinctiveness of their own auditory-based experiences into philosophical arguments that have served as guidelines for preparing deaf children and young adults to participate in a larger (Hearing) society. As a consequence, the Deaf

This chapter is a revised version of a keynote address paper entitled "Our Voices, Our Vision: Politics of Deaf Education" that was presented at the Convention of American Instructors of the Deaf and Conference of Educational Administrators Serving the Deaf on June 28, 1993, at the Omni Inner Harbor Hotel in Baltimore, Maryland.

Please note that Preston's (1994) terms, *Deaf community* and *Hearing* community will be used in this paper to indicate "the more generalized group of community has been excluded from decisions about the education of deaf children.

This paper also explores how the mechanism of language policy arbitrarily gives importance to ASL and English in deaf education by providing background information allowing for a better understanding of the ways deaf students are treated, dominated, and represented by English-only educators, who are generally considered outsiders by the Deaf community. (See Cohen 1994; Jacobs 1989; Nover 1993; Nover and Moll 1994; Nover and Ruiz 1992, 1994; Padden and Humphries 1988; Preston 1994.) Specifically, this paper shows (1) how American Sign Language and English are perceived by these educators and the Deaf community in terms of reflection, creation, and maintenance of power in deaf education; particularly, how both languages convey sociocultural information in the Deaf community; (2) how English-only educators produce and structure modes of thinking and acting in deaf and hard of hearing students and how they then promote, reproduce, and maintain dominant-subordinate relationships within the framework of deaf education; (3) how English-only educators legitimize, disseminate, promote, reproduce, and maintain auditory-based doctrines through the established political and educational practices in deaf education. Finally, this paper concludes by analyzing the history and current trends of deaf education in an attempt to determine its future and offer some directions for change and policy formulation with respect to ASL and deaf education. It is hoped that this article will serve as a springboard for the development of policy changes and new program initiatives that will more appropriately and effectively serve the Deaf community and will provide an impetus for an ongoing dialogue within the Deaf community in its quest for educational excellence.

ENGLISH-ONLY EDUCATORS

Within the field of deaf education, the term "English-only" educator refers to those who espouse the use of English as the only language to

---

persons who are culturally and usually functionally deaf: the Deaf world, Deaf culture, and the Deaf," and " 'Hearing' in a similarly generalized way: the Hearing world, Hearing culture, and Hearing people (as a group)" (p. 16).

be used in the education of deaf and hard of hearing students, regardless of whether they themselves are hearing, hard of hearing, deafened, or deaf. Historically, these educators have generally monopolized political power over Deaf people's needs, preferences, and conduct in all social interactions. On the one hand, they have usually "medicalized" Deaf people as deficient, and, on the other hand, they view hard of hearing, oralist, and deafened people as superior to Deaf people who lack competence in spoken and written English skills. They also view American Sign Language as "a crutch, refuse to learn it and discourage its use; [while] the deaf [and many hearing people] believe it is the equal of English and superior for instructing and communicating with the deaf" (Lane 1987, 6).

Historically, the terms "hearing professionals" and "deaf professionals" were commonly used in any literature relating to Deaf issues. However, because these terms are both ambiguous and ambivalent, two replacement terms, "English-only educators" and "ASL/English bilingual educators" (who may be hearing, deafened, hard of hearing, or deaf), will be used in this paper for the sake of clarification. The focus is not on the individuals or their audiological status as deaf or hearing, rather on the language policies they support and promote. The term English-only educators reflects the attitudes and behaviors of English-only advocates as described by James Crawford (1992) in his controversial book entitled *Hold Your Tongue: Bilingualism and the Politics of English Only.* He observes that English-only advocates exhibit an attitude of ethnic intolerance and extreme paranoia about the spread of other languages in the United States; as a result, they have increased their efforts to legislate English as the official language of the United States.

Similarly, within the context of deaf education, English-only educators of deaf and hard of hearing students are threatened by the recognition and respect that ASL and Deaf culture are gaining in society. Such paranoia is illustrated, for example, in a warning letter sent to the administrators of programs serving deaf and hard of Hearing students in September 1992 by Edward L. Scouten, a well-known Hearing leader and educator of the deaf. Scouten has been one of the English-only gatekeepers of the deaf education system; he is a well-known advocate for the use of the Rochester Method (use of fingerspelling exclusively). The English-only gatekeepers tend to withhold information and decision-making positions from the Deaf community by using their internal networks. In fact, English-only educators such as Scouten repeatedly advise deaf students that they must learn to accommodate to the Hearing world, especially their hearing parents and educators, because the world is a Hearing place into which they must conform.

In his letter, Scouten warned school administrators of the deaf in the United States about a two-day conference at Gallaudet University planned for October 1992. As Scouten explained,

> the specific subject will be "ASL in Schools: Policies and Curriculum." This conference marks a dangerous trend in American education of the deaf. It diverts attention from the long established goal of providing prelingually deaf children with the full opportunity to learn and use the English language as a practical mode of receptive and expressive communication, i.e., reading and writing and, if possible, speech. As educators, we must remember that English is the key to all academic, technical, economic and social disciplines in the workaday world which awaits our prelingually deaf students. (see Appendix B for the complete letter.)

Actually, the purpose of the conference, at which the Deaf author of this paper was a keynote speaker, was simply to examine issues arising from theories, research findings, and current practices in bilingual education for deaf and hard of hearing students from a Deaf perspective.

This attitude of intolerance and irrational fear toward the spread of ASL in the United States and lack of respect for ASL and Deaf culture is widespread among English-only educators. For example, similar concern over the spread of ASL was indicated in a resolution made by the Board of Directors of the Alexander Graham Bell Association of the Deaf (AGBAD) in November 1992. This association exists to promote the exclusive use of speaking and listening via hearing aids in deaf education; it also advocates that deaf and hard of hearing students receive cochlear implants. The association is one of four voting organization members of the Council on Education of the Deaf (CED) which oversees fifty-three universities providing teacher-training programs in deaf education in the United States; the three other organization members are the Conference of Educational Administrators Serving the Deaf (CEASD), the Convention of American Instructors of the Deaf (CAID), and the Association of College Educators of the Deaf and Hard-of-Hearing (ACEDHH). On November 7, 1992, the AGBAD board voted unanimously to pass a resolution stating the board's opposition to the use of ASL in programs for deaf students. The resolution was forwarded to Kathee Christensen, CED President, who announced the results of the AGBAD vote at the CED board meeting on December 5, 1992, in Washington, D.C.

WHEREAS the accreditation of teacher training programs by the Council on Education of the Deaf is based mainly upon self evaluation of those programs as to how well they meet their objectives; and

WHEREAS the Alexander Graham Bell Association for the Deaf does not support the potential proliferation of the use of pure ASL as the preferred mode of communication in educational programs for deaf students;

NOW, THEREFORE BE IT RESOLVED that the Alexander Graham Bell Association for the Deaf reiterates its opposition to the standard on sign language proposed by the special Council on Education of the Deaf Task Force. (Patrick Stone, AGBAD President, November 12, 1992)

THEORETICAL AND METHODOLOGICAL PERSPECTIVES

This section draws from Richard Ruiz's (1984) insights regarding the politics of bilingualism and biculturalism within educational institutions. Ruiz proposes that three language orientations—language-as-problem, language-as-right, and language-as-resource—underlie the language planning process (cf. Baker 1993; Eastman 1983; Haugen 1971; Lucas 1992; Nover and Ruiz 1994; Rubin 1971; Rubin & Jernudd 1971; Ruiz 1984; Tollefson 1991). They explain how ASL and English are perceived in terms of reflection, creation, and maintenance of power within deaf education. The definitions of the three language orientations proposed by Ruiz are presented in table 1.

Language as Problem

English-only educators of deaf students embody the complexity of dispositions that view the use of and teaching of ASL as a social, economical, and educational disadvantage. Such beliefs lead to a devaluation of ASL and the Deaf community and favor English-only groups (Nover & Ruiz 1992, 1994). This ASL-as-problem orientation has been present in

TABLE 1. *Three Basic Perspectives on Languages*

Language-as-Problem	Language-as-Right	Language-as-Resource
Where language differences are seen as determinants of social, economic, and educational disadvantage, this orientation leads to a devaluation of minority languages and their communities and favors the dominant language group.	A reaction against the problem, it construes the expression in one's community language as a natural, human, moral, and legal right; the conflict with the predominant orientation is often played out in court.	This sees language differences, including languages, language varieties, and their corresponding communities, as a resource that is conceptualized both intrinsically and extrinsically.

Note: Further information on language orientations underlying language planning can be found in Baker (1993); Nover and Ruiz (1992, 1994); and Ruiz (1984).

all aspects of deaf education for years. Because English-only educators have encouraged and sustained the ASL-as-problem orientation along with attitudes of auditory superiority, they have negatively affected the daily well-being of deaf children and young adults along with the social forces that have shaped the way Deaf people interact in the Hearing world. They have done so by supplying ideologies that justify this English-only orientation in a mostly auditory-based society. Also, this orientation has contributed to the creation of a systematic form of discrimination labeled "audism," that will be discussed in the next section. Such discriminatory practice may threaten the welfare and rights of Deaf children and adults as citizens; it also fragments the political struggle against such varied forms of oppression and weakens the intellectual influence of the ASL/English, bilingual/bicultural movement.

This ASL-as-problem orientation has led English-only educators to develop and shape theories, policies, and practices involved in deaf education that are not based on logical and empirical considerations of deaf children and adults. Actually, these educators have an intense, auditory-based sentiment system. Specifically, they focus on "fixing" any hearing loss rather than on maximizing the natural abilities of deaf children who may easily develop cognitive abilities through American Sign Language. In fact, most deaf and hearing children of Deaf parents usually are proficient in two languages very early: Many hearing children of Deaf parents are bilinguals and enjoy the cognitive and cultural advantages of that status; many Deaf children use ASL as their natural language and English as a second language. Most deaf children of Deaf parents also function better in academic settings than deaf children of hearing parents, who are forced to imitate English as a first language and lack exposure to their natural language, ASL (Nover and Moll 1994). Experience indicates that deaf children, for example, often are forced to spend hours and hours of meaningless training to learn skills using weaker or less developed abilities (i.e., hearing and speech, and a manual code of English), rather than being encouraged to use more natural strengths in acquiring a visual/spatial language, ASL, which could easily facilitate their learning of English as a second language (Nover and Moll 1994).

This language-as-problem orientation is an example of the misguided efforts of English-only educators to help deaf students learn a spoken language and/or a manual code of English that may never really be their own. English-only educators' preferences become the rationale for and legitimizers of the educational direction aimed at deaf students. For example, a common assumption of English-only educators such as Van Uden (1968), Miller (1970), and Northcott (1981) is that deaf "children will acquire spoken English through seeing and hearing it, and that this language acquisition will lead to more complete integration with the 'hearing world' " (quoted in Johnson et al. 1989, 4). English-only educators overemphasize the importance of the English-only philosophy in various communication methods, including "oralism" (see Paul and Quigley 1990), "total communication," and "sign-supported speech" (SSS) (see Johnson and Erting 1989). Two camps of English-only educators maintain the ASL-as-problem orientation. The oralists advocate for the exclusive use of residual hearing and the teaching of speech and speechreading. The manualists endorse the exclusive use of an invented, imposed, manual code of English word order (total communication or sign-supported speech philosophy) in most schools for the deaf (e.g., Maxwell 1990). The main argument used to support this total communication policy held that, since the oral-only method was ineffective, a manual code of English would logically facilitate the learning of English. Since English-only educators have the notion that English is superior to ASL, they perceive that the learning of English tends to bring refinement to the Deaf community and its culture.

The ASL-as-problem orientation explicit in the attitudes and behaviors of English-only educators is formed partly during the educators' training and partly during their experiences as teachers. For instance, they usually are not encouraged to learn and use ASL as a resource in the classroom and to interact with Deaf adults in the Deaf community; therefore, they do not always understand the realities of what it means to be Deaf. These educators, due to their traditional view of Deaf people as pathologically impaired, have long felt that they alone have the competence, education, and certification or license to provide assistance in deaf education. They claim that only they are capable of defining, appropriating, taking control of, and manipulating Deaf realities and providing the remedies needed to "fix" the problem (i.e., making deaf children and young adults "normal"). They always legitimate their actions through the argument that only they know what is in the best interest of a deaf child.

Assessments of deaf students given by English-only educators have produced somewhat distorted analyses. These distortions may stem from English-only educators' failure to properly understand the concepts of ASL and the Deaf experience. Consequently, English-only educators, especially administrators, have maintained and reproduced a model orientation that has been proven deficient within the deaf educational system. Giroux (1983) provides significant discussions on theories of reproduction (i.e., Althusser 1971; Apple 1990; Bourdieu and Passeron 1977; and Bowles and Gintis 1976) by focusing on how power is used to mediate between schools and the interests of the dominant society. Nyberg (1981) argues that "power is unavoidable in all social relations that involve at least two people related through a plan for action. Power is a part of everybody's daily life. It concerns not just the rich and greedy, the armed and forceful, the elected (or appointed) and official; but everybody" (p. 16). Similarly, when applied to deaf education, a theory of reproduction can explain how and why English-only educators perpetuate (or reproduce) the language-as-problem orientation and how schools for the deaf function in the interest of the English-only society. It also explains as well the socially asymmetrical relationships of power needed to sustain the current connection between Deaf and Hearing people in deaf education. Study in this area of power and ideologies between Deaf and Hearing people is badly needed.

The current policy of English-only educators strongly advocates the concept that deaf children should be either exclusively educated in oralism or exposed to spoken English and signed English simultaneously for the acquisition of English skills. In addition, experience indicates that educators tend to advocate the notion that each deaf child must be given a chance to become like a hearing person. Consequently, English-only educators attempt to coerce Hearing-conformity by suppressing (and/or by delaying) the learning and use of ASL and the recognition of the importance of lived experiences, needs, and preferences within Deaf culture (cf. Lane 1992; Lucas 1992). Unfortunately, the implication of such a policy for deaf children is that a very high proportion of their interactive experiences will not be particularly well adapted to their communicative needs. Rather, these interactions will be structured toward the communicative needs of the parents, educators, and/or caretakers who have unconsciously internalized the attitude of English-only superiority. Accordingly, parents and educators do not take into account deaf children's changing abilities and consequently modify their behavior to that of deaf children; instead, deaf children are expected to be like hearing persons.

Sadly, most Hearing (and some Deaf) parents typically gain their pathological attitudes about the right way to handle their deaf children from English-only professionals such as audiologists, speech therapists, doctors, health visitors, and special education teachers and administrators who know little about the significant experiences of Deaf people. Ironically, until recently, English-only educators have not been able to explain or justify the current realities of deaf children and adults in terms of why they, historically, have had difficulty in acquiring auditory-based English and becoming enculturated into the auditory-based culture. In fact, the current deaf education system has been recognized as a "failure" in two federal reports (Babbidge Report 1965; Commission on Education of the Deaf 1988).

Language-as-Right

In the 1990s, we are witnessing an escalation in the persistent tug-of-war between English-only and bilingual educators within the education of deaf and hard of hearing children. The deeply held assumptions formulated by the English-only educators have been increasingly challenged by bilingual educators and researchers both Hearing and Deaf. In fact, more and more bilingual educators involved in deaf education are beginning to wage a campaign of resistance to ASL-as-problem policy by taking an active role in preserving their heritage, including use of ASL and a knowledge of Deaf culture. This active role derives from what Ruiz (1984, 1990) calls "language-as-right" orientation. Increasingly, the Deaf community is reacting against the ASL-as-problem orientation and demanding that the use of ASL be recognized as a natural, human, moral, and legal right and that English be used as a second language in all classrooms of deaf children and young adults. They also want the deaf education model reformed to make it relevant to the needs of the Deaf community. Of course, the Deaf community acknowledges the importance of English and basic academic competencies as vital skills needed for success in education and employment, but it also advocates the need for the Deaf community to set its own educational agenda based upon the actual needs and concerns of Deaf people.

According to Dr. Roslyn Rosen (1993), the former president of the National Association of the Deaf, "the number of deaf superintendents of schools for the deaf has increased dramatically, from about 3 in 1987 to about 15 today" (p. 3). Consequently, more and more bilingual educators (deaf, deafened, hard of hearing, and hearing) and parents are supportive of the "changes in the [deaf education] system which recognizes deaf children's need for early natural language (ASL) competence and for communicative access to curricular material" (Johnson et al. 1989, 1). A year ago, Eddy Laird, Deaf and a former English teacher, was appointed as superintendent of the Indiana School for the Deaf. Laird (1993) acknowledges the emergence of the new bilingual/bicultural movement as a "relatively new concept to deaf education, appearing less than a decade ago. Basically, it recognizes ASL as a language in its own right" (p. 12). Bilingual educators such as Laird endorse the idea that "English should be taught according to the principles of teaching a second language (ESL) and that the ultimate goal of the system is well-educated, bilingual children" (Johnson et al. 1989, 15). These educators feel that schools for deaf students must give ASL the same respect traditionally given to English. As a result, deaf children and young adults will have the opportunity to utilize their first language and learn English as a second language. Conversely, deafened and hard of hearing children should have the opportunity to learn ASL as a second language when English is their first. Children and young adults must be able to use both languages fluently and confidently; bilingualism comes hand-in-hand with biculturalism.

Language-as-Resource

ASL is slowly beginning to be recognized as a cultural and social resource in the classrooms of deaf and hard of hearing students as well as in those of hearing students. A growing number of reforms that have previously been branded antiHearing and nonconstructive favor the abandonment of a manual code of English and English-only monolingual education for a bilingual/bicultural (ASL and English) educational alternative. This alternative fits nicely into Ruiz's third language orientation, "language-as-resource" (cf. Baker 1992; Nover and Ruiz 1992, 1994; Ruiz 1984).

In 1990 two groups of Deaf leaders from The Learning Center for Deaf Children in Massachusetts and the Indiana School for the Deaf in Indiana, with the support of Hearing allies, made significant history by (1) reacting against ASL-as-problem, (2) demanding that ASL is the right of deaf and hard of hearing children and must be used in the classroom, and (3) installing an ASL-as-resource orientation within their educational schools for the deaf (Philip and Small 1991, Titus and Reynolds 1992). More and more schools for the deaf are now considering the development of ASL-as-resource policies. In short, the current policies of these schools emphasize that deaf children and young adults must be prepared to function effectively in both worlds, not just one world; they need bridges between their own Deaf culture and the Hearing culture. Interestingly, Laird (1993) and others argue against the age-old assumptions of English-only educators by claiming that "ASL doesn't destroy or limit the English abilities of our deaf children. Quite the contrary, ASL enhances English in both spoken and written forms" (p. 12).

Until recently, English-only educators have taken the leading role in shaping deaf education, particularly through the established standards of the CED, which are based on pathological and medical perspectives. However, due to political pressure from the Deaf community and bilingual researchers, English-only educators and policy makers are now being forced to reassess their assumptions, ideals, beliefs, and desires in light of new information and perspectives. The CED and English-only educators must consider more Deaf-centered research and language planning that takes into full account the Deaf community and the elaboration of an "ASL-as-resource" orientation within deaf education.

This section begins by examining the concepts of audism, hearization, and protests that provide an analytical basis for understanding how, historically and politically, Deaf people have come to be dominated by English-only philosophies. Concerns over discrimination against Deaf people and English-only influences are not new. In fact, Deaf people from all over the country convened in Cincinnati in 1880 to establish the National Association of the Deaf (NAD), the oldest advocacy organization in the United States. The purposes of the convention were to address such issues as the ASL-as-problem orientation, auditory-based domination, prejudices, and discrimination imposed by the English-only educators who devalued ASL and the experiences of Deaf people (Benderly 1990; Gannon 1981; Nover 1993). The NAD has existed for 115 years, providing support and education and promoting the acceptance, the well-being, and the freedom of Deaf children and adults. For 115 years, much of the Deaf community has insisted that "audism" has been continually detrimental to the social, economic, political, and psychological well-being of the Deaf community.

The term audism was possibly coined first by Tom Humphries (1975), coauthor with Carol Padden of *Deaf in America: Voices from a Culture* (1988). The meaning of audism is attached to institutionalized prejudices and biases that perpetuate discrimination based on the idea of the superiority of auditory and speech competency over ASL. This attitude of superiority perceives hearing and speech as the developmental norm for humans; conversely, signing is considered to be a deficiency. In fact, audism is a problem constantly confronted by Deaf people throughout their lives. The concept of audism eludes Hearing people because they take hearing and speaking skills for granted, and they conform to societal norms and biases, often unaware that they are contributing to the oppression of Deaf people. For example, some Hearing people may feel superior to Deaf people because they can hear (Humphries 1975). Audism, like racism or sexism, reflects beliefs, attitudes, behaviors, or institutional arrangements that favor one (majority) group over another (minority) group (cf. Farley 1982). Specifically, Hearing people constitute a majority group that tends to dominate, restructure, and exercise authority over the minority group of Deaf children and adults (Baynton 1992; Benderly 1990; Jacobs 1989; Lane 1992; Nover 1993).

Audism first came into focus as a problem during the Second International Congress held in Milan, Italy, for educators of deaf children in September (6-11), 1880. More than 160 educators of the deaf from various countries assembled, including 87 participants from Italy, 56 from France, 8 from England, 5 from the United States, 3 from Scandinavia, 3 from Germany, 1 from Belgium, and 1 from Switzerland (Boatner 1959; Brill 1984). The five Americans were Edward Miner Gallaudet, president of the National Deaf-Mute College; the Rev. Thomas Gallaudet, and Episcopalian minister to the deaf and rector of St. Ann's Church in New York City; Issac Lewis Peet, principal of the New York Institution; Charles A. Stoddard, a member of the Board of Directors of the New York Institution; and James Dension, principal of the Columbia Institution in Washington, D.C. James Dension was the only deaf participant at the second International Congress (Gannon 1981).

The same Congress opened the eyes of Edward Miner Gallaudet (and the other four American representatives) to "the real power of publicity and public relations" (Boatner 1959, 110) in terms of the proliferation of audism. For example, Abbé Guilio Tarra, the president of the Congress, was the most prominent Hearing leader of the "pure oral method" in Italy, where he generated a growing enthusiasm for teaching speech to Deaf people (Bender 1981; Boatner 1959). From him, American representatives experienced real audism when they saw that he had "so inspired the delegates with his eloquence that the whole audience rose as a body and shouted *'Viva la parola!'*" ("Long live speech") (Boatner 1959, 110). After long and animated discussion, this Congress passed two significant resolutions that marked the beginning of the worldwide spread of audism. The first resolution was passed by a vote of 116 to 16 with loud applause from the representatives. The resolution states:

The Congress—
Considering the incontestable superiority of speech over signs in restoring the deaf-mute to society, and in giving him a more perfect knowledge of language.

Declares—
That the oral method ought to be preferred to that of signs for the education and instruction of the deaf and dumb. (Bender 1959, 154)

Apparently, the members wanted to further strengthen the first resolution by adopting the second resolution. The second resolution states:

The Congress—
Considering that the simultaneous use of speech and signs has the disadvantage of injuring speech, lip-reading and precision of ideas

Declares—
That the Pure Oral Method ought to be preferred. (Ibid.)

The delegates also passed a resolution regarding the preferred teaching method. The first part of the resolution states,

The Congress—
Considering that the teaching of the speaking-deaf by the Pure Oral method should resemble as much as possible that of those who hear and speak

Declares—
1. That the most natural and effective means by which the speaking-deaf may acquire the knowledge of language is the 'intuitive' method, viz., that which consists in setting forth, first by speech, and then by writing, the objects and the facts which are placed before the eyes of the pupils. . . . (Ibid.)

Clearly, these resolutions reflected the control of a group of Hearing-only educators and the perpetuation of audism. The purpose of these resolutions was clear: to eliminate signed languages (e.g., American Sign Language, Italian Sign Language, French Sign Language, and Spanish Sign Language) in order to introduce and maintain oral superiority. As a consequence, these resolutions prompted the development of educational policies that banned the use of sign languages in the classrooms of deaf children the world over.

In keeping with this view, many educational programs for deaf children have since implemented a coercive assimilation policy aimed at destroying signed languages and Deaf cultures (Deaf American culture, Deaf Italian culture, Deaf French culture, and Deaf Spanish culture). Architects of assimilation targeted deaf children and young adults for hearization, thus denying them the opportunity to acquire their own natural signed languages and to become enculturated into their own Deaf cultures. On the whole, over the last hundred years, English-only educators have successfully reproduced, maintained, and promoted auditory-based values and English-only beliefs within their own ranks. Consequently, they have had the capacity to maintain considerable control over Deaf people and modify their behaviors accordingly. This process is called "hearization," a term that I have coined.

CONCEPTUALIZATION OF HEARIZATION

English-only educators have tended to promote their own auditory-based views about how deaf and hard of hearing children and youth become competent participants in the English-only society. Because these educators have had a significant impact on how deaf and hard of hearing children are to speak/sign to one another in the course of their communications with each other, these children have become locked into an auditory-based language and cultural system. Psychologically speaking, the implicit message that deaf children and young adults receive from English-only educators is that Hearing people are normal and Deaf people are deficient.

Ochs (1990) and Schieffelin (1990) have conducted extensive and significant anthropological research on the concept of the "language socialization" that significantly applies to deaf children and adults. Ochs and Schieffelin state that "[l]anguage socialization entails both socialization through language and socialization to *use* language (Ochs 1990, 287). Ochs emphasized that the importance of "a basic tenet of language socialization is that language must be studied not only as a symbolic system that encodes local social and cultural structures, but also as a tool for establishing (i.e., maintaining, creating) social and psychological realities" (p. 288). She further emphasized that "[b]oth the symbolic and the tool-like properties of language are exploited in the process of language socialization. Language socializes, and in this sense, it is a social tool." (Ibid.)

Within this framework of language socialization, deaf and hard of hearing children undergo a process of language socialization in an auditory-based manner; this is what I term "hearization." Hearization is a process whereby deaf children are forced to imitate and then are directed to repeat the unnatural language behaviors, preferences, expectations, values, perspectives, ethos, and characteristics of an auditory-based culture through spoken or a manual code of English. This process thus delays deaf children's acquisition of a natural language (ASL) and prevents them from fully understanding their own Deaf culture. In other words, this process not only delays acquiring ASL, but wastes valuable learning time and may be cognitively damaging to some degree. For example, in oral schools, children are taught to imitate how English-only educators talk and are also directed to repeat the appropriate way of talking; they are repeatedly taught not to use hands or pointing and not to make facial expressions. Additionally, students are repeatedly told to use voice when talking with their deaf peers even though these peers cannot hear. The practice motivates deaf children (and their hearing family members) to treat other deaf children and adults differently (i.e., in a subordinate manner). Furthermore, hearization leads many deaf children into wishing or thinking they will become hearing some day. Some prefer to be called "hearing impaired" or "hard of hearing" rather than deaf. Unfortunately, deaf and hard of hearing children may learn to view Hearing people as superior to those who are Deaf.

As an illustration, the television program *60 Minutes* presented a story on cochlear implants in November 1992 that angered many members of the Deaf community because of its proimplant bias (see the debate between Apicella 1993 and Fleischer 1993). Ed Bradley, the anchorperson, asked seven-year-old Caitlin, who is deaf, "if someone said, 'Caitlin, you could have the implant, or no implant,' what would you say?" Caitlin responded, "That I want to have the implant. And, also I wish I was like everyone else, you know, but I think I should have the implant" (quoted in Coffey 1992). Caitlin is an excellent example of hearization. (See Lane 1992, for an extensive discussion on risks and limitations of childhood cochlear implants.) Other good examples of hearization can be found in *What's That Pig Outdoors?* in which the author, Henry Kisor (1990), relates his constant struggle in a hearing world. In *Children of Silence: The Story of My Daughters' Triumph over Deafness* (Robinson 1991), a mother describes her journey from heartbreak to triumph in dealing with two deaf daughters. In *Deaf Like Me* (Spradley 1985), the author writes about a family's desperate fight to teach a deaf daughter to speak so she would be considered "normal."

In short, hearization policies dictate that the function of schools for the deaf is to employ English as a means of social control. These schools socialize deaf children and young adults, through English, into the ideology of the auditory-based world and teach them to imitate and repeat certain aspects of auditory-based behaviors in order to conform to the expectations of the Hearing world. In keeping with this, English-only educators place a heavy emphasis on auditory-based knowledge, which is constructed so as to maintain a power base for English-only educators and policymakers. However, Deaf people resent the fact that English-only educators fail to recognize these discriminatory attitudes and inappropriate behaviors and that they permit deaf children and young adults to suffer needless humiliation and psychological pain that negatively reinforce feelings of disentitlement and marginalization in society (cf. Grosjean 1982, Nover and Moll 1994).

THE HISTORICAL PATTERNS OF DOMINATION

The 1880 Milan Conference still profoundly affects daily life in the American Deaf community. The ideas put forth at that conference still foster the illusion that Deaf people agree with the concept that every deaf child should be given a chance to be like a hearing child. Therefore, English-only educators' dominance has been accomplished through the power of illusion.

However, ever since 1880, many Deaf people have protested the way English-only educators and policymakers have organized deaf education toward their own auditory-based interests. In fact, deaf leaders have long been indignant that their concerns and efforts to defend deaf children against ASL-as-problem orientation, audism and its abuses and indignities have been suppressed by English-only educators. Examples presented by six Deaf leaders are provided below.

In 1904, Dr. James L. Smith, the sixth president of NAD, alerted Deaf people at the seventh convention of the NAD in St. Louis, Missouri, that

> The enemies of sign language are not confined to those who decry it and call for its abolition entirely. Its most dangerous enemies are in the camp of its friends, in the persons of those who maltreat it and abuse it by misuse. The sign language, properly used, is a language of grace, beauty, power. But through careless or ignorant use it may become ungraceful, repulsive, difficult to comprehend. (quoted in Gannon 1981, 363)

Between 1904 and 1910, George W. Veditz was the seventh president of NAD. In 1913, he delivered a significant lecture entitled "Preservation of the Sign Language," relating his bitter experiences with auditory-based and English-only domination of deaf education.

[W]e American Deaf are rapidly approaching some bad times for our schools. False prophets are now appearing with news to the people that our American means of educating the Deaf are all wrong. These men have tried to educate people and make people believe that the oral method is really the one best means of educating the Deaf. But we American Deaf know, the French Deaf know, the German Deaf know that in truth, the oral method is the poorest. Our beautiful sign language is now beginning to show the results of their attempts. They have tried to banish signs from the schoolroom, from the churches, and from the earth. Yes, they have tried, so our sign language is deteriorating. . . . A new race of pharaohs that knew not Joseph are taking over the land and many of our American Schools. They do not understand signs for they cannot sign. They proclaim that signs are worthless and of no help to the deaf. Enemies of sign language—they are enemies of the true welfare of the deaf. (quoted in Padden and Humphries 1988, 35–36)

In the 1920s and 1930s, Dr. J. Schuyler Long was a strong advocate for Deaf children and adults; he was the Deaf principal of the Iowa School for the Deaf. He was also the first Deaf person to publish a sign language book, which included five hundred illustrations (Gannon 1981) and for many years was the only such book. In 1931, at the Convention of American Instructors of the Deaf (CAID) Convention in Winnipeg, Canada, he strongly criticized English-only educators for promoting the speaking-only method. He also criticized the fact that there was no certification plan for Deaf teachers and that CAID's certificate was a "blanket" certificate requiring the same training for kindergarten teachers as for those teaching at the secondary level. Long and others suggested that CAID should transfer its responsibility for the certification system to the Convention of Executives of American Schools for the Deaf (CEASD) (Long 1931).

In the 1930s, Albert Ballin, a painter, actor, writer, and also a Deaf man, wrote to rage against the oralist institutional domination of deaf education and Deaf people. For example, he condemned educational institutions for the deaf in *The Jewish Deaf* magazine in May 1923 because these institutions were totally controlled by boards of directors that were composed of Hearing men who never invited "any deaf (person) to their councils to give them the benefit of his (deaf adult's) experiences or views in bettering the education or welfare of the deaf" (quoted in Ballin 1930, 29).

In 1938, Tom L. Anderson, the fifteenth president of NAD, published a significant article entitled "What of the Sign Language?" In the article, he expressed concern over the fact that young Hearing educators "have little respect for the language [ASL] as a noble means of communicating noble thoughts" and the fact that Hearing educators "have taken it up without proper grounding in theory and practice" (p. 120). "Many of them use it in the spirit of the young man of my acquaintance who asks for the tomato catsup by making the sign for 'cat' and the sign for 'up' and expecting a laugh" (p. 121). However, Anderson was concerned that "many of these young [Hearing] people [are] sincere enough, in a way, but just not knowing any better" (ibid). As a consequence, he claimed, "sign language [ASL] is deteriorating" and since "the number of deaf teachers is decreasing," Deaf people "have lost many of the influences which formerly tended to standardize the manual language" (1938, 120). He decried the fact that "the loss of these influences, and the substitution of several more or less unwholesome influences, is tending to bring forward an inferior sign language which we refer to as 'a sign language' more correctly than as 'the sign language'" (p. 121). He sadly observed that sign language "[has] suffered the loss of its idiomatic grace and rhythm by being forced to trail along behind the spoken word" (p. 121). At the time, the policy of "our schools . . . is to address assemblies bilingually (in this case, speaking and signing simultaneously) for the benefit of the hard-of-hearing students, thereby placing "the non-oral, non-aural pupils at a grave disadvantage, not only in the classrooms but in group activities" (Anderson 1938, 125).

In the 1970s, Frederick C. Schreiber, a well-known international Deaf leader, painfully observed how sign language was being repeatedly abused by English-only educators.

The sad truth is that we have chaos. Today in this country there are four major sign languages, and hundreds of people—both professional and nonprofessional—are busily adding to the confusion . . . What matter that a teacher-training program needs to teach four different versions of sign language in order to be sure its graduates can be employed anywhere in the U.S. or that a family with a deaf child moving from one part of the country to another will have not only to learn a new system but also to unlearn the old? This is what is happening. To be precise, it has already happened. (p. 6)

As of this writing, in the United States, there exist seven manual codes of English none of which express the real, authentic perspective of the Deaf community. These were developed and implemented by those who lacked knowledge and expertise in general linguistics, the linguistics and sociolinguistics of American Sign Language, or language planning processes. Research (cf. Lucas 1989; Maxwell 1990; Ramsey 1989; Stokoe 1992; and Supalla 1991) indicates that these invented, ad hoc codes have inadequate bases in the systematic conventions for representing manually either oral or written English, yet are widely recognized by English-only educators for instructional purposes (see Bornstein 1990). These seven manual codes of English (see Bornstein 1990) include: (1) the Rochester Method (speech and fingerspelling, but no signs); (2) Seeing Essential English (SEE 1); (3) Linguistics of Visual English (LOVE); (4) Signing Exact English (SEE 2); (5) Signed English (SE); (6) Morphemic Sign System (MSS), the most recently developed invented code (see *A New Tower of Babel,* 1992); and (7) Cued Speech (CS) (a manual system to provide cues for spoken English). Figure 1 provides the names of the English-only developers or contributors and the years when each code was recognized and implemented by deaf education.

Research (cf. Maxwell 1990; Nover and Ruiz 1992, 1994; and Ramsey 1989; Woodward 1973) indicates that these language development and planning processes do not take into account the expressions of the Deaf community. For example, Nover and Ruiz (1992, 1994) and Woodward (1973) emphasize the importance of sociolinguistic assessment as preparation for policy formulation that has yet to take place within the Deaf community. Additionally, Woodward (1973) argues that the developers of manual codes of English have failed to adequately create a visual system that parallels English. For example, they have not addressed such significant issues as (1) "the existing sociolinguistic language situation in the [D]eaf community"; (2) "some characteristics of American Sign Language"; (3) "successes and failures in language standardization and planning in [H]earing and [D]eaf communities"; (4) "linguistic problems of Manual English"; and (5) "sociological-attitudinal problems of Manual English" (p. 1). Nevertheless, perhaps out of ignorance, manual codes of English are often installed by English-only educators without appropriate language planning.

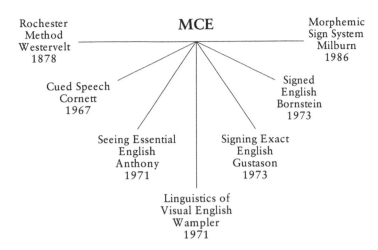

FIGURE 1. *Seven invented manual codes of English, their developers or contributors, and dates of acceptance.*

From this author's experience, many Deaf children's and adults' complaints toward such manual codes center on the idea that the representation of English is more alienating and less human-oriented than ASL; these complaints are often ignored by English-only educators. "Native ASL speakers find manual English awkward and unnatural, and its use is disfavored by the Deaf community" (Jackendoff 1994, 84). Such manual codes of English are only arbitrary and conventional systems. In fact, most Deaf community members feel that one of the goals of developers of these manual codes of English has been to invent codes that are easily learned and used by English-only educators and hearing parents of deaf children. Additionally, one of the reasons many Deaf persons contest the use of manual codes of English is that the cultural beliefs behind them reflect the language practices, choices, and attitudes of English-only dominant educators. However, it appears that English-only educators and policy makers still assert the superiority of manual codes of English and disregard ASL as representative of the values and attitudes of the Deaf community. Evidently, this ASL-as-problem policy is often markedly at odds with the perception of the Deaf community that ASL is participatory and closer to the human world of Deaf people.

The message emanating from the concerns of Deaf leaders and people is clear: Deaf people simply do not feel represented. They want control over educational institutions serving deaf children, curriculum reform to make Deaf cultural retention an important factor in their education, and Deaf community empowerment to strengthen the three-way partnership between the Deaf community, parents, and educational systems. Future research on the impact of ASL-as-problem, audism, and hearization is needed to examine the biases of the English-only educators and to learn how English-only educators influence deaf children and young adults— and how to reduce, or even eliminate, ASL-as-problem, audism, and hearization.

THE PROCESS OF POLITICAL CHANGE

Educators and public officials, along with government representatives, and their studies, reports, and educational research have recognized that deaf education has been a failure. Two major federal reports and a working research paper on deaf education have revealed a persistent and disturbing pattern in the area of deaf education in the United States.

In March 1964, Secretary of Health, Education, and Welfare Anthony J. Celebrezze established an eleven-member advisory committee to make the first investigation of education in the United States under Public Law 88–136. Secretary Celebrezze appointed nine Hearing (H) and two Deaf (D) members (see table 2). Each person was selected for their input and not for whom or what interests they represented. The two Deaf members were Leroy Duning, an architect, and Robert Lankenau, a senior chemist at Firestone Tire and Rubber Company. Duning and Lankenau also were involved with the NAD board. Lankenau was a secretary of NAD while serving on the advisory committee. He was also eighteenth president of NAD (1968–1972). According to Lankenau (personal communication, May 15, 1993), Duning represented deaf-oral groups, and Lankenau represented the Deaf-signing groups.

The advisory committee met eight times over a period of sixteen days. Lankenau states that Hearing members knew very little about Deaf people and deaf education and so spent much time asking the Deaf members questions regarding the lives of Deaf people. The first federal report was made to Secretary Celebrezze by the Advisory Committee on the Education of the Deaf on February 11, 1965. The report, entitled "The Babbidge Report," included "an analysis of the problems of educators of the deaf and . . . a number of constructive recommendations for both

TABLE 2. *The 1964 Advisory Committee on the Education of the Deaf*

Homer Babbidge, Jr., Chair (H)	Robert Lankenau (D)
Leroy Duning (D)	Edgar L. Lowell (H)
G. Franklin Edwards (H)	Kenneth E. Oberholtzer (H)
Winfred L. Godwin (H)	Margaret Hall Powers (H)
Miriam Pauls Hardy (H)	J. R. Rackley (H)
Leroy D. Hedgecock (H)	

administrative and legislative action" (Brill 1971, 75). All in all, the Babbidge Report indicated dissatisfaction with the overall results of deaf education; it clearly indicated a failure to educate deaf children effectively.

In 1988, twenty-three years later, the President of the United States established a twelve-member Commission on Education of the Deaf (COED) to study Public Law-99371 (August 4, 1986). Six hearing (H) and six deaf (D) members were appointed to serve on the COED Commission (see table 3). The COED was authorized to assess the quality of education of deaf students and make a report of its findings and recommendations. The Commission submitted their report in 1988 to the president and the Congress of the United States. The COED report stated that, "[t]he present status of education for persons who are deaf in the United States is unsatisfactory. Unacceptably so. This is the primary and inescapable conclusion of the Commission on Education of the Deaf" (COED 1988, viii).

Interestingly, on the surface, an even number of Hearing and Deaf members were appointed; however, English-only members still represented the majority of COED. Lucas (1989) observes that "the linguistic status of ASL is also repeatedly questioned by laymen, both hearing and deaf individuals who may have personal or professional stakes in the sign language. This includes professional educators and the parents of deaf children" (p. 4). Lucas (1989) provides an excellent example of how the majority of COED viewed ASL-as-problem by including in their report the observation that "the Commission on Education of the Deaf recognizes American Sign Language as a legitimate language"; this statement is immediately followed, however, by the qualification that "the commission has not reached full consensus on this recommendation" (pp. 4–5).

In 1989, a group of three hearing researchers made a proposal at

TABLE 3. *Commission on Education of the Deaf (1988)*

Frank Bowe, Chair (D)	William P. Johnson (D)
Gary Austin (H)	Henry Klopping (H)
William Gainer (H)	David Nelson (D)
Gertrude Galloway (D)	Gary W. Olsen (D)
Dennis B. Gjerdingen (H)*	Sharon J. Speck (H)
Peter Greenough (H)	
Patty Hughes (D)	

*Nanette Fabray MacDougall served from September 1986 to April 1987 and was replaced by Dennis B. Gjerdingen in June 1987.

Gallaudet University directed toward the need to reform deaf education. Their working paper, "Unlocking the Curriculum: Principles for Achieving Access in Deaf Education," addressed relevant research issues and needs regarding effective and appropriate pedagogy for deaf children. Their proposal stirred up old debates and shook up the existing pedagogy of deaf education. In their paper, these researchers stated, "These results represent a failure of the system that is responsible for educating deaf children" (Johnson, Liddell, and Erting 1989, 1).

Today, the concerns of the Deaf community remain the same. These two reports and the working research paper represent the prevailing view that the current practice of educating deaf and hard of hearing children and young adults according to an English-only philosophy is clearly inappropriate. Two significant items of the fifty-two COED recommendations are related to the next question of how the standards of the Council on Education of the Deaf (CED) are perceived. The items are that "the Department of Education set up guidelines that would minimally be no less stringent than CED's" (COED 1988, 97) and that "new teacher-training programs be established, and some re-established, with a built-in requirement for aggressive recruitment, and priority given to qualified members of minority groups and people who are deaf" (COED 1988, 97). Evidently, the COED holds a high regard for CED; in fact, many states look to CED for guidance and have adopted CED's standards as part of their state's Department of Education regulations. However, COED did not adequately critique the impact of the standards of CED on English-only educators who have reproduced and perpetuated their traditional views toward how deaf and hard of hearing children are taught.

The persistence of protests by the Deaf community, along with the failure of deaf education and the underlying issues of power and control, leads to a multitude of questions: Who really makes policy decisions? Has CED perpetuated the failure of deaf education? Are the problems in schools/programs for the deaf a result of the failing of CED? What exactly are the ideological assumptions of CED? Is deaf education still in crisis? If so, are teacher-training programs responsible for such crises? Is the poor quality of instruction the result of some failure on the part of deaf students and their teachers, or of the educational system, or a combination of both the system and the individuals? What are the concerns of the Deaf community today? The following section explores several of these questions with an eye to determining whether CED is responding to the changing needs of deaf children and adults.

HISTORICAL PERSPECTIVE ON CED

The Council on Education of the Deaf (CED) was organized on January 20, 1960 (Brill 1971; Scouten 1984), by representatives who were "mostly oralists (English-only educators) or patronizers of deaf people" (Merv Garreston, personal communication, April 24, 1993). The three constituent organizations included the Alexander Graham Bell Association for the Deaf (AGBAD), the Conference of Educational Administrators Serving the Deaf (CEASD), and the Convention of American Instructors of the Deaf (CAID). At the meeting, the representatives of these organizations agreed to make an effort to "cooperate in such areas as practices, legislation, scheduling of meetings, approaches to lay and peripheral groups, teacher certification and public information" (Brill 1971, 35). At the time, Byron B. Burnes, the sixteenth president of the NAD was not aware of the three organizations' efforts to establish CED (personal communication, May 16, 1993). A few months later, on April 3, 1960, nine participating members met at the CEASD conference in Evanston, Illinois, to discuss the feasibility of establishing CED (see table 4). David Mudgett, a math teacher, was the only Deaf member. At this second meeting, the representatives from each organization discussed and adopted a constitution and bylaws, which were then sent to the three

TABLE 4. *CED Planning Committee Members*

AGBAD Representatives	CEASD Representatives	CAID Representatives
Dr. George Pratt	Dr. Marshall Hester	Dr. Richard Brill
Mr. J. Donovan	Dr. William J. McClure	Mr. Lloyd Ambrosen
Dr. Clarence O'Connor	Dr. Hugo Schunhoff	Mr. David Mudgett

constituent organizations for ratification (Brill 1971; Scouten 1984). The first CED assembly took place on October 24–25, 1960, at Gallaudet College (now Gallaudet University) in Washington, D.C. Dr. S. Richard Silverman, Director of the Central Institute, was elected the first president of the CED; he was considered to be an extremely, indeed, overly zealous, oralist leader (Merv Garreston, personal communication, April 24, 1993.)

Historically, until 1935, CAID was the only professional organization accrediting teacher-training programs and certifying teachers of the deaf. In the 1930s, CEASD took over the certification responsibility. However, on June 24, 1969, "CEASD officially transferred responsibility for the certification of teachers of the deaf to the CED" (Brill 1971, 118, 123). Currently, CED is the national association that establishes certification standards and accredits approximately fifty-three college and university programs (Harold A. Johnson, personal communication, April 13, 1993) for the preparation of teachers of deaf children and youth. It also certifies graduates of approved programs. The CED executive board is charged with the responsibility of developing and validating the knowledge base and skills needed by all entry-level deaf education educators to ensure that they meet the minimum requirements. As of September 1, 1987, the twelve-member CED executive board consisted of four representatives from each of the three member organizations, the Alexander Graham Bell Association for the Deaf (AGBAD), the Conference of Educational Administrators Serving the Deaf (CEASD), and the Convention of American Instructors of the Deaf (CAID). The term of office for representatives is two years or until successors are designated; the terms are staggered to provide for termination of one of the two terms each year. Importantly, each member organization has veto power.

Behind the Scenes at CED

A historical snapshot of CED shows a professional organization whose traditions, structure, and operations adhere to English-only philosophies and disallow any flexibility in accommodating the changing demands of the Deaf community. This author has studied the structuring process of CED by analyzing the standards that currently shape the training programs for educators of deaf children and youth. An analysis of these standards indicates that CED's English-only orientation is maintained through concepts of audism and hearization that continue to support the asymmetrical relation of power.

This asymmetrical relation of power was illustrated by the fact that all nine Ad Hoc Revision of Standards Committee members who attended the meeting in Tucson, Arizona, in November 1983 were Hearing. This committee made the latest revision of the certification standards and submitted it to the CED executive board. At the time, the president of CED was Dr. Edgar L. Lowell, a strong advocate of the English-only philosophy. The representatives from each participating organization are listed in table 5. The CED board approved the revised standards in December 1984, with ratification by the three member organizations in June 1985. The revised standards became effective on September 1, 1987.

Content Analysis of CED Standards

This content analysis provides a means for discerning the ideological patterns of the English-only educators—patterns that are deeply embedded in the current CED standards. For example, English-only educators simply make assumptions concerning social norms, values, and beliefs of auditory-based culture. Such assumptions are described in the CED standards.

The standards contain an introduction and twelve sections that cover such areas as certification definitions, procedures, and requirements (see Appendix C). However, only the introduction and Section 7.0 (Competencies for Provisional Certification of Academic Teachers) are analyzed for their relevancy to the issues of audism, hearization, and power structure. Section 7.0 contains seven main sections and forty-six subsections (see Appendix D). Forty-nine references of Section 7.0 are analyzed. It should be noted that Section 7.0 is significantly emphasized by the CED board through its program evaluation procedure. Harold A. Johnson, who provided information on the most recent CED program information (personal communication, April 13, 1993), is the CED-appointed, volunteer director of the CED program evaluation; he oversees the evaluation panel, which is composed of two qualified and actively employed teacher educators. Like Johnson, teacher educators from the approved list of the CED are also asked to volunteer their time to make site visits every ten years and examine evidence that programs are providing students with the minimal competencies as stated in Section 7.0 of the CED standards.

Review of Section 7.0 of the CED standards reveals three categories: (1) English-only-centered orientation, (2) Deaf-centered orientation, (3) nonrelevant. The review indicates that the Introduction and Section 7.0 prescribe knowledge, skills, and attitudes of English-only-centered culture. The introduction states that CED does not endorse "any one method, combination of methods, or particular philosophy of teaching as being superior or more productive than another" (CED 1985, 5). However, even though CED claims that it maintains a neutral stance, a comparison of this statement with Section 7.0 (the competencies for certification of academic teachers) reveals a contradiction. Forty-six (94 percent) of the competencies refer to an English-only-centered orientation category, 2 percent reflect a Deaf-centered orientation (Section 7.4.5), and 4 percent are nonrelevant (Sections 7.5.2, 7.6.1) (see Appendix D).

An assessment of the impact imposed on the training of educators of deaf children by the CED standards is illustrated here using one of the fifty-three university deaf education teacher-training graduate programs. The program philosophy indicates that the graduate program is based on "the premise that specialized preparation for teachers of deaf and hard-of-hearing children should focus on the understanding of the result of hearing loss on communication development, and the interrelationship of communication with all other areas of development." The program's curriculum has satisfied the standards of CED since 1987.

On the basis of an interview with a hearing professor who is the director of the deaf education program at a research university in the Southwest (for details, see Appendix A) and readings of the data, the data were categorized into three areas: English-only-centered orientation (E), Deaf-centered orientation (D), and nonrelevant (O). An analysis of the courses reveals that 75 percent have an English-only orientation, 12 percent have a Deaf-centered orientation, and 13 percent are nonrelevant (see table 6).

TABLE 5. *Ad Hoc Revision Committee Representatives (1983)*

AGBAD	CEASD	CAID
Garl R. Garber	Henry E. Klopping	Virginia Heidinger
Sandra Ball	Carl Kirchner	Ruth Seth Funderberg
Kathleen Gabe	Carolyn L. S. Bullard	Mary Delaney

Clearly, a majority of the courses represent the promotion of an English-only orientation, with a particular emphasis on the continuation of the use of speech and hearing in educational programs. This curriculum manifestly represents both audism and a continuation of the language-as-problem orientation. Further content analysis of the university's program demonstrates how these courses reflect Section 7.0 of the CED standards.

SECTION 7.1: FOUNDATIONS OF EDUCATION OF THE HEARING IMPAIRED

The university's graduate students in the deaf education teacher preparation program are required to take two, 3-unit courses: (1) SER 530—Education and Rehabilitation of Deaf and Hard of Hearing Individuals and (2) SER 575—Observation and Participation. The program information emphasizes that students should have a knowledge of

1. the physical, psychological, and educational needs and characteristics of deaf and hard of hearing individuals;
2. the effects of hearing loss on all aspects of development;
3. the effects of hearing loss on the psychological, educational, occupational, and economic aspects of life;
4. the impact of a deaf or hard of hearing child on the family unit;
5. current legislation concerning the rights and responsibilities of deaf and hard of hearing children, their families, and the professionals who work with these children; and
6. the history of and current issues in the education and rehabilitation of deaf and hard of hearing children.

Interestingly, both classes at the university are taught by Hearing professors. Also, most textbooks used in these courses are written by those who view Deaf people as outsiders and who believe that deaf children and young adults should behave like Hearing persons. This is illustrated through the use of many pathological terms such as hearing impaired, special education, disorders of language development, diagnosis, correction, improvement, hearing loss, and adaptations of regular curriculum (Nover and Ruiz 1994). In short, these two courses clearly demonstrate an auditory-based, English-only philosophy, along with a pathological orientation toward deaf children.

SECTION 7.2: SPEECH SCIENCE AND AUDIOLOGY

Students are required to complete fourteen units of the following courses: SER 532—Oral/Aural Communication Development and Assessment: Deaf and Hard of Hearing Children; SER 538—Methods for Oral/Aural Communication Development: Deaf and Hard of Hearing; SPH 583—Principles of Audiology; SPH 585—Aural Habilitation: Children; SER 594—Practicum, Communication Development: Deaf and Hard of Hearing Children. With these courses, students are expected to demonstrate knowledge in the following areas:

1. the effect of hearing loss on speech reception and production;
2. the development of auditory and speech skills in children with normal hearing;
3. the range of communicative functions that audition and oral communication can assume in the lives of deaf and hard of hearing children;
4. the function of hearing aids and strategies of selection, maintenance of, and troubleshooting for these devices;
5. the advantages and limitations of group amplification systems;
6. strategies to develop oral/aural communication skills with deaf and hard of hearing children in classroom and clinical settings.

In addition, students are expected to demonstrate the ability to

1. analyze and interpret aided and unaided audiological findings;
2. evaluate and make recommendations for optimal environments for development of oral/aural communication;
3. monitor individual and group amplification systems;
4. use formal and informal means of assessing oral/aural communication skills of deaf and hard of hearing children;
5. design and implement individual instructional programs for speech and auditory (oral/aural) functioning based on assessment information;

6. plan and implement individualized programs of instruction to enable deaf and hard of hearing students to acquire and refine oral/aural communication skills;

7. work with audiologists, speech pathologists, and regular classroom teachers to ensure that deaf and hard of hearing children have opportunities to generalize oral/aural skills learned in clinical settings.

Again, fourteen of these courses clearly indicate English-only and pathological orientation.

SECTION 7.3: LANGUAGE AND COMMUNICATION

The competencies of Section 7.3, Language and Communication, are met through four courses: SER 534—Language Development for the Exceptional Child; SER 537—Language and Reading Intervention: Deaf and Hard-of-Hearing Children; SER 594B—Practicum, Communication Development: Deaf and Hard-of-Hearing Children; and SER 593—Internship. Interestingly, SER 433a/533a "Structure of American Sign Language" is not required but is optional. In addition, the program information emphasizes that students are required to take two, 4-unit intermediate ASL courses to satisfy the program competencies. Students who enter with intermediate sign language competency are encouraged to complete the intensive ASL course (SER 544a) during the summer; however, students who enter with beginning ASL skill are not expected to complete the intensive sign courses, despite the fact that the National Association for Bilingual Education has a standard on language proficiency that requires students to pass the advanced-level exam for spoken language.

In short, twenty-three to twenty-six units of language and communication coursework are related to an English-only-centered orientation. On the other hand, only eight units represent a Deaf-centered orientation category: two intermediate ASL courses. However, a Deaf-centered curriculum could include, for example, courses such as Teaching English as a Second Language, Teaching Reading Skills in a Second Language, Second Language Writing, Language Transfer, ASL Literature, Deaf Culture, Deaf History, Cross-Cultural Issues, Bilingual Education, and First and Second Language Acquisition and Teaching.

SECTION 7.4: CURRICULUM AND INSTRUCTION

The university's program information indicates that three courses (twenty-four units) satisfy Section 7.4 of the CED standards. These

TABLE 6. *An Analysis of Orientation of the University's Courses*

Department and College Courses
(E) SER 500 Foundations of Special Education and Rehabilitation (3)
(O) SER EDUC 500 Disciplined Inquiry in Education (3)

Subtotal: 6 units

Concentration Core
(E) SER 530 Education and Rehabilitation of Deaf and Hard of Hearing Individual (3)
(D) SER 531a (intermediate) American Sign Language (4)
(D) SER 531b (intermediate) American Sign Language (4)
(E) SER 534 Language Development Exceptional Child (3)
(E) SER 537 Language and Reading Intervention: D/HH Children (3)
(E) SER 582 Principles of Audiology (3)
(E) SER 585 Aural Habilitation: Children (3)
(E) SER 532 Oral/Aural Communication Development: D/HH (3)

Subtotal: 29 units

Practicum
(E) SER 575 Observation and Participation (3)
(E) SER 594 Communication Practicum (2)
(E) SER 593 Internship (15-18)

Subtotal: 20–22 units

Electives (O)
Six units in the area of specialization (early childhood education; education of multihandicapped children; bilingual/bicultural education with a focus on minority children and those deaf children whose first language is American Sign Language; elementary education with a focus on literacy.

Subtotal: 6 units

Total: 61–63 units

(E) = English-only-centered; (D) = Deaf-centered; (O) = Other

courses are SER 593—Internship and Internship Seminar; SER 537—Language and Reading Instruction: Deaf and Hard-of-Hearing Children; SER 538—Methods for Aural/Oral Communication Development: Deaf and Hard-of-Hearing Children. These courses provide students with a knowledge of:

1. the different kinds of assessment instruments used with deaf and hard of hearing children;
2. the reliability and validity of these instruments;
3. methods of modifying assessment instruments for use with deaf and hard of hearing students;
4. the effects of modification on the interpretation of assessments results;
5. the effects of the evaluator's and child's communication skills on assessment results and interpretation of these;
6. how to use assessment results to plan instruction;
7. modifications to be made as necessary to the regular curriculum for deaf and hard of hearing children;
8. current educational technology and its uses in the education of deaf and hard of hearing children.

In short, twenty-four units of these courses are related to an English-only-centered orientation.

SECTION 7.5: PROFESSIONAL DEVELOPMENT

The university program information indicates that two courses meet the CED standards on professionalism, professional development, and ethical practices. The two courses (nineteen–twenty-one units) are SER 593—Internship and Internship Seminar and SER 575—Observation (fifteen–eighteen units), and Participation Seminar (three units). These courses provide students with a knowledge of ethical standards in the education of deaf and hard of hearing children and of their own cultural biases and how these may affect their teaching and communication with professionals, deaf and hard of hearing children, and their parents. In addition, graduate students are expected to demonstrate the ability to

1. communicate with deaf and hard of hearing children, other professionals, and parents of deaf and hard of hearing children;
2. participate in interdisciplinary teams;
3. regard positively and sensitively the cultures, religion, gender, and sexuality of their students;
4. be involved in professional activities that benefit deaf and hard of hearing children and their families;
5. be involved in professional activities that develop their own professional skills.

Twenty-one units of these courses have an English-only orientation because the interaction is primarily with English-only professionals.

SECTION 7.6: PRACTICUM

The Section 7.6 practicum requirement is met through four semesters of practicum experiences. The four courses are SER 576—Observation and Participation (first semester); SER 593—Internship and SER 594b—Communication Development Lab (second semester); SER 593—Specialization Internship and SER 594b—Communication Development Lab (third semester); and SER 593—Specialization Internship (fourth semester). These courses allow students to transfer theoretical information obtained in previous and concurrent coursework to an applied setting; sequentially acquire skills in the areas of assessment, classroom management, instruction, evaluation, and professional collaboration; and continuously refine skills acquired during the previous practicum experience.

Analysis reveals that the content of these courses is closely tied to the requirements of the standards of CED. Although the direction is still based on English-only-centered orientation, the particulars of implementation differ. For example, requiring beginning ASL skills as an admission requirement have been emphasized, whereas the standards of CED do not require them. The analysis in the study illustrates that the courses associated with the standards of CED were developed primarily to serve English-only educators and parents. It is clear that English-only educators maintain dominant-subordinate relations by disseminating, promoting, reproducing, and maintaining auditory-based doctrines in deaf education. In short, English-only educators protect their status quo by legitimizing established political and educational practices in deaf education. However, by changing the standards of CED, perhaps this English-only orientation can gradually be revised to emphasize an orientation that will, in the long run, better serve the needs of the population these teachers are being trained to educate.

Behind the CED Boardroom Door

The Association of College Educators of the Deaf and Hard of Hearing (ACEDHH), an organization of almost all Hearing members, was admitted to CED in 1988. The National Association of the Deaf (NAD), however, was denied membership then because of its lack of educational status. NAD was formed by Deaf people in 1880 because "[they] were concerned about the educational conditions in schools for the deaf and about the method of instruction. Pure oralism was threatening the learning freedom of deaf children and the employment of deaf teachers" (Gannon 1981, 62). NAD has been a strong advocate for the educational rights of deaf children for years. NAD again applied for membership in CED in 1993, which was approved on December 4, 1993; their membership became effective in June 1994.

In 1992, two CED board meetings were held. The first meeting took place in San Diego, California, on June 28, 1992, and lasted four hours and twenty minutes. Seven board members were present: two AGBAD representatives, two CAID representatives, one CEASD representative, and two ACEDHH representatives. Five members were absent; Bill Johnson was the only Deaf person who served on the board. (See table 7 for a list of the CED board members.) Dr. Harold Meyers, a CAID representative, chaired the meeting. Dr. Fred Weintraub, Associate Executive Director of the Council for Exceptional Children (CEC), was invited to discuss the possibility of establishing a partnership between CED and CEC. A study was considered on the feasibility of combining the CED standards with the CEC standards. Significant issues included ASL standards and the Deaf Initiative Project.

The CED board had appointed a task force on ASL standards in December 1990 and instructed it to review Section 7.0 (Competencies for Provisional Certification of Academic Teachers) of the CED standards. The board also suggested that only revisions of Section 7.0 and a new

TABLE 8. *CED Task Force on ASL Standards*

Kathee Christensen, Chair (H)	David Updegraff (H)
Joe Fischgrund (H)	Jay Innes (D)
Larry Fleischer (D)	Ben Bahan (D)
Ellen Schneiderman (H)	David Reynolds (D)
Harvey Goodstein (D)	Roberta Traux (H)
Clarie Bugen (H)	Robert Mobley (H)
Michael Strong (H)	

(H=hearing; D=deaf)

addition, 7.3.2 (d) (Communication), be made; these were to incorporate visual-spatial communication in the preparation of teachers of children/youth who are deaf.

The first meeting of the CED Task Force on ASL Standards took place in New Orleans on June 30, 1991. Five Deaf and eight Hearing members attended this meeting (see table 8 for a list of the CED task force members). At the conclusion of the meeting, the following philosophical statement was proposed:

> All programs that require Sign Language proficiency must demonstrate how they use ASL or signed systems in the instructional environment to facilitate bilingual communicative competence.

The second task force meeting was held at Gallaudet University on December 6, 1991. Kathee Christensen, professor at San Diego State University, and Jay Innes, associate professor at Gallaudet University, cochaired the meeting. The proposed standards on ASL were presented by Christensen and Innes to the CED board; the proposal contained the following language, which the task force approved on December 6, 1991:

> In programs preparing teachers for Sign Language environments, students must demonstrate proficiency in American Sign Language (ASL) including both production and comprehension, as measured by a validated instrument or procedure specifically designed for that purpose.

With the task force presentation, the CED board voted to modify the task force proposal and, on December 7, 1991, approved the following language for presentation to the four CED constituent organizations (ACEDHH, AGBAD, CAID, and CEASD):

TABLE 9. *CED Members Attending December 5, 1992, Board Meeting*

Kathee Christensen, President	Sandy Ball, AGBAD
David Updegraff, CEASD	Stephanie Polowe, CAID
Olga Welch, CAID	Patrick Stone, AGBAD
Shirin Antia, CEASD	Oscar Cohen, CEASD
Mary Campbell, AGBAD	Marilyn Sass-Lehrer, ACEDHH
Roberta Truax, ACEHDD	

In programs preparing teachers for sign language environments, students must demonstrate proficiency in American Sign Language (ASL) *which is defined to include one or more varieties of the language of signs commonly used in the Deaf community in America.* Both production and comprehension proficiency in ASL must be demonstrated.

On March 2, 1992, ACEDHH was the first to vote to reject the CED-approved ASL standards. In April 1992, the CEASD membership voted to approve it. In June 1992, the CAID board approved it. In June 1992, the AGBAD rejected it. Thus, in June of 1992, the CED board received two approvals and two rejections. As a result of the two rejections, the board voted to instruct the CED Task Force on ASL Standards to reconvene to make the language of the proposed standards acceptable to all constitutent organizations.

The task force, co-chaired by Jay Innes and Stephen Nover, reconvened on December 4, 1992, to resolve the language of the proposed statement on ASL. The CED board instructed representatives from each of the four constituent CED organizations to serve on the task force; however, the AGBAD representative never attended. The task force members prepared a new proposal for the CED board. This proposal emphasized the following issues:

1. that teachers with ASL skills be aware of Deaf culture and be able to communicate with the Deaf community;
2. that ASL skills are important in teaching language;
3. that use of ASL will provide greater access to content;
4. that a shortage of adequately trained teachers exists.

On December 5, 1992, the CED board meeting was held at Gallaudet University. Eleven of twelve members of the CED were present: two

ACEDHH representatives, three AGBAD representatives, three CEASD representatives, and two CAID representatives. All members present were hearing. Table 9 lists the attending members.

The meeting began at 9:10 A.M. with the newly elected president, Kathee Christensen, welcoming and introducing new members and visitors. Four Deaf visitors attended the CED board meeting: Jay Innes, Washington, D.C.; Stephen Nover, Tucson, Arizona; Barbara Kannapell, Washington, D.C.; and Paddy Ladd, England. Only one interpreter was provided for the meeting, which ran from 9:10 A.M. to 5:35 P.M.; interestingly, the interpreter approached one of the deaf visitors to apologize that he was not an ASL-qualified interpreter.

In the early afternoon, ASL Standards Task Force members Jay Innes, Stephen Nover, Michael Strong, and Kathee Christensen reported to the CED board that: (1) the task force had met to discuss options of how to address the objections of the two organizations (AGBAD and ACEDHH) that had rejected the proposal; (2) the CED board should reaffirm ASL in the same language that had already been approved the year before (Dec. 7, 1991); (3) the CED board should advise ACEDHH and AGBAD to reconsider their votes; and (4) the task force members should be invited to the meetings of ACEDHH and AGBAD. A heated discussion that lasted at least two hours followed, and a modified motion was made and passed by the CED board.

> In programs preparing teachers for sign language environments, students demonstrate proficiency in American Sign Language (ASL), which is defined to include one or more varieties of the language of signs commonly used in the United States. Both production and comprehension proficiency in ASL must be demonstrated *under 1.2.4.A Bilingual/Bicultural, ASL Programs.*

However, the task force members were not made aware of the modified proposal until they met in Gleneden, Oregon, for the ACEDHH Convention, "Building Bridges: From Theory to Research to Practice," on the last weekend of February 1993. The members of ACEDHH voted to approve CED's modified proposal. Although it is not clear whether the intent of the modification was to weaken the task force's original proposal, it does appear that the 1.2.4.A bilingual, bicultural, ASL Program could apply to only two programs: those at Boston University and California State University, Northridge, which provide training in ASL/English bilingual and bicultural education. The question arises, therefore, as to what happens to the other fifty-one programs in the United States. In the late afternoon, Olga Welch made the motion to invite NAD to join the CED board as a fifth organizational member, subject to the action by constituent organizations. Ten members voted to accept the motion; one AGBAD member voted against it.

Mervin Garretson, former president of NAD (1976–1978), recalls NAD's many long years of battle with CED over the admittance of NAD as a member. He states that while CAID and CEASD voted several times to admit NAD as a member, AGBAD always vetoed the proposal (personal communication, March 29, 1993). However, on December 4, 1993, CED's four organization members unanimously voted to admit NAD as the fifth organization member.

In contrast, the inclusion of ASL in the CED Standards has not been brought to a vote. Since each organization has veto power, it may be a long time before ASL is included in the CED Standards because AGBAD will probably not vote for such an inclusion. The situation will not change until major changes are made in CED's by-laws or until the member organizations change.

The CED board meeting in Washington, D.C., on December 5, 1992, marked the beginning of a historical change because "the CED board voted to completely revise the CED standards. The committee, which is charged with the revision process, will be made up of four Deaf persons and four board members (Hearing or Deaf). That means that the Deaf Community will have at least four and possibly more representatives on the standards revision committee" (Christensen, personal communication, March 9, 1993).

Fortunately, Kathee Christensen, the former CED president, advocates the change from ASL-as-problem policy to ASL-as-resource policy by including the Deaf-centered orientation, particularly the ASL/English philosophy, within the CED structure. For example, during her tenure, she appointed six Deaf and six Hearing members to serve on the CED Standards Revision Committee. In fact, six Deaf persons will be involved in the decision-making process for the first time in CED's history. Dr. Christensen asserts that the "CED standards are now in the process of being revised to reflect research and inform future practice" (personal communication, March 9, 1993). She also adds that "the by-laws are being revised, NAD is being promoted for a permanent membership, and

TABLE 10. *CED Standards Revision Committee Members*

Kathee Christensen, Chair (H)	Gerilee Gustason (D)	At-large members:
Roberta Truax (H)	Sandra Ball (H)	Doin Hicks (H)
Richard Stoker (D)	Larry Fleischer (D)	Jay Innes (D)
Oscar Cohen (H)	Olga Welch (H)	Stephen M. Nover (D)
Gerry Bateman (D)		

(H=hearing; D=deaf)

the standards committee will have its first meeting in June 1993) (personal communication, 1993). In fact, the first CED Standards Committee met at the Baltimore Omni on June 25, 1993. The names of the CED Standards Revision Committee are shown in table 10.

SUMMARY AND CONCLUSION

Three basic language orientations (language-as-problem, language-as-right, language-as-resource) have been discussed in order to reveal how ASL and English are perceived by English-only educators. The past 115 years of deaf education indicate that audism, hearization, and domination adversely affect Deaf people. An examination of the parties who play significant roles in the development of deaf education, particularly CED, reveals exactly what ideology controls this institution. In addition, history indicates that CED has not been effective in addressing the concerns of the Deaf community about deaf education. The CED standards have been a key factor in producing English-only educators and maintaining auditory-based ideology and deficit orientation, which are overemphasized at all levels of educational programming for deaf children and young adults. This ideology perpetuates educational practices that convince deaf and hard of hearing children and adults to regard ASL as language-as-problem. In short, CED exercises strong control on the structure of deaf education.

In other words, the deaf education establishment continues to impose an English-only position and "hearization," reflecting audism and a pathology-only view of Deaf people. This is in fact a political position that perpetuates the power of these educators. It manifests a position in language planning known as "language-as-problem." However, Deaf and Hearing bilingual education advocates are beginning to become powerful forces behind political and social change. In fact, bilingual deaf educators have a better understanding of their own social issues, needs, and problems than many English-only educators. The bilingual education position now emerging takes the position that ASL should be recognized as the natural language of Deaf and hard of hearing people and that English competence should be built on a strong ASL foundation. This manifests a position in language planning known as "language-as-resource."

It is time that Deaf bilingual educators take control. The CED structure and standards must be overhauled, and a revision of deaf education must also be considered within the Deaf community. For example, Deaf bilingual advocates suggest that the Deaf community, parents, and educators must work together in developing and implementing "the idea of the Deaf person as a fully integrated and well-developed cultural person by means of ASL and a community of Deaf people [which] is now the point from which to begin, as well as the base from which the Deaf person can achieve biculturality and even multiculturality" (Humphries 1993, 4). Ultimately, all deaf children and young adults deserve complete and consistent accessibility to ASL and to English. This can be modeled only by competent bilingual/bicultural teachers. Additionally, policy mandating ASL as the first language and English as the second language must first be implemented and then utilized to maintain educational excellence. It is hoped that, twenty years from now, if not before, excellence in deaf education will be collaboratively achieved by the Deaf community and CED working together to shape the future of deaf education.

REFERENCES

Althusser, L. 1971. Ideology and ideological state apparatuses. In *Lenin and Philosophy, and Other Essays*. London: New Left Books. 127–86.

Anderson, T.L. 1938. What of the sign language? *American Annals of the Deaf* 83(2):120–130.

Anthony, D. 1971. *Seeing essential English*. Anaheim, Calif.: Educational Services Division.

Apicella, R. 1993. The debate: Cochlear implants in children, Part II: A parent's right. *Hearing Health: The Voice on Hearing Issues* 9(3):18–23.

Apple, M. 1990. *Ideology and curriculum*. New York: Routledge.

Babbidge, H. 1965. *Education of the deaf in the United States*. Report of the Advisory Committee on Education of the Deaf. Washington, D.C.: U.S. Government Printing Office.

Baker, C. 1993. *The politics of bilingualism: Foundations of bilingual education and bilingualism*. Philadelphia: Multilingual Matters, Ltd.

Ballin, A. 1930. *The deaf mute howls*. Los Angeles: Grafton Publishing Company.

Baynton, D. 1992. A silent exile on this earth: The metaphorical construction of deafness in the nineteenth century. *American Quarterly* 44(2):216–243.

Bender, R. 1981. *The conquest of deafness: A history of the long struggle to make possible normal living to those handicapped by lack of normal hearing*. 3d ed. Danville, Ill.: Interstate Printers and Publishers.

Benderly, B. L. 1990. Reprint. *Dancing without music: Deafness in America*. Washington, D.C.: Gallaudet University Press. Original edition, Garden City, N.Y.: Doubleday 1980.

Bilingual considerations in the education of deaf students: ASL and English, June 28–July 1, 1990. 1992. Washington, D.C.: Gallaudet University College for Continuing Education.

Boatner, M. T. 1959. *Voice of the deaf: A biography of Edward Miner Gallaudet*. Washington, D.C.: Public Affairs Press.

Bornstein, H. 1976. A description of some current sign systems designed to represent English. *American Annals of the Deaf* 118:454–463.

———, ed. 1990. *Manual communication: Implications for education*. Washington, D.C.: Gallaudet University Press.

Bourdieu, P., and J. C. Passerson. 1977. *Reproduction in education, society and culture*. Translated by Richard Nice. London: Sage.

Bowles, S., and H. Gintis. 1976. *Schooling in capitalist America: Educational reform and the contradictions of economic life*. New York: Basic Books.

Brill, R. 1974. *The education of the deaf: Administrative and professional developments*. Washington, D.C.: Gallaudet College Press.

Brill, R. 1984. *International congresses on education of the deaf: An analytical history, 1878–1980*. Washington, D.C.: Gallaudet University Press.

Coffey, R. 1992. Caitlin's story on *60 Minutes*. TBC News 53. Riverdale, Md.: The Bicultural Center.

Cohen. L. H. 1994. *Train go sorry: Inside a Deaf world*. Boston: Houghton Mifflin.

Cornett, R. O. 1967. Cued speech. *American Annals of the Deaf* 112:3–13.

———. 1989. *Cued Speech News* 22:2.

Council on Education of the Deaf. 1985. Standards for the certification of educators involved in the education of hearing impaired children and youth. *The Volta Review*. (Washington, D.C.: Alexander Graham Bell Association.)

———. 1988. Constitution and by-laws of the council on education of the deaf.

———. 1990. Approved programs for the preparation of teachers of the hearing impaired. Committee on Professional Preparation and Certification. Washington, D.C.: Gallaudet University.

Crawford, J. 1992. *Hold your tongue: Bilingualism and the politics of English only*. Reading, Mass.: Addison-Wesley.

Eastman, C. M. 1983. *Language planning: An introduction*. San Francisco: Chandler and Sharp.

Farley, J. E. 1982. *Majority-minority relations*. Englewood Cliff, N.J.: Prentice-Hall.

Fleischer, L. 1993. The debate: Cochlear implants in children, part II: Whose child is this? *Hearing Health: The Voice on Hearing Issues* 9 (April/May):18–23.

Gannon, J. 1981. *Deaf heritage: A narrative history of deaf America*. Silver Spring, Md.: National Association of the Deaf.

———. 1989. *The week the world heard Gallaudet*. Washington, D.C.: Gallaudet University Press.

Garretson, M., ed. 1990. *Communication issues among the deaf*. Monograph, vol. 40. Silver Spring, Md.: National Association of the Deaf.

———. ed. 1991. *Perspectives on deafness*. Monograph, vol. 41. Silver Spring, Md.: National Association of the Deaf.

———. ed. 1992. *Viewpoints on deafness*. Monograph, vol. 42. Silver Spring, Md.: National Association of the Deaf.

Giroux, H. 1983. *Theory and resistance in education: A pedagogy for the opposition*. New York: Bergin and Garvey.

Grosjean, F. 1982. *Life with two languages: An introduction to bilingualism*. Cambridge, Mass.: Harvard University Press.

Gustason, G. 1973. Signing exact English. In *Recent developments in manual communication*, ed. G. Gustason and J. Woodward, 38–48. Washington, D.C.: Gallaudet College Graduate School.

Gustason, G., D. Pfetzing, and E. Zawolkow. 1973. *See supplement II*. Rossmoor, Calif.: Modern Signs Press.

Haugen, E. 1971. Instrumentalism in language planning. In *Can language be planned? Sociolinguistic theory and practice for developing nations*, ed. J. Rubin and B. Jernudd, 281–289. Honolulu: University of Hawaii Press.

Humphries, T. 1975. *The making of a word: Audism*. Unpublished manuscript.

———. 1993. Deaf culture and cultures. In *Multicultural issues in deafness*, ed. K. M. Christensen and G. L. Delgado, 3–15. New York: Longman.

Jackendoff, R. 1994. *Patterns in the mind: Language and human nature*. New York: Basic Books.

Jacobs, L. M. 1989. *A deaf adult speaks out*. 3d ed. Washington, D.C.: Gallaudet University Press.

Johnson, R. E., and C. Erting. 1989. Ethnicity and socialization in a classroom for deaf children. In *The sociolinguistics of the Deaf community*, ed. C. Lucas, 41–84. San Diego: Academic Press.

Johnson, R., S. Liddell, and C. Erting. 1989. Unlocking the curriculum: Principles for achieving access in deaf education. *Gallaudet Research Institute Working Paper* 89(3). Washington, D.C.: Gallaudet University.

Kisor, H. 1990. *What's that pig outdoors?* New York: Penguin Books.

Laird, E. 1993. Quoted in *Education: The deaf Michigander* by Marvin T. Miller.

Lane, H. 1984. *When the mind hears: A history of the deaf.* New York: Random House.

———. 1987. Is there a psychology of the deaf? Address to the OSEP Conference of Research Project Directors, July 13, 1987.

———. 1992. *The mask of benevolence: Disabling the deaf community.* New York: Alfred A. Knopf.

Long, J. S. 1931. The certification of teachers. *American Annals of the Deaf* 76:378–88.

Lucas, C. 1989. *The sociolinguistics of the Deaf community.* San Diego: Academic Press.

———. 1992. Official English: Implications for deaf education. In *Language loyalties: A source book on the official English controversy*, ed. J. Crawford, 381–383. Chicago: University of Chicago Press.

Maxwell, M. 1990. Simultaneous communication: The state of the art and proposals for change. Simultaneous communication, American Sign Language, and other classroom modes using signs. *Sign Language Studies* 69 (winter):333–390.

Milburn, W. 1986. *1986 morphemic list.* Amarillo, Tex.: Amarillo Independent School District Regional Educational Program for the Deaf.

Miller, J. 1970. Oralism. *Volta Review* 27:211–217.

Moores, D. 1987. *Educating the deaf: Psychology, principles, and practices.* Boston: Houghton Mifflin.

Neisser, A. 1990. Reprint. *The other side of silence: Sign language and the deaf community in America.* Washington, D.C.: Gallaudet University Press. Original edition, New York: Alfred A. Knopf, 1983.

A new tower of Babel? 1992. *Deaf Life* (March): 24–27.

Northcott, W. 1981. Freedom through speech: Every child's right. *Volta Review* 83:162–181.

Nover, S. 1992. Deaf education promotes audism. *TBC News* 37:3. Riverdale, Md.: The Bicultural Center.

Nover, S. 1993. Who will shape the future of deaf education? In *Deafness 1993–2013*, ed. M. Garretson. *A Deaf American* Monograph, vol. 43. Silver Spring, Md.: National Association of the Deaf.

Nover, S. and L. Moll. 1994. Cultural mediation of deaf cognition. In *Post-Milan: ASL and English literacy: Issues, Trends, and Research*. Washington, D.C.: Gallaudet University College of Continuing Education.

Nover, S., and R. Ruiz. 1992. ASL and language planning in deaf education. In *ASL in schools: Policies and curriculum*. Washington, D.C.: Gallaudet University, College of Continuing Education.

Nover, S. and R. Ruiz. 1994. The politics of American Sign Language in deaf education. In *The use of sign language in instructional settings; Current concepts and controversies*, ed. B. Schick and M. P. Moeller. Omaha, Neb.: Boys Town National Research Hospital.

Nyberg, D. 1981. *Power over power: What power means in ordinary life, how it is related to acting freely, and what it can contribute to a renovated ethics of education*. London: Cornell University Press.

Ochs, E. 1990. Indexicality and socialization. In *Cultural psychology*, ed. J. Stigler, R. A. Shweder, and G. Herdt, 287–308. Cambridge: Cambridge University Press.

O'Rourke, T. J., K. Christenson; A. Goodstein; T. Humphries; M. Kuntz; A. Titus; and M. Strong. 1990. Teaching English to deaf students and English as a second language: Psychological considerations. *Teaching English to Deaf and Second-Language Students* 8 (summer):5–19.

Padden, C., and T. Humphries. 1988. *Deaf in America: Voices from a culture*. Cambridge, Mass: Harvard University Press.

Paul, P. V., and S. Quigley. 1990. *Education and deafness*. New York: Longman.

Philip, M., and A. Small. 1991. The path to bilingualism and biculturalism at the learning center for deaf children. In *Perspectives on deafness*. Monograph, vol. 41, 121–123. Silver Spring, Md.: National Association of the Deaf.

Preston, P. 1994. *Mother father deaf: Living between sound and silence*. Cambridge, Mass.: Harvard University Press.

Programs for training teachers. 1992. *American Annals of the Deaf* (April):194–199.

Ramsey, C. 1989. Language planning in deaf education. In *The sociolinguistics of the Deaf community*, ed. C. Lucas, 123–146. San Diego: Academic Press.

Robinson, K. 1991. Reprint. *Children of silence: The story of my daughters' triumph over deafness*. New York: Penguin Books. Original edition, London: Gollancz, 1987.

Rosen, R. 1993. The president signs on. *The NAD Broadcaster* 15(3):3.

Rubin, J. 1971. Evaluation and language planning. In *Can language be planned? Sociolinguistic theory and practice for developing nations*, ed. J. Rubin and B. Jernudd, 217–252. Honolulu: University of Hawaii Press.

Rubin, J., and B. Jernudd, eds. 1971. *Can language be planned? Sociolinguistic theory and practice for developing nations*. Honolulu: University of Hawaii Press.

Ruiz, R. 1984. Orientations in language planning. *NABE Journal* 8(2):15–34.

———. 1990. Official languages and language planning. In *Perspectives on official English*, ed. K. Adams and D. Brink, 11–24. Berlin: Mouton de Gruyter.

———. 1994. Language policy and planning in the United States. *Annual Review of Applied Linguistics* 14:111–125.

Schiefflin, B. B. 1990. *The give and take of everyday life: Language socialization of Kaluli children*. Cambridge: Cambridge University Press.

Schreiber, F. 1974–75. New signs . . . the pros and cons. *Gallaudet Today* 5(2):5–6.

Scouten, E. 1984. *Turning points in the education of deaf people*. Danville, Ill.: Interstate Printers and Publishers.

Smith, J. L. 1923. Quoted in *Deaf heritage: A narrative history of deaf America*, by J. Gannon (1981). Silver Spring, Md.: National Association of the Deaf.

Spilman, J. B. 1988. Quoted in *The week the world heard Gallaudet*, by J. Gannon (1989). Washington, D.C.: Gallaudet University Press.

Spradley, T. S., and J. P. Spradley. 1985. Reprint. *Deaf like me*. Washington, D.C.: Gallaudet University Press. Original edition, New York: Random House, 1978.

Stokoe, W. 1992. *Simultaneous communication, ASL, and other classroom communication modes*. Burtonsville, Md.: Linstok Press.

Strong, M., ed. 1988. *Language, learning and deafness*. Cambridge: Cambridge University Press.

Supalla, S. 1991. Manually coded English: The modality question in signed language development. In *Theoretical issues in sign language research* Vol. 2, ed. P. Siple and S. Fischer. Chicago: University of Chicago Press.

Titus, A., and D. Reynolds. 1992. *Bilingual/bicultural education for deaf students: Changing the continuing education*. Washington, D.C.: Gallaudet University.

Tollefson, J. W. 1991. *Planning language, planning inequality*. New York: Longman.

Toward equality: Education of the deaf. 1988. Commission on Education of the Deaf. Washington, D.C.: U.S. Government Printing Office.

Van Uden, A. 1968. *A world of language for deaf children (Part 1: Basic principles)*. St. Michielsgestel, The Netherlands: The Institute for the Deaf.

Veditz, G. 1913. Quoted in *Deaf heritage: A narrative history of deaf America*, by J. Gannon (1981). Silver Spring, Md.: National Association for the Deaf.

Walworth, M., D. Moores, and T. O'Rourke, eds. 1992. *A free hand:*

Enfranchising the education of deaf children. Silver Spring, Md.: T. J. Publishers.

Wampler, D. 1971. *Linguistics of visual English: An introduction*. Santa Rosa, Calif.: Early Childhood Education Department, Aurally Handicapped Program, Santa Rosa City Schools.

Westervelt, Z. F. 1878. The early years. Quoted in *Deaf heritage: A narrative history of deaf America*, by J. Gannon (1981). Silver Spring, Md.: National Association for the Deaf.

Woodward, J. 1973. Manual English: A problem in language standardization and planning. In *Recent developments in manual English*, ed. G. Gustason and J. Woodward, 1–12. Washington, D.C.: Gallaudet College.

———. 1982. *How you gonna get to heaven if you can't talk with Jesus: On depathologizing deafness*. Silver Spring, Md.: T. J. Publishers.

APPENDIX A
Research Design and Methods
Interview and Content Analysis

The Council on Education of the Deaf was chosen partly as a source for document analysis because of its significant role in shaping the direction of deaf education, that is, professional standards for the preparation and hiring of teachers of deaf and hard of hearing children. For example, the state regulations of the Department of Education and the universities' teacher education preparation programs serving deaf and hard of hearing children in the United States are established by the standards of the Council on Education of the Deaf (CED); also, CED created an English-only group identity, which significantly functions in the certifying, classifying, and identifying of professionals and teacher preparation programs. This paper also analyzes the underlying ideologies held by English-only educators that become apparent upon examination of documents such as (1) the standards of CED; (2) CED's constitution and by-laws; (3) minutes from the last two meetings (June 28, 1992, and December 5, 1992) of the CED executive board; (4) internal documents of CED, including letters, memoranda, and meeting agendas; (5) the Certificate of Activity Report Summary of CED programs from July 1, 1991, to June 30, 1992; (6) participant observation by the author at the CED executive board meeting on December 5, 1992; (7) information relating to a program for educating deaf and hard of hearing individuals at a university in the Southwest; and (8) selected articles in professional journals and books that describe the prevailing policy trends for deaf education.

The purpose of the interview is to present the author's findings and interpretations on the content analysis of the standards of the Council on Education of the Deaf (CED) that the author has conducted. Specifically, the purpose of this interview was to assess the graduate coursework offered by a university teacher preparation program and compare it to the coursework required by the standards of the CED. The professor chosen for the interview is presently the director of the teacher preparation program serving deaf and hard of hearing children. This professor is also a good representative of the various teacher education programs around the country, has served on the CED board for three years, and indicated a good understanding of the structure and standards of the CED.

The professor was interviewed for an hour and a half on April 2, 1993; this interview was audiotaped, and a sign language interpreter was used. The interview was designed using a question-and-answer format that encouraged the professor to explain and comment on the existing standards of the CED; being confirmatory in nature, it was structured to discover how the standards of the CED shape the teacher preparation graduate program at the university. First, the interviewer asked general questions about the professor's professional background. The professor's career includes experience as a lower school classroom teacher at a school for the deaf for four years and two summers; coordinator for practicums for the Hearing Impaired Program at the university for two years; senior teaching fellow at the university for one year; and professor and director of teacher education serving deaf and hard of hearing children for thirteen years. Professional training for these positions emphasizes learning disabilities, mental retardation, audiology, teaching language and speech, and curriculum and supervision.

Then the professor was asked questions about the CED Section 7 competencies to see whether the university program is closely guided by the standards of CED. Analysis of this ethnographic case involved reading and rereading the twenty-five typed pages of interview transcripts; a five-page description of the general program, including (1) admissions requirements, (2) concentration philosophy, (3) required coursework and practicum, (4) practicum experiences, (5) roles and positions for which students are prepared, (6) financial assistance, (7) support services, and

(8) seven pages of programs relating to education of deaf and hard of hearing individuals, containing program philosophy, program competencies, and practicum experiences.

The professor's program philosophy indicates that the graduate program is based on "the premise that specialized preparation for teachers of deaf and hard of hearing children should focus on the understanding of the result of hearing loss on communication development and the interrelationship of communication with all other areas of development." The professor also discussed the program courses that satisfy the standards of the CED.

APPENDIX B
Letter to School Administrators

September 27, 1992
7017 Basswood Road
Frederick, MD 21701

Dear School Administrator:

Enclosed is my keynote address which was given last June at the Conference of Teachers of English and Language Arts for the Deaf in Harrisburg, Pa. The presentation entitled, "Let's Not Reinvent the Square Wheel," may strike a note of interest, particularly, if it applies to the school or program under your administration.

As you probably know, Gallaudet University will sponsor a bilingual conference to be held on campus October 28–30, 1992. The specific subject will be "*ASL in Schools: Policies and Curriculum.*" *This conference marks a dangerous trend in American education* of the deaf. It diverts attention from the long established goal of providing prelingually deaf children with the full opportunity to learn and use the English language as a practical mode of receptive and expressive communication, i.e., reading and writing and, if possible, speech. As educators, we must remember that English is the key to all academic, technical, economic and social disciplines in the workaday world which awaits our prelingually deaf students.

In my 16 years of teaching Preparatory English at Gallaudet College, our average entering student, at that time, had a minimal reading achievement score of 9th grade, while many exceeded that level. Today, the average entering students, of 17 or 18 years of age, have a 3rd to 4th grade reading level. These young people also have great trouble writing simple sentences.

It was a similar circumstance in 1868 that prompted Dr. E. M. Gallaudet to present his thoughts on English instruction to the Conference of Principals, our present day CEASD. It is, indeed, my belief that Dr. Gallaudet's message is as relevant to the English reading and writing predicament of today's prelingually deaf students as it was for those students of 124 years ago.

While I am no longer an active educator of the deaf, my interest in prelingually deaf children and their English learning environment possibilities, is as strong as ever. With a thoughtful and concerted effort, school for the deaf administrators could raise the English reading and writing levels of their pupils through environmental assistance and thereby, at the same time, raise the whole of their academic standards as well. As an aside, Gallaudet University and the National Technical Institute for the Deaf would be eternally grateful.

Should you deem the effort urged by Dr. Gallaudet to be "worth the salt" today, I would like to be a voluntary part of your effort, in any way possible.

Sincerely yours,

Edward L. Scouten
Professor Emeritus
NTID at RIT

Council on Education of the Deaf Standards

Section 7 of the CED Standards

7.0 *Competencies For Provisional Certification of Academic Teachers Addendum to 7.0* (December, 1990)
Teacher training programs will ensure that courses and curriculum on both the undergraduate and graduate levels reflect ethnic and multicultural issues related to deafness, education, and general development.

7.0 *Competencies for Provisional Certification of Academic Teachers.*
In order for teachers to work effectively with hearing-impaired children, they must possess knowledge and skills in several core areas. The development and evaluation of these skills and knowledge are the responsibility of approved teacher preparation centers. The following outline contains the basic areas of knowledge and the competencies within those areas required for provisional certification.

7.1 *Foundations of Education of the Hearing Impaired*

    7.1.1 Historical and current developments in education of the hearing impaired in the United States and other countries and the influence of historical developments upon the current state of the field.

    7.1.2 National and local issues, trends, and events that influence the education of hearing-impaired children.

    7.1.3 The purposes and services of national, state, and local organizations and government agencies concerned with the education and welfare of the hearing impaired.

    7.1.4 National, regional, and local education programs for the hearing impaired; the variety of educational settings and service delivery models; and the roles and responsibilities of personnel in the various settings.

    7.1.5 The status of hearing-impaired people in today's society and their specific needs in the affective domain.

    7.1.6 Implications of hearing impairment for the psychological, sociological, vocational, and educational development of hearing-impaired individuals; and the range of support services available for use in educational planning.

    7.1.7 Techniques for responding to questions, problems, and issues as described by parents of hearing-impaired children.

    7.1.8 Methods for giving basic guidance and providing a support system for referrals for additional

assistance needed by
parents.

7.1.9 Content and nature,
issues, and trends of fields
and professions related to
education of the hearing
impaired, such as regular
education, special
education, audiology, and
educational psychology;
and the contributions of
these fields to education
for the hearing impaired.

7.1.10 Methods for locating and
utilizing resources,
reference materials, and
professional literature in
the education of the
hearing impaired and in
related fields.

7.2 *Speech Science and Audiology*

7.2.1 *Speech Science*

7.2.1 (a) Human speech,
auditory, and visual
mechanisms and related
brain and central nervous
system structures;
anatomy of these mecha-
nisms, their interrelated-
ness, common pathologies
affecting these mecha-
nisms, and the functioning
of these mechanisms in
communicative and other
types of behavior in both
intact and defective
organism.

7.2.1 (b) Production, transmis-
sion, and reception of
speech sounds and other
sounds; physical and
psychophysical character-
istics of sound; and
methods of displaying and

graphically representing
these characteristics.

7.2.1 (c) General and specific
effects of hearing impairment upon the production
of speech and the recep-
tion of speech and other
sounds.

7.2.2 *Audiology*

7.2.2 (a) Various procedures for
testing hearing and
interesting hearing test
results.

7.2.2 (b) Characteristics of
various types of amplification equipment and their
application to learning and
instructional processes.

7.3. *Language and Communication*

7.3.1 *Language*

7.3.1 (a) The structure of the
English language (linguistics), the acquisition and
use of language
(psycholinguistics), and
the implications of these
areas for education of
hearing-impaired infants,
children, and young
adults.

7.3.1 (b) Research and other
literature on language of
the hearing impaired.

7.3.1 (c) Acquisition and
development of language
in normal-hearing and
hearing impaired infants,
children, and youth.

7.3.1 (d) Disorders of language
development.

7.3.1 (e) Commonly used
methods and procedures
of language instruction for
hearing-impaired children

and youth.

7.3.1 (f) Techniques for utilizing appropriate instructional procedures to effect language learning in hearing-impaired students and for diagnosing, correcting, and improving language.

7.3.2 *Communication*

7.3.2 (a) Communication processes and the effects of hearing loss on communication.

7.3.2 (b) Research and other literature on communication of the hearing impaired.

7.3.2 (c) Various modes of communication (e.g., reading, writing, speechreading, auditory perception, speech, fingerspelling, sign language) used in teaching hearing-impaired individuals; methods, procedures, and materials used in teaching these modes of communication, including the use of techniques and materials appropriate to individuals or groups in the development, diagnosis, correction, and improvement of communication.

7.3.3 *Reading*

7.3.3 (a) Methods of teaching reading in general education.

7.3.3 (b) Special assessment and instructional procedures for teaching reading to hearing-impaired students.

7.4 *Curriculum and Instruction*

7.4.1 The purpose and nature of curriculum and its relation to learning and instructional processes.

7.4.2 Curriculum and instructional procedures common to education of the hearing impaired and regular education; adaptations of regular curriculum and instructional procedures for the hearing impaired; and aspects of curriculum and instruction unique to education of the hearing impaired.

7.4.3 Methods for planning, implementing, and evaluating learning experiences for individuals and groups in order to:

7.4.3 (a) identify learner entry level;

7.4.3 (b) conceptualize and formulate objectives in behavioral terms;

7.4.3 (c) design methods of evaluation based upon measurable objectives and utilize data collection procedures;

7.4.3 (d) select, design, produce, and utilize media, materials, and resources appropriate to learner behavior and lesson objectives;

7.4.3 (e) implement appropriate instructional procedures; and

7.4.3 (f) evaluate learner responses and revise

instruction appropriately.

7.4.4 Use of diagnostic instruments in programs for the hearing impaired to order to:

7.4.4 (a) interpret assessment and diagnostic information; and

7.4.4 (b) translate the diagnostic information into curriculum.

7.4.5 Current educational technology, such as computers and TDDs, applicable to the hearing impaired.

7.4.6 Behavior management techniques.

7.4.7 Methods of planning and organizing curriculum content in an area of specialization for effective learning by individuals and groups of hearing-impaired students.

7.5 *Professional Development*

7.5.1 Ethical behavior and the application of ethical standards in the education of the hearing impaired.

7.5.2 Effective use of paraprofessionals (teacher aides, volunteers, students, parents, and other assistants).

7.5.3 Methods of effective participation within a team of professionals.

7.5.4 Communication skills effective with other professionals, hearing-impaired children and youth, and parents of hearing-impaired students.

7.6 *Practicum*
Observation participation, clinical practice, and student teaching to develop familiary with:

7.6.1 facilities, services, and programs available for the education and counseling of hearing-impaired children and adults;

7.6.2 effective interaction strategies to use in learning situations with hearing-impaired individuals or groups at one or more teaching levels.

Language and Learning in a Deaf Education

Classroom: Practice and Paradox

Mary Ann La Bue

The relationship between language and learning is interwoven in any classroom, but for deaf students it has most often functioned to impede academic success, not secure it. This ethnographic microanalysis focuses on the language practices of one hearing teacher and the educational and linguistic context within which they take place in a middle school for the deaf. I have attempted to tease apart the rationale that drives a teacher to make particular linguistic and curricular decisions in a reading lesson. My findings reveal a chain of ideological paradoxes and circular thinking that make it possible for a teacher to continue a linguistic practice that she acknowledges as inherently flawed, limiting her students' access to meaningful content.

These paradoxes include situations in which well-intentioned teachers speak to deaf students, who in turn, are expected to understand and appreciate the complexities of a spoken and written language they do not adequately know. Underlying these incongruities is a misguided logic that upholds these practices. In order to understand these paradoxes, I have examined three principal domains: (a) the context of deaf education from the viewpoint of one classroom; (b) the linguistic interaction, particularly the interplay between speech and sign; and (c) the incongruities embroiled in a teacher's practice that exist as a result of the interplay.

The purpose of this paper is to highlight one teacher's dedication and determination to teach reading to deaf children and to underscore the linguistic and contextual obstacles that constrain even the most honorable and well-intentioned efforts to improve the quality of education for deaf children. Anne MacKenzie[1] worked to make the best out of existing realities embedded within disturbing paradoxes of deaf education.

1. I have used pseudonyms for the school and persons discussed in this paper.

Anne, like most teachers of the deaf, is charged with a futile task: to teach deaf children in a language they do not understand because they cannot hear it. We shared the belief in the importance of clear and competent communication. Anne admitted that she has often observed teachers who are neither clear nor competent:

Communication with the kids in the classroom is *so* important, and a *big* part of that is signing. I don't see a lot of competence. . . . I don't see the awareness that it is important to communicate with kids in a clear way. . . . I see teachers teach, and I would probably say the same things about myself sometimes, unless I try to be really aware that if this kid is not picking up my (or whoever's teaching) voice, how in the hell are they understanding what is going on with just looking at those sign[s]? Those signs. No voice is carrying the expression. I don't even think that people are aware of it.

I argue in this paper that a simple awareness of the importance of clear and effective communication is not sufficient to change long-standing language practices in the classroom. One reason seems to be that there is little support for alternative approaches at hand. There are a few schools across the United States beginning to implement versions of bilingual/bicultural programs in ASL and English.[2]

Speaking and signing simultaneously is supported in the school in which Anne teaches. Allen and Karchmer (1990) report that an average of eighty percent of teachers in schools for the deaf sign and speak during academic instruction. Ninety-one percent of students in residential programs speak and sign in class. Allen and Karchmer found that "virtually none of the students, except those in residential schools, had signing teachers who did not use simultaneous communication. In residential schools, 11 percent had teachers who reported [signing only without lip movements]. Linguistically, these findings imply a low rate of possible ASL use in the classroom" (p. 54).

Speaking English with supporting signs is routine practice in virtually

2. The California School for the Deaf in Fremont, the Learning Center in Framingham, Massachusetts, and the Indiana School for the Deaf are in advanced stages of implementing bilingual/bicultural programs for deaf children. Teacher education programs at Gallaudet University and Boston University incorporate ASL and deaf studies into their curriculum.

every school for the deaf in the United States. Anne is by no means an isolated case. A detailed look at what goes on in one teacher's classroom, then, will provide useful insight into common practice in deaf education today.

The history of deaf students' poor academic achievement (Allen 1986) indicates a problem in the definition of appropriate academic and linguistic classroom environments for these students. I believe it will be teachers like Anne MacKenize who will pave the way for reform. She opened her classroom to me and my videocamera, knowing that she and I would later discuss and analyze her methods and language practices in teaching deaf children to read. She spoke openly and honestly about her own strengths and concerns as a teacher of deaf children, knowing that the present state of educating deaf children is largely unacceptable. She is working within a system that is slowly trying new ways to address the relatively low achievement levels of deaf students and is dedicated to improving the quality of her students' education.[3]

What is the pedagogical and linguistic context within which a teacher of the deaf functions? How does the linguistic system that Anne uses work to convey specific curricular content? How does Anne make sense of the linguistic system that she uses, given the educational context within which she works? In order to answer these questions, I provide a broad description and analysis of the school, the classroom, and the literature lesson within which Anne's linguistic practice occurs. In this section, I describe and discuss my method qualitatively and my linguistic data collection and analysis.

METHODS

Entry to the Field

Anne participated in a preliminary study in which I examined students' access to curricular content. My findings revealed bits and pieces of con-

---

3. For the purposes of this paper, it was not necessary to test the students for their reading achievement levels. They are not doing the work of hearing students their age. Although many factors contribute to any child's academic achievement, one factor that is usually taken for granted is that the child and the teacher are using a common language in the classroom. In general, deaf children do not enjoy this condition.

tent that students received given Anne's use of a mixture of signed and spoken English. By the end of the study, I wanted to look more closely at *how* Anne presented curricular content and what she thought about her own language practices.

Data Collection

OBSERVATIONS

I observed six one-hour literature lessons over two months, five of which were videotaped. I wrote detailed field notes and analytic memos of each observation as I watched the replay of Anne's lessons. These fieldnotes and memos informed each interview session.

INTERVIEWS

Anne and I met for eight hour-long semistructured interviews. I audiotaped, transcribed, and wrote analytic memos on each interview. During the interviews, Anne and I watched portions of the videotape of the reading lesson in which Anne provided description, interpretation, and analysis of events. For each interview, I prepared an interview guide based on issues and questions of classroom language that surfaced as I observed her lessons and read our transcripts. This interview setting also helped us to compare and contrast her ideas about language and literacy with her actual classroom practice.

DOCUMENTS

I obtained handouts and notes from weekly middle school literacy meetings. These were helpful in understanding basic ideas behind story grammar (the middle school's approach to teaching literature) and the emphasis that the middle school teachers placed on language learning. I used two of these handouts, "Minimal Ingredients for a Good Story" and "Narrative Devices [and corresponding] Linguistic Representation," as a guide for the microanalysis of Anne's signing.

Data Analysis

OBSERVATIONS AND INTERVIEWS

I examined observation fieldnotes, interview transcripts, and analytic memos throughout the data collection. This initial analysis shaped the content of our interviews from which emerged Anne's perceptions of deaf and hearing children's acquisition of ASL and English, their acquisition of written English, her own role in creating a natural language environment for her students, and the influences of her educational and professional background. Naturally, these perceptions are deeply connected and interwoven throughout her practice and philosophy of teaching.

I compared and contrasted Anne's thinking about language with her actual practice during lessons. As a result of studying her thinking based on these interviews, I traced what I found to be circular logic that seemed to explain how Anne could maintain and facilitate her language practices even though she may not wholly believe in their value.

LINGUISTIC ANALYSIS

One of Anne's primary objectives in her literature lessons was to make episode structure of stories explicit to her students. Based on her definition of episode structure (a set of events whose meaning is linked and encoded within the grammatical structure of the verb phrase), I looked specifically at tense differences, which indicate scene setting and scene moving within stories (Gordon 1989, 56).

This three-part descriptive analysis focused on the lexical and syntactic contributions to event structure of the same segment of written, spoken, and signed narrative text. For each modality, I mapped out the event structure of the narrative in a tree diagram. I then traced each part of the event structure to its grammatical representation in the sentence (see Appendix A). This design permitted me to do a systematic comparison across different modalities representing the same text. The analysis provided a basis from which to investigate the relative transferability of linguistic representation of narrative devices from spoken English to a signed representation of English. I was then able to understand more fully the inherent linguistic variables and obstacles present as Anne attempted to teach episode structure.

My claim in this paper, generated from a working hypothesis from my own teaching experience and current research,[4] is that the linguistic structure of sign—when used while speaking—is constrained and overruled by the speech to the extent that its capacity for presenting systematic syntactic structure and conveying complex curricular content is significantly limited. My analysis supported this hypothesis.

4. The attempt to systematically sign a spoken language dates back as early as 1776 to the work of Abbé Charles Michel de l'Epée in France. This method

Anne's second year in the classroom brought with it the trials and tribulations of most new teachers. She volunteered to talk about how the perceptions of language and literacy that she had brought with her were maintained and/or altered as she gained teaching experience. In addition, she volunteered to take a close look at what she presented to her students and how she presented it. She literally saw herself on video, continually questioned her assumptions about how deaf children acquire and develop language and learn to read. I admired her openness to this project as she struggled with me to think beyond her own—and her school's—good intentions as we examined her linguistic performance, questioned its value, and considered why she maintains these language practices.

This methodology, which allowed us to identify links between teaching philosophy and practice, also produced emotional tension. As Anne and I scrutinized her language practices and rationale for them, Anne could see that many of her intentions were not conveyed in her signs, the primary modality accessible to her students. In this process, I also tacitly scrutinized Anne's professional self: it is her language practice that contributes to deaf children's low achievement: they cannot learn adequately from the signs that they see, and they cannot make enough sense of the spoken language that she uses because they cannot hear it. I believe Anne perceived this experience by recognizing, with trepidation, as getting at the heart of whether she was a good teacher as we explored the consistency of her intentions and her practice. Anne and I both felt the emotional weight of this detailed scrutiny. We both felt it critical, then, to explore not only specific language practices, but also the context within which she works, the influences of her school and colleagues, and her prior education. Next, I explore this context and provide a glimpse into the nature and substance of literature lessons.

---

has been abandoned and rediscovered throughout the centuries. Linguistic studies show that pieces of both modalities are dropped, resulting in neither one being very comprehensible (see Johnson, Liddell, and Erting 1989; Kluwin 1981, on junior high teachers; Marmor and Petitto 1979, on high school teachers; Strong, Charlson, and Gold 1987, on elementary school teachers; Swisher 1984, on hearing parents).

The purpose of this section is to provide a context for understanding the nature of the literature lessons within which Anne's linguistic performance occurred. I include a brief description of (a) the school, (b) Anne's professional and educational background that contribute to her language practice, (c) the format, focus, and intent of her literature lessons, and (d) Anne's mixed views about how to best present stories to her students.

Imagine, now, entering the long, one-story cement building that is the New England School for the Deaf (NESD).

The School

When I first entered NESD and walked down the narrow, carpeted halls with their low ceilings, I was struck by the extraordinary murals displayed throughout the school. Near the building entrance was a three-dimensional mural consisting of an accordion-like arrangment of long pieces of wood. Looking at it from one angle the message is: THE DEAF CAN DO ANYTHING. I moved around to the other side to see the rest of the message: EXCEPT HEAR. This now-famous quote from I. King Jordan, the deaf president of Gallaudet University,[5] became significant to me as I explored the linguistic paradox of speaking to deaf children who do not hear.

On my way to the middle school, I passed the lower school and heard the familiar, though disturbing, sound of teachers talking to their students. Trying to sign while speaking most often slows down and distorts speech, particularly if the speaker is a new or struggling signer. The tendency is to elongate the vowels in every word in order for the hands to "catch up" with what is being said. The result is something like, "Okaaaay, nooow weee aaare reaaadyy fooor luunch. Pleeease staaand uuup." Not all teachers talk like this, but it was prevalent as I walked down the hall toward the middle school and reminiscent of the many deaf schools I have worked in and visited.

5. I. King Jordan is the first deaf president of Gallaudet University, the only four-year liberal arts university for deaf people in the world. He was appointed in 1988 after a week-long student revolt protesting the appointment of a hearing woman with limited knowledge of the language and culture of deaf people.

The Middle School

Passing the lower school, I turned the corner and negotiated my way through a group of several preschool children riding tricycles in the middle of the hallway. Opposite the preschool was the entrance to the middle school. Located between the preschool and elementary school areas, the middle school was one large, carpeted room divided into four class areas: one class in each corner of the room, enclosed by four-foot-high portable dividers. The center served as a common space for middle school meetings. A computer lab featuring four Macintosh computers and a printer was located in one end of the room. On the wall above the computers was a bulletin board display of students' poems and stories.

Anne MacKenzie

I was interested in working with a teacher who was considered a good signer, communicates well with her students, and was willing to explore language and communication issues in her class. Anne had the ability to sign fast enough so that her speech is barely distorted. As a graduate student at Gallaudet University in parent-infant guidance, Anne took classes in signed English and American Sign Language. After one year in the Parent-Infant Guidance program at NESD, Anne requested to teach in a classroom setting, and the principal placed her in the middle school. This study took place during Anne's second year at the middle school.

To my knowledge, Anne had not had specific training in how to teach at the middle level. What she had learned about appropriate expectations, curricula, social, and emotional development of her students had been mostly on the job. She had relied on her intuitions, conferred with and observed her colleagues, and consulted with the language and writing specialists at the school. I do not know the specific details around which Anne moved into the middle school but feel that many of the language and literacy dilemmas that Anne faced were complicated by not having been trained more specifically for classroom teaching. This said, Anne remained, without doubt, a central character in the lives of her students.

Together with two specialists in language and writing, the middle school teachers were constructing a new literature curriculum based on story grammar at the time of this study. Anne found these literacy meetings essential in building a shared vision of literature instruction. She was enthusiastic about learning new methods of teaching literature and welcomed guidance from those around her.

Anne's construction of what it means for deaf children to acquire language and literacy skills stemmed from strong influences from her personal, educational, and professional experiences:

> [It's] what I hear Lynn [a fellow teacher] talking about and Anna, and Joan, pulling all that [into my work]. That's a big part of [what] comes into the classroom. And it's what I hear from deaf awareness meetings. And it's [what] I heard at Gallaudet . . . it's partly Signing Exact English class, where I heard the teacher saying this does work to do it this way. And I guess it's from when I grew up, too. I'm always thinking back to how [my] teachers did it. And how I felt about that.

Anne often expressed her willingness to learn and the importance of not feeling as though she was forced into anything new. She valued curricular changes that included her own views and recognized the importance of her colleagues' support while she tried to implement changes. Anne trusted those around her as they confirmed her own belief that a change in teaching reading was necessary. She supported the change from a more integrated approach to reading to separate literature classes. All of these factors played a part in how Anne constructed literacy and literature lessons within her classroom.

The Classroom

Anne's class was in one corner of a large, carpeted room. Students' desks were usually arranged in a semicircle in front of a blackboard. There was a round table in the corner of their area where they met for literature and group work.

At the time I videotaped, Anne had five students, four girls and one boy. These fourteen-year-old students were from hearing families where there was minimal signing at home. One student was visually impaired and used a magnifying glass to read. To my knowledge, the students had no other physical impairments.

There was writing everywhere, on and above the chalkboards, inside and outside the bulletin board dividers, and on the cement wall that bordered their class. The writing was mostly representative of math (fractions), science (human development), literature (quest stories), and spelling

resolution	nursery
problem	hospital
similar	appointment
different	triplets
teenager	nervous
common	reproduction
search	quest
narrative	journal
through	project
delivery	environment

FIGURE 1: *Vocabulary from subject areas studied.*

words taken from each unit. Most, if not all, of these vocabulary words (Figure 1) were from the various subject areas under study.

Anne occasionally referred to these words as they reappeared in print and in her discussion of the literature. My initial impression was that one would expect hearing fourteen-year-old students to know most of these words. Later, this impression was confirmed through personal communication by a middle school teacher of hearing children and a specialist on middle schools. More age-appropriate vocabulary, reading materials, and other student work is difficult for any child who has not had exposure to a natural language from birth. For deaf children of hearing families, knowledge of the world around them is often limited because they lack the important contributions of family and peer language interaction. Thus, the acquisition of literacy becomes complicated, and teachers like Anne are faced with presenting information about the world that most children acquire at a very early age.

Scaffolds and Story Grammar

According to the developing literacy curriculum in the middle school, a good story met the following criteria:

- exhibits an episode structure
- is motivated by character actions, plans, and goals
- includes a conflict or concern-causing event
- contains inside views of characters' thoughts
- contains specific narrative use of language.

Anne felt that the books the middle school chose fit these criteria. The books were at a much lower reading level than one would find in a middle school literature curriculum for hearing students. Some of the books in the series had one or two sentences per page accompanied by a full-page picture. The class spent several days, sometimes more than a week, on one very short story. In contrast, examples of literature in the eighth-grade curricula in two school districts near Boston, Massachusetts, include *The Pearl,* by John Steinbeck, *Oliver Twist,* by Charles Dickens, and *The Fledging,* by Jane Langton. Although the deaf students in Anne's class could not read books at this level of difficulty, the comparison is useful to show the relative difference between the academic levels of hearing and deaf middle school students.

"Quest" stories were the focus of literature lessons throughout the middle school during my observations. Common among these stories is a character who travels to a far-off place seeking fortune or pursuing a desire. The thrust of the lessons emphasized three components of a larger scheme of narrative organization of the story: the plan, the problem, and the resolution. The curriculum loosely referred to this approach to teaching literature as story grammar.

Anne and her students illustrated the plan, problem, and resolution as a visual scaffold: three separate boxes, one box connected to the next by a straight line. This was to show that each component worked together to frame a story. During our first interview, Anne said that she was skeptical at first that scaffolding was too simplistic and could become a crutch for her students. After trying this method with one or two stories, she observed that the scaffold could help them predict meaning by citing a problem (or conflict) and a resolution. She felt, then, that reading would be more enjoyable because the students would have a better and deeper understanding of stories. She also felt the scaffold could be applied to and improve the students' creative writing. Anne hoped that using these scaffolds would move students to independent reading—as she said, "[to] have a book and know how to deal with it."

On large sheets of construction paper, students had written under three side-by-side boxes what the plan, the problem, and the resolution were for each quest story they had read. These posters were displayed around the room.

Description of a Literature Lesson

By her own report, Anne prepared her lessons by reading the story and asking herself, "What do you need to know on this page to understand this book?" Anne flipped through one book and pointed out the words and phrases that she selected as important in one quest story, *The Buried Treasure:*

Lazy
They do not care for hard work
They didn't bring much money home
Secret
Treasure
Buried
In my garden
If you keep digging you will find the treasure
He died
Now we'll get the garden
Now we'll dig
He gave them seeds
They planted seeds
They began to love their work
Wives waited on them
They were tan
They loved their work
They talked less and less about the treasure
They had a fine harvest
Pride
Reaped a rich crop
Brothers realized how wise their father had been

Indeed, reading through these lines, it is possible to get a sense of the story. After Anne had picked out the words and phrases she felt were integral to understanding the story line, she filled in an event scaffold, finding places in the story that indicated the characters' plan, their problem or conflict, and their resolution.

FORMAT

Literature class met three times a week for approximately one hour. The students sat at the back of the room, all seated around a round table, usually sharing books. During my six observations from late September to mid-November, 1991, the class covered three short quest stories. The format for reading these stories varied from round-robin reading aloud, to Anne reading the entire story to the students, to a combination of silent reading and reading aloud. When Anne or the students read aloud, they would also try to sign according to the syntax of the printed page. Most of the time Anne told the story, and the students watched her. Each book had approximately fifteen to twenty pages, with a few sentences on each page accompanied by an illustration.

The students often watched Anne reading the story to them: Anne and the writing specialist read *The Buried Treasure*, Anne read part of *The Inch Boy* and all of the *Frog Prince*. She said that she experimented with the kind of signing that she did with each story. With some stories she followed English syntax closely, with others she used a mixture of English and ASL-like signing. Later in this paper, I explore Anne's thinking about experimenting with different kinds of signing.

FOCUS

Within the lessons, Anne paid particular attention to story structure, that is, to the overall plan, problem, and resolution that spanned the book. After each page, Anne recapped what she read, then asked the students questions. Occasionally she asked them to find answers to her questions within the text. Anne's questions were most often about the main character's motivation.

Although she had mixed feelings about interrupting the flow of the story to ask these questions, Anne felt that the students' responses indicated whether they were following the story. What I observed, however, was a tremendous attempt from Anne to tell, and then retell, the story line as she questioned the students whose responses were rarely more than a few words. When students did respond, Anne shaped their answers to fit what she was looking for. Here is an excerpt of one question-and-answer period after Anne had read a page from *The Inch Boy:*[6]

6. The line designated ANN refers to Anne's spoken message. The line designated SGN is Anne's corresponding signed message. See Appendix B for additional transcription conventions.

ANN: They're really big men.
SGN: BIG MEN.

ANN: Why would these big men listen to him?
SGN: WHY   BIG MAN LISTEN TO [POINT TO FLOOR]?

ANN: And go and get the lord?
SGN: GO   GET   LORD?
The students did not answer.

ANN: Why would they listen to a   little guy?
SGN: WHY   LISTEN [POINT TO FLOOR] LITTLE MAN?

ANN: What do you think?
SGN: 0.

ANN: Why would this little bitty [pause] guy +. . .
SGN: WHY   LITTLE
act: Anne picks up the inch boy cut-out from the table

ANN: Okay.
SGN: 0.
act: Begins to put paper cut-out on the floor

After receiving no answers from the students, Anne began to retell the events on the page that she had just read to them. Here, she used direct speech in ASL. Direct speech involves a body shift to indicate who is speaking.

ANN: He's down here.
SGN: 0.
act: Anne puts paper cut-out of the inch boy on the floor

ANN: And he's knocking.
SGN: KNOCK   .

ANN: And the guard   opens the door.
SGN: #GUARD OPEN DOOR——.
rle: Guard
act: stands up, turns left

ANN: And he's looking.
SGN: [CL: 1P-LOOK-STRAIGHT-AHEAD]. 7

ANN: And there's nobody there.
SGN: NO ONE POINT-LOCATIVE.
rle: Narrator

act: turns center

ANN: and Issunboshi is waving and waving for a long time.
SGN: #I   WAVE———————————————LONG TIME.
rle: Issunboshi
act: turns right

ANN: and finally   he sees him
SGN: PAH   [CL: 1P-LOOK-DOWN-2P][8] POINT-LOCATIVE.
rle: Narrator   Guard
act: center   turns left

Anne explained that she asked the students questions after each page "to see if they're understanding to the point of what's gone on so far so that when they read farther, they're going to get that. Plus they're going to get what the story's about." Anne talked of students' comprehension of stories when she read to the students in the same way she would if they were actually reading the stories themselves. The students were not getting information about the story by reading it; they were getting information through watching her tell the story and a second time through her questions. Anne explained that when she went on to read the next story to the students, she changed her questioning strategy and read the book straight through:

> I went back and I talked about the princess who promised to do things . . . what words said that she had promised and if she intended on keeping the promise? So that's the next step. It's a little bit deeper. And you couldn't get that while you're reading it, but once you're finished, then you go back and you kind of reflect on it and you know that she never intended on keeping that promise.

Anne was talking about two kinds of hypotheses related to comprehension of text: interpretations (hypotheses that already happened in the

7. This sign is an ASL classifier predicate indicating the first person, the speaker, is looking straight ahead.

8. This ASL classifier predicate indicates first person looks down at second person.

text) and predictions (hypotheses about what is going to happen in the text (Collins and Smith, 1982). Both skills are important. Anne seemed to struggle over the types of questions she asked the students rather than the fact that the students were not reading the books. Reading the story straight through seemed more natural to her: "I felt a clearer picture was made of the story. And it was just natural, . . . like how stories should be told. I don't know how to describe it. Not beat [it] to death with comprehension questions or the teacher checking to see if they got that."

Anne described how she now would read *The Inch Boy* in a different manner since reading *The Frog Prince:*

> Now, once [Issunboshi] got [to Kyoto] I would say, "So he's here. What's he doing here?" Just talk about it. Not for comprehension questions but as a part of the story. He's here because this was linked back to his plan . . . so, more after the fact, instead of before the fact. I think that's more natural again. . . . It's what you do when you're reading, too.

Her focus on interpretation instead of prediction seemed more natural to her—what she might do among her friends when talking about books. In her efforts to create a more natural reading environment for her students, Anne experimented with different questioning techniques. She relied more on her own intuitions and personal experience than on more formal knowledge of reading instruction.

This does not necessarily set Anne apart from others who teach students with limited proficiency in English and/or who have poor reading skills. McDermott (1976) found reading lessons for poor readers are often organized in ways that provide students with few opportunities to read during the lessons, answer questions, or participate in discussions. Teacher interruptions in reading lessons for low-achieving students were twenty times more frequent than for higher achieving groups.

INTENT

Anne strived to create a natural environment for reading and improving her students' reading skills. It seemed to me, however, that she did not make the distinction between the students' understanding of a story that was told to them and their understanding of one that they had read themselves. In effect, she gave them credit for understanding her signing, not for understanding information they gleaned from the written story, but yet believed this was reading comprehension.

Anne believed that comprehension skills could be separated from learning the structure of the story and that the task of practicing comprehension skills during the lesson dragged the story down. She thought that if she asked fewer questions, questions that to her indicated that students were following the story line, then she could concentrate on the literature portion of the lesson—that is, explicitly teaching the structure of the story though story grammar. I asked, "If you aren't teaching 'reading skills,' what are you teaching?" She answered:

> The literature. The story. . . . there's episodes that happen . . . and to pretty much follow that scaffold. And [to show that] the characters are motivated by plans and goals through the events they make things happen. There's usually the climax [which] is the complication or the problem, or is the promise kept or broken.

Anne, influenced and supported by other teachers and administrators, perceived reading to be more than a compilation of tiresome, isolated, reading skills. She was concerned that the students not simply learn that a story has three parts—a plan, a problem, and a resolution—but that any story contains deeper, richer information. She wanted to get the students inside the characters, to discuss their motivations and how these shaped the events in the story. Anne knew that reading skills are important but had not learned how to fit these skills into the discussion. She provided time for students to use worksheets to cover isolated skills.

The paradox is that on one hand, Anne was dedicated to making the story clear. She was committed to presenting a rich experience around literature: providing good stories in a positive learning environment, with attention to the structure of stories, character perspective, and motivation. She strived to get at a deeper level of understanding and move students beyond tedious reading skills. Anne was willing to attend meetings, to try new and alternative approaches to teaching reading that felt natural to her and most natural for learning.

On the other hand, her practice of talking about books to her students undermined the processes of learning to read. Anne read at least three stories to the children (*The Buried Treasure, The Inch Boy, The Frog Prince*), but the students did not read the stories on their own. I observed the students reciting words, but I am unclear if they could read. But as Anne and her colleagues knew, the students' ability to read was not at the point where they could grab a book and read it on their own.

The words of I. King Jordan ("The deaf can do anything except hear.") displayed at the entrance of the school reflect this paradox on a larger scale. On one level, it seems obvious that deaf people cannot hear. Yet, inherent in the language practices that make talking to deaf children primary, is the assumption that they *can* hear.

Unearthing the paradox around Anne's efforts to make the story clear, yet maintaining an environment that does not permit students to read, was a critical point in this study. There does not seem to be a positive connection between Anne's good efforts at creating a stimulating reading environment and students' reading competence. Within this paradox, Anne struggles over the best way, if there is such a thing, to present stories to her students.

ANNE'S DILEMMA

Although Anne spends much of the literature lessons reading the stories to her students, she has mixed views about doing so for at least two reasons. One has to do with exposing the students to what she calls "the language of stories," the other with how she decides to sign the story. She wanted to preserve the integrity of the author's words (the language of stories), but she knew that her students did not know many of the words in the story. Because of this, she struggled between signing the story word-for-word—a kind of transliteration—and a kind of signing that she calls "more meaningful." The latter combined features of ASL with the basic signs in English syntax, which provided more of an interpretation of the story, rather than word-for-word signing. What often happened, in fact, was that Anne signed a combination of English syntax and features of ASL.

Because the students are deaf or hard of hearing, they could not make enough sense of Anne's *spoken English* to get the event structure as she told the story. They were not reading the story because they are watching Anne. What they *were* doing was watching her sign. What exactly were they seeing? How did Anne's signing carry the event structure of the story? How did the signs compare with the written and her spoken version of the story? These are the questions that shape the next section.

Anne felt her students would understand *The Inch Boy* better if she read it to them than if they tried to read it themselves. I sought to understand to what degree the students had access to event structure from Anne's presentation of a story. This section is intended to critique the linguistic form available to the students for the purpose of teaching episode structure. I examine some linguistic layers beneath the communicative function of a mixture of signed English and features of ASL. It is important to remember that Anne is considered a good signer who, on many levels, communicates well with her students. Working from the assumption in the middle school curriculum that episode structure is encoded in changes in the verb phrase, I analyzed the variability of verb phrase with a focus on word order, tense, and temporal modifiers across the written, spoken, and signed modalities to see how each modality conveyed the plan, the problem, and the resolution. I also analyzed the presence and function of ASL features within the signed sample. I discuss the spoken and signed versions below within the same subsections because, in theory, the signs are intended to complement the speech. Finally, I conclude with a brief discussion of the story's resolution and some comments.[9]

It may seem peculiar to analyze Anne's spoken message, given that her students are deaf. However, spoken English was the only natural language in the classroom. As her signs were meant to support what she said (as opposed to being able to stand alone, as a natural signed language could do), it was necessary to analyze all of Anne's attempts to communicate with her students.

At the end of the lesson from which I took this sample, the students were up on their knees on their chairs, leaning toward the middle of the table, hunched over the book Anne was reading, genuinely interested in the story. Ultimately, the students had access to a series of basic events in the story through Anne's signs. However, their access came not from

---

9. Although there are several layers of narrative structure that occur within one episode—for example, a character's internal state, actions, reactions, and outcomes—I have considered only the narrative episode structure that is closely tied to the plan, problem, and resolution, as that is Anne's main teaching objective for the lesson.

TABLE I. *Readability, Sentence, and Word/Sign Statistics*

	Entire Book	Sample Episode		
		Written Sample	Spoken	Signed
Grade level	5	6	3	–
Number of sentences	75	14	34	38
Average length of sentence (words)	9	11	7	5
Question forms	0	0	1	2
Passive voice	4	3	2	0
Number of words	682	150	275	181

grammatical shifts in verb phrases and tense but from elaboration, repetition, and additions as Anne talked *about* the text.

Statistical Overview of *The Inch Boy*

The statistics in table 1 show the variability among the written, spoken, and signed versions of a narrative episode, compared with the entire story. According to the Flesch-Kincaid Grade Level Index, *The Inch Boy* is recorded at a fifth-grade level. The book has a total of seventy-five sentences; the average length of each sentence is nine words. There are four passive voice sentences and no question forms. The narrative episode I used in the microanalysis is recorded at grade six reading level.[10]

This overview is meant to provide a general sense that Anne's spoken and signed versions of the written sample are syntactically much simpler than the written version. There are thirty-four spoken sentences compared

10. The readability, sentence, and word level statistics are rather low, considering reading lists in middle schools for hearing children. Additional examples from one eighth grade curriculum include *Light in the Forest*, by Conrad Richter; *The War of the Worlds*, by H. G. Wells; and *A Gathering of Days: A New England Girl's Journal, 1830–1832*, by Joan Blos. *The Inch Boy* could conceivably be used to discuss complex components and structure of literature. My point is not the potential of the book to bring out the complex structure of literature, but that Anne feels that the students would not be able to adequately understand the text if they were to read it silently.

to fourteen used in the text, because in telling the story, Anne elaborated on the written text and included descriptions, repetition, additions, elaboration, illustrations (props), questions, and answers.

It was inappropriate to assign a reading level to the signed sample as signs are inherently incomparable to English written text. The signs referred to in this paper are glosses—labels for signs—not translations. I ran the English glosses through a computer-generated program called Grammatik to receive the statistics in table 1. I knew of no way to account for some ASL features that Anne used with these signs, for example, the grammatical feature of body shift in direct speech. Although the features add to the complexity of the sign, their inclusion did not affect the sentence type, length, or word-count statistics. Anne explained that one of her premises for trying to map each sign for each word spoken was to expose deaf students to English syntax. It is the signs in English syntax that Anne hopes will convey the "language of stories" (in this case, the plan, problem, and resolution) to the students through her signing, not through the enhanced meaning that features of ASL may bring to the story. Thus, it was important to analyze the syntax of the signed string for its syntactic ability to convey the language of stories.

Comparison across Modalities

The next section presents an analysis of "the confrontation" as it illustrates linguistic features common throughout the episode, as well as features present only during this segment. Anne and her students sat around the round table in the back of their room, some students sharing books. At this point in the story, one-inch-tall Issunboshi is standing before the large wooden doors of a palace in Kyoto, Japan, seeking to fulfill his dream of becoming a samurai.

The confrontation between Issunboshi and the guards is one in a series leading up to the major crisis in the story. In the written version, the confrontation is expressed in four sentences, compared to nineteen sentences in Anne's telling of the story.

In this segment of the episode, Anne used direct speech in ASL called role shifting (shifting her body to indicate who is speaking). Anne conveyed direct speech in two ways, encoded by lexical and prosodic (intonational) features of her oral utterances and by her body movements.

(38) It took some time before he managed to attract the attention of the guard at the huge wooden gates.

(39) "I am Issunboshi," he announced.

(40) "I have heard many tales of the great Lord Sanjo and it is my wish to serve such an honourable man.

(41) "Please sir, announce my arrival."

In the first sentence of this section (38), there are two minor outcomes as a result of Issunboshi's plan to become a samurai: first, the boy's arrival at the palace, and second, attracting the attention of the guard. The reader must make several inferences from this sentence; that is, the character is at his destination because palaces have guards and big wooden gates, and guards are positioned at big wooden gates. The text does not tell us how the character attracted the guard's attention, only that it "took some time" (a temporal marker) until he did. The boy takes a forceful stand in front of the guard as he announces his presence (39) and in (40) his plan (to serve the lord and thus become a samurai).

There is a tense shift to present perfect (have heard) in (40), taking the reader back in time and indicating a cause and effect. It is tense shifts such as these that move a reader between events. In the past, Issunboshi has heard great stories, which presented the lord as an honorable man, and thus, it is his wish to serve such [a] man. The character's actions—announcing his arrival and plan and using a (polite) direct command for the guard to announce his arrival—are effective for him, as the next segment demonstrates.

SPOKEN AND SIGNED VERSION

In Anne's spoken and signed version of this part of the episode, she simplified sentences, provided many intertextual comments, and made use of some ASL features to emphasize the character's dilemma (see Appendix B for transcription conventions). Part two of the spoken narrative episode is nineteen sentences (the written text is four sentences). Anne split the first sentence of the written text into thirteen shorter sentences, making explicit the presuppositions in the original text. Anne began reading this segment by repeating the last sentence on the preceding page. She was able to then state explicitly that Issunboshi had reached the palace.

(42) TXT: **Issunboshi immediately set off for the palace.**

(43) ANN: It [say]s, [Issunboshi] [set off] [right away].
(44) SGN: o [SAY]o [#I=name sign] [LEAVE] [FAST].

(45) TXT: o.

(46) ANN: He [went] [straight] [to] the [palace].
(47) SGN: o [GO] [STRAIGHT] [TO] o [P-A-L-A-C-E PALACE].

(48) TXT: o

(49) ANN: you [know] [like] a [castle] [for] [king]s?
(50) SGN: o [KNOW] [LIKE] o [CASTLE] [FOR] [KING]o.

(51) TXT: o.

(52) ANN: A palace [where] the [famous] [Lord] [Sanjo] [live]d.
(53) SGN: o o [WHERE] o [FAMOUS] [LORD] [S-A-N-J-O] [LIVE]o
[LIVE] [LIVE].

The last sentence of the first part of the episode is, "Issunboshi immediately set off for the palace of the famous Lord Sanjo." In part two of the spoken version, Anne rephrased the sentence and broke it into two parts (43) and (46). She substituted *"immediately set off for the palace"* with *"Issunboshi set off right away."* but she signed, LEAVE FAST. "Immediately," "right away," and FAST express similar temporal moves. In (49) and (53), Anne defined and repeated an explanation of the function of the palace.

In the next nine spoken and signed sentences, Anne went to great lengths to describe tiny Issunboshi's dilemma as he stood in front of the high wooden doors. Anne's elaboration made explicit the written text, "it took some time before he managed to attract the attention." In this explanation, Anne used many ASL features, including classifier predicates and role shift, to indicate direct speech.

(54) TXT: **It took some time before he managed to attract + . . .**

(55) ANN: there was a [big] [guard] [stand]ing there.
(56) SGN: o o o [BIG] [GUARD] [STAND] o o .

Anne began to create a picture of what it was like for the boy standing before the big gates. She stood up and made her signs big, with her face and body adding to the animation. At this point, she departed from the text completely as she took on the role of Issunboshi, waving her arms, trying to attract the guard's attention. While telling the story, her English was, of course, complete. Her signs did not match her speech but rather captured the gist of what she was saying (*BIG GUARD STAND*). In effect, she created a set of spatial and temporal relationships much more like those that would be created in ASL. The paradox is that Anne attempted to make the story clear to aid the students' comprehension, but no reading was happening.[11]

(57) TXT: **the attention of the guard at the huge wooden gates**

(58) ANN: [and he opened the door].
(59) SGN: [o— o—OPEN-O- o—DOOR].

(60) TXT: o

(61) ANN: [and he stood there].
(62) SGN: [o———o—o———OFIST-ON-HIP———].

Anne used direct speech in ASL in (59). She shifted to the right, taking on the role of the guard, used the ASL sign for OPEN DOOR, and used a big, sweeping movement. The personal pronoun "he" in Anne's speech (58) referred to the guard. The role shift made clear the meaning of the pronoun.

In (62), Anne shifted her body position to the left taking on the role of Issunboshi. She put her fists on her hips and looked up at the imaginary guard. The personal pronoun "he" in (61) referred to Issunboshi. Again, using direct speech in ASL, Anne made these referents explicit by

11. At least one student was confused at this point. He signed SAME STORY? although Anne did not see him. He kept looking back and forth between his book and watching Anne sign and looking at Anne's book. Anne had told them that she was going to read the story to them, and this student could not match the signs to the print. He has a lot of hearing, and Anne had felt that among the five, he was one of the better readers. He continued to alternate between looking at his book and watching Anne sign throughout the lesson. It was unclear to me whether he was confused by Anne's signing or not clear that she was telling the story rather than reading it.

using her body position and facial expressions. It is not clear to me why Anne chose to use direct speech when it was not in the story, other than perhaps the effect of explicating the pronouns, making the story easier to follow and also making the story more interesting to watch.

In Anne's spoken lines, she used the simple past tense. There were no overt indicators for tense in her signs.

(63) TXT: o.

(64) ANN: for a [long] [time] [Issunboshi] [o   ].
(65) SGN: o   o [LONG] [TIME] [I (name sign)] [LITTLE].

(66) TXT: o.

(67) ANN: [was   down   here].
(68) SGN: [o   o   o   ].
(69) act: bends down to floor

In these two sentences, Anne elaborated the point that Issunboshi was waiting outside the door for a long time (stated in the written version in the first sentence "It took some time before he managed. . . . "). She repeated the fact that Issunboshi is little (65) and, in (69), bent down to the floor to show how small Issunboshi appeared.

(70) TXT: o.

(71) ANN: and he was [wave] and   [waving].
(72) SGN: o   o o   [WAVE—o———o———].

Here, Anne presented conflicting information. She simultaneously spoke as narrator, using the third person pronoun and staying within past tense, while using the direct speech in ASL, which requires first person. She turned to the same location where she had stood before as Issunboshi, crouched low to the ground, waved her arms, and looked up as if looking at the guard.

(73) TXT: o.

(74) ANN: and he's [try]ing to get the [guard].
(75) SGN: o   o o [TRY]o o o   o   [GUARD].

(76) TXT: o.

(77) ANN: to [pay attention].
(78) SGN: o [PAY ATTENTION].

During these two sentences, Anne shifted her body to the center, in the narrator position. She spoke as the narrator, again referring to Issunboshi in the third person, although the third person was not indicated in her signs. From her signs (TRY GUARD PAY ATTENTION] and by standing in the center or in neutral space as narrator, Anne expected the students to infer that it was Issunboshi who was trying to attract attention.

(79) TXT: o.

(80) ANN: to [look down   ].
(81) SGN: o [o———oCL:V 3P-LOOK-DOWN-1P].

Anne used ASL in (81) to elaborate what it was that Issunboshi hoped the guard would do. Again, Anne simultaneously spoke as narrator but shifted to the role of Issunboshi (turned slightly to her right) and signed from the position of the character. She spoke in the third person (trying to get the guard to pay attention [to him], to look down), but her signs used different pronoun referents. Using the classifier predicate, Anne's spoken English reflected the role of the narrator, her body shift indicated the character, and her sign, the directional verb, indicated that a third person (the guard) looked down at the first person (Issunboshi but could also be Anne herself).

(82) TXT: o.

(83) ANN: [wave-ing and wave-ing] for a [long] [time] [nothing].
(84) SGN: [WAVE-o— o— o———o] o o [LONG] [TIME] [NOTHING].

(85) TXT: o.

(86) ANN: [finally] the [guard] [see-s   him   ].
(87) SGN: [PAH   ] o [GUARD] [o—o—o CL:V 3P-LOOK-DOWN-1P].

In (83), Anne maintained the role of Issunboshi, waved her arms, repeated that he tried to attract attention and "for a long time" nothing happened. In (87), Anne made it it clear that at last, the guard saw the boy. The use of the classifier predicate in (87) is an inaccurate use of the pronoun referent.

(88) TXT: "I am Issunboshi," he announced.

(89) ANN: and [Issunboshi] [announce]s, [I] [am] [Issunboshi].
(90) SGN: o   [#I   ]   [ANNOUNCE] [I] [AM] [#I   ].

Anne's spoken and signed message almost matched the written text, except that she changed the direct speech in the book to indirect speech in both her speech and signs. She did not role shift when she signed *I am #I.*

(91) TXT: I have heard many tales + . . .

(92) ANN: [I] have [heard]   [many] [tales   ]+..
(93) SGN: [I] o   [OLISTEN] o [MANY] [STORY+*plural marker*]

(94) TXT: +, of the great Lord Sanjo.

(95) ANN: of the [great] [Lord] [Sanjo   ]+ . . .
(96) SGN: o   o   [GREAT] [LORD] [S-A-N-J-O].

(97) TXT: +, and it's my wish to +,

(98) ANN: [and] [it's] [my] [wish] [to]+ . . .
(99) SGN: [AND] [IT] o [MY] [WISH] [TO]

(100) TXT: +, serve such an honorable man.

(101) ANN: [serve] [such] [an] [honor]able [man   ].
(102) SGN: [SERVE] [MUCH] o   [HONOR-o] [GENTLEMAN].

Anne stayed with the text almost word for word, although she changed the tense from present perfect (have heard) to present. Anne stayed in neutral space during this sentence, not taking on the role Issunboshi. She kept her spoken sentences in the present tense although she left the present tense markers out of her signs.

(103) TXT: o.

(104) ANN: I wanna [work].
(105) SGN: o o   [WORK].

(106) TXT: o.

(107) ANN: I wanna try to [protect] [him].
(108) SGN: o o   o   o [PROTECT] [HIM].

Anne departed from the written text and repeated Issunboshi's purpose and plan to become a samurai.

(109) TXT: **Please sir, announce my arrival.**

(110) ANN: So [please] [announce] [my] [arrive]al.
(111) SGN: o [PLEASE] [ANNOUNCE] [MY] [ARRIVE]o.

(112) TXT: o.

(113) ANN: [Inform   ] [somebody] [to come   ].
(114) SGN: [1P-INFORM-2P] [SOMEONE] [CL:1 3P-COME-UP-TO-1P].

Anne continued to stay in neutral space in the position of narrator, although she spoke in the first person. In (114), Anne repeated in ASL-like signing the meaning of "Please announce my arrival." This marked the end of the second part of the episode.

CONCLUSION

In Anne's effort to convey narrative event structure to her students, the retelling of the story became primary and the written text secondary. Anne talked about the text. As a result, she invited the students into the world of the story rather than the world of the text.

The data indicate that the events of the story were encoded in both the spoken and signed versions. Anne helped her students make sense of the story by making it lively, improvising in parts, elaborating, and reinforcing her objective to teach the structure of events in a story. She was aware that this text may have been too hard for all of her students to read and understand on their own and that handing the book over to them to read on their own may have been intimidating and/or fruitless. As a result, Anne's spoken message varied from the text; it simplified more complex constructions, elaborated, repeated key points, and made almost all presuppositions explicit.

The data also demonstrate that Anne's efforts did not reinforce the student's efforts to learn to read. Anne's spoken English was complete and often an accurate rendition of the text. But the students could not make useful sense of her speech because they cannot hear. Thus, the fidelity of the spoken text to the written text was of little help to the students, as it might have been if there were hearing students engaged in a reading aloud exercise.

Her signs were also problematic. The signed intention was often incomplete with respect to the information presented vocally and textually, and her ASL often did not express what she intended. In at least three cases, the English words in the written and spoken versions differed in function from the signs produced to represent these words: the written and spoken word *heard* is produced as LISTEN; the written and spoken noun *arrival* is produced as the verb ARRIVE; the written and spoken adjective *honorable* is produced as the noun or the verb HONOR. This discrepancy between the function of the written and spoken words on the one hand and the ASL signs produced for these words on the other contributes to the creation of a confusing message. Therefore, the students were not getting an accurate representation of the text in either language. The students were left, on the one hand, with a watered-down version of an elementary text and, on the other, with more information about the text than the story itself provided. Anne was aware of her students' limited competence in English and compensated by giving them a linguistically simplified version of the story. She was also quite interested in having the students learn and so compensated for their inabilities by giving them an informationally enriched version of the story. Thus, the stated purpose of the activity was not accomplished. The children were not reading, nor were they learning to read.

Anne, like all teachers, practices within the limits of her knowledge. By looking aggressively at her own practice, Anne tested the boundaries of these limits. In the next section, I return to my interview data and explore Anne's assumptions about the relationship between written, spoken, and signed text.

LOGIC: MANAGING THE LIMITS OF KNOWLEDGE

> When they read [part of the story] the other day, I didn't know if they got the meaning out of it. So I thought if I told it to them they would. But I still wanted to get back to the print. That same old thing. So I wrote down how I would sign it to two [hearing] girls, but I tried to stay true to the print. At least in the word order and the vocabulary. . . . To keep it as much the same as I could, but not to stay restricted to [the print].—Anne

This quote captured Anne's cyclical thinking between language form and teaching reading. Because the students could not gain enough information from reading the book on their own, Anne decided to sign the remainder of *The Inch Boy* to them but was uncertain about how to sign it. "Staying true to the print" (signs that match the text in a one-to-one correspondence) was a problem because, from her experience, Anne knew that signs presented in a one-to-one correspondence with speech make little sense. Anne did not stay true to the print but did stay true to the content of the story, using some of the same vocabulary and word order of the written text but changing the text in places to make the events in the story clear. Anne felt her students needed to learn the story from the print, but they did not understand print well enough to make the story meaningful. And so Anne was caught in a struggle that pits language of instruction against access to content.

Anne's concern about how best to teach reading to deaf students probably stemmed, in part, from her limited experience as a new teacher and in part from her training in parent guidance. The problems cited here as a result of language practice are not specific to Anne but concern the more general and ineffective philosophy of educating deaf children inculcated throughout most teacher education programs and schools. The tension between language practice and teaching content extends far beyond Anne's classroom.

In this section I (a) identify the struggle between language form and teaching content, (b) explain the logic that sustains the struggle, and (c) begin to build a theory that explains Anne's continued adherence to speaking to deaf children in spite of her intuitive sense that it is ineffective, both as a means of acquiring English grammar and providing reasonable access to curricular content. In order to understand the broader educational context in which Anne worked, I provide a philosophical framework that has in part influenced Anne's thinking about how deaf children acquire English.

Circular Logic in Deaf Education

The literature on deaf education that supports Sign Supported Speech (SSS, also referred to as simultaneous comunication, or signed English) is based on the underlying assumption that deaf students have sufficient residual hearing to learn English aurally (Hyde and Power 1991; Luetke-Stahlman and Luckner 1991; Moores 1987; Evans 1982). In this view, parents and teachers are encouraged to speak to deaf children. The literature on teaching deaf students often presents guidelines on what to say and how to say it. For example, Luetke-Stahlman and Luckner suggest adults talk to deaf children about the significance, importance, and enjoyment of reading (1991, 261):

> A parent might express ideas such as, "I need to make a shopping list so I remember to buy milk and eggs," or "I'm going to write the name of this movie on the VCR box so we can remember which one it is."
> . . . . Many of the functions and uses of *oral*, signed, and written language are absorbed by students simply by virtue of their membership in our literate society. . . . *Hearing*/seeing stories offer *hearing-impaired* students the opportunity to experience the joys of *playing with vocabulary, listening* to or *seeing rhythmical English patterns,* and encountering ideas that stimulate and reinforce imagination and curiosity. [Italics are mine.]

These suggestions do not seem necessarily inappropriate in language and literacy learning environments where children can hear. However, the authors are referring to children who cannot hear. It is contradictory, at best, to assume that deaf children can listen to or see rhythmical English patterns. How is this possible when rhythmical English patterns are carried through sound? This perspective supports the disturbing pretense that deaf children will hear if they are exposed to enough spoken English.

In the philosophy of signed English, the signed portion is valued insofar as it supports the spoken message. This philosophy is also based on the assumption that a sign on the hands can carry the same linguistic information as the spoken word it is mean to represent. According to signed English, if a string of signs has a one-to-one correspondence to the spoken word, then the deaf child can *see* all the linguistic information carried in the speech on the signer's hands. For example, Luetke-Stahlman claims that "the more closely the sign system input . . . corresponds to written English, the better students are able to read. . . . [Therefore] adults need to encode completely the vocabulary, figurative English, inflected verb forms, and affixes that are read and written . . . " (p. 261). The assumption is that a signer can take individual signs and manipulate them so that they follow spoken word order. Then, by virtue of a one-to-one correspondence to the spoken words, the signs absorb syntactic, semantic, phonological, and pragmatic rules encoded in the underlying structure of language, beneath word-level meaning. The curve in the logic underlying this assumption is that deaf children have already acquired the grammatical rules of English, so that when they see English signs in English word order, they understand those signs as if they were hearing English.

For deaf children, the signed portion of the message is the means by which they have access to information. Signs that are meant to accompany speech are useful only insofar as the child knows the underlying rules of English grammar. Anne reported that she, her colleagues, and some parents were mystified when her students did not understand simple commands or wh-questions (*who, what, when, where,* and *why*). One reason may be that they have never acquired the underlying rules of how commands and questions work in English because these rules are acquired by hearing them. Simply substituting a sign for a word is not sufficient to transfer the rules of a language from the mouth to the hands. If one pays attention only to word-level meaning and believes that grammar exists only at the word level of language, then learning English by using a string of signs may make sense. But we know from linguistic theory that language does not work that way.

Anne, like most teachers in deaf education, was taught that signed English (or SSS) can convey the grammar of English, that if she signs every word and morpheme she speaks, the students will be exposed to English three times, once by hearing it, once on the lips, and once on the hands.

But Anne faces the incongruence of this logic every day: if this were true about signed English, her fourteen-year-old students, exposed to this for years, would be able to understand simple wh-questions or commands. But her students have difficulty understanding the most basic forms of English. The incongruence between language input and its effect on students' ability to acquire language is difficult to change, despite evidence that students' control of syntax affects their reading achievement (Chomsky 1972).

Creating a congruence with the language of instruction and a language most accessible to deaf students requires that teachers shift from using spoken English as the language of instruction to ASL, the language that Anne drew upon when wanting to make her points clearer. At NESD, ASL is neither readily accessible to hearing teachers, nor—as Anne explained—readily acceptable in deaf schools. For teachers and administrators interested in improving the education of deaf children, importance has been placed on other areas of change. For example, emphasis on reading changed from a social studies-based literature approach to a story-grammar approach, such as Anne described. Without alternatives related to reform in language practices, there is a kind of suspension of its importance in how curricular content is delivered. The result is that even the most innovative curricular reforms can be constrained by the inability to present the new information in a fully comprehensible and understandable language.

Instead, the literature on deaf education, represented in Anne's own perspective, demonstrates an adherence to a system in which one places faith that somehow, someday, students will eventually learn to read if they continue to "see English on the hands." It is not unlike what Geertz (1973) calls "the religious perspective" within a cultural system. The religious perspective "moves beyond the realities of everyday life to wider ones which correct and complete them, and its defining concern is not action upon those wider realities but acceptance of them, faith in them" (p. 112). I make the comparison to those people in deaf education who continue to have faith that signed English will somehow be the answer to teaching English to deaf children in spite of compelling scientific evidence against it. But science often has no bearing on firm religious beliefs. And those trained within a belief system, with little access or availability to alternatives, are not easily swayed by contradictory scientific evidence. Thus, the effectiveness of signed English is deemed irrefutable. The circular logic preserves the status quo: English continues to remain the language of instruction, content is conveyed essentially independently of formal language, and the pretense remains that deaf children will acquire English by hearing it and seeing it on the hands.

Circular Logic in the Classroom: Language Form versus Content

As I demonstrated in the microanalysis, Anne's students are exposed to consistent patterns of linguistic and narrative structure of written text, but they do not read it, nor does Anne believe they are able to understand it sufficiently if they do read it. The linguistic pattern of vocal presentation of narrative structure is consistent but is not accessible to the students because they cannot hear it. The pattern of linguistic and narrative structure of sign is communicative, though lexically, morphologically, and syntactically incomplete and inconsistent. Yet, the signs are the only modality that could provide the students complete access to the information. Anne accomplishes her objective of teaching the content and event structure, essentially independently of using a standard language form.

Current Form: "Not a Full Language"

I know you never sign what you think you are signing. Because your voice takes up so much of it. And sometimes . . . I stop and think, "What did I just now actually sign?"

—Anne

As Anne and I watched the videotape of her lesson that included the portion of the story I analyzed in the previous section, she immediately focused on the extent to which her speech and signs followed the story. The sound on the TV monitor was off, as Anne requested, so that she could pay attention to what she was signing. Aloud, she interpreted her own signing into English as we watched:

ANNE: Issunboshi was so excited when he finally arrived. He was on the river for a long trip. He finally got to Kyoto. He said to himself, "This is where I belong. This feels good." I broke this down.

MAL: Why did you do that?

Language and Learning in a Deaf Education Classroom : 197

ANNE: I'm experimenting . . . you can't get a recipe from anybody on how to do literature, on how to do stories with kids. Do you let them read it? Do you read it? Do they take turns reading it? So the only way is to listen to what other teachers do and to do it myself. Try different things. It's my first year of really doing literature. It's my chance to experiment . . . I don't go, "Issunboshi was very excited when the river finally brought him" [reads from text]; I paraphrase it [like] when I tell my nieces stories.

Anne's view on how to teach content was directly related to her decisions about choice of language form. She seemed to approach the presentation of content from two directions. The first was to use signs that closely follow the printed page (more English-like signing). The second was to use a mixture of signs from signed English and ASL, which required her to deviate from the print but added meaning and clarity to the story. In our interviews, Anne spoke sometimes from one perspective and sometimes from the other.

English-like Signing

When Anne was at Gallaudet University, her professor said that it is possible to use Signing Exact English (SEE) and add the ASL features to the English signs. Anne wondered, "Why is that different [from hearing kids]—if deaf kids see that in their home, at school, a [signed] full representation of English? But it can't be the same [as spoken English] because it's sound versus visual. But [she said that signed English] could be used successfully [to acquire English]."

Anne was told that signed English is the same as spoken English. If the child had exposure to English-like signing from birth, Anne felt that the child would have a good chance of acquiring English. This is the assumption embedded within the philosophy of signed English, even though there is no evidence that supports this claim.

The problem with this logic is both its circularity and the irrefutable tenet of cause and effect. The circularity is thus: (a) teachers must use English so that students can acquire it; (b) they change to ASL features so students can undertand; (c) the result is not English anymore, so what the students are understanding and learning is not English; (d) so the students do not know English; (e) so the teachers try harder to use English because they (a) must use English so that students can acquire it. . . . In the wake of this logic is the everyday reality of fourteen-year-old students who are well beyond the optimal age of acquiring a first language and are still learning to read.

Anne's professor said that it is appropriate to use some ASL along with signed English. This implies that signed English alone is not adequate to fully represent the spoken portion of the message. This also implies that ASL can be deconstructed and arbitrarily drawn upon as a language, making it useful to a degree, but not suitable or worthy of its full use in an educational setting. This belief in mixing two languages with the intent of presenting a clearer English message to deaf students was embedded in Anne's perspective on her language practice largely as a result of her training.

Modifying the Form: The Mix

Signed English theory claims that signing in English word order will eventually make sense to deaf students. Although Anne may believe this at some level, her experience has been contrary to the theory. Anne recalled the time a (hearing) school counselor came to talk to her class about Sarah, a student in class who was visually impaired:

> I think the way [the counselor] was signing was the natural way you talk to people. . . . She would say [and sign], NOW WHO WANTS TO GET UP AND WALK AROUND AND PUT THE CUPS ON AND SEE WHAT IT FEELS LIKE TO SARAH? WHO WANTS TO TRY THAT? That seemed pretty straightforward. But they didn't get it. And I [signed] something like, WHO? YOU WANT TO VOLUNTEER? YOU TO STAND UP [says 'get up'] AND WHAT-DO FEEL LIKE? It was the same idea. . . . I remember 'volunteer,' I knew that they would know that word. She didn't use "volunteer."

The counselor signed and spoke at the same time in a natural way that hearing people would speak to each other, but the students did not understand. They just sat there. Anne interpreted for the counselor when the students did not react to her question. Anne said she signed without using her voice, added some ASL features, and presented the counselor's idea so that the students would know what to do. Anne said that even though the counselor signed and talked at the same time, "they didn't understand what she was talking about." "Why?" I asked. Anne replied:

> Because it's those [commands]. . . . That happened so much last year

and even in the beginning of this year, they would give me a blank stare. And now they appropriately respond by moving or by starting work or by waiting . . . it's more social behavior . . . [they] seem more socially appropriate. The speech teacher works on it with them so that they can predict what they think a teacher wants by using context, too.

When the students were given a directive signed exactly as it is spoken, for example, "Open your books to page twenty-three," many students did not understand what to do. Sometimes they just sat there and did nothing. Sometimes they responded inappropriately. These students did not know what was expected of them. Anne raised and explicated this phenomenon that has confounded many teachers of deaf students who use signed supported speech. Anne believed that the students could not predict the social response to the directive. Not understanding the command form of a language seems to me a reflection of the students' limited competence in a first language. The underlying message is that something is wrong with the students, not the form used to convey the message.

This is one small but powerful illustration that word order and vocabulary are only the outward symbols of language. But word order and vocabulary are the levels at which signed English places its importance. What Anne does know is that her students often do not understand the meaning of simple directives. If the students understood English, then they should have understood the counselor. The speech teacher tried to teach the social and cultural cues for behavior explicitly through speech without the students having a firm foundation in the language. Their responses and behaviors were deemed a social problem, not a linguistic one:

> I would jump in there so many times after [the counselor] said something. [Then] they would know to move. I was trying to think, 'How am I changing it?' and it would always be that my voice would be turned off right after she would say something. [Otherwise] they would just sit there.

The students reacted (appropriately) when Anne turned off her voice, changed around some signs, and added some ASL features. In a sense, this supported her theory that mixing two languages is more communicative. The students understood the mix better than when they received spoken English accompanied by signs. Anne drew upon her theory in literature class:

That's why I talk about adding the ASL because if I stood up in a class and did ISSUNBOSHI WAS VERY EXCITED WHEN THE RIVER FINALLY BROUGHT HIM TO KYOTO [signing word-for-word], that's just not enough. It might be true English, but it's not true meaning . . . I don't know how to say it. It's not the same thing as if you said it.

Anne felt she was dutiful in presenting English to her students by signing in English word order. She also knew that by doing only that, the meaning of her message would get lost. Her evidence was in the blank stares the students often gave her when she signed word-for-word. Yet she felt word-for-word signing was true English.

In Anne's view, the signed representation of English is English, though devoid of meaning. In order to give students the meaning embedded in English, she borrowed from ASL features. ASL features (classifier predicates, linguistic use of space, certain facial features, etc.), she felt, provide the English meaning. The print was English, so the students were exposed to it. Anne knew that in reality, when the students were exposed to signing in English word order, they did not understand. To make the story understandable and enjoyable, Anne drew from ASL. The ASL features made the English portion of the message clearer.

How can components of ASL be used to make English clearer? Because of the different modalities used in ASL and English, it is possible to overlay some features of ASL onto spoken English. For example, if one asks a question in English, "How are you?" it is possible to use two nonmanual linguistic features in ASL for yes/no-question formation (head raised and slightly forward, eyebrows raised) simultaneously with the spoken English sentence. The problem is, of course, how can the addressee process the rules of two languages at once?

Anne strove to sign in English word order and use ASL features for meaning. As she watched the videotape, she realized that she departed from the print and signed something that was similar in meaning but not the exact words on the page:

What I left out, though, is the reading of this in English. [I didn't] follow it. Like, "Issunboshi was very excited," and go ahead with, "when the river finally brought him to Kyoto,"—exactly. . . . I don't know. I've seen deaf people do it . . . when you can match up the signs, to not just sign it but to sign it ASL within the English.

This was something that Anne believed was linguistically possible, although it could not work with two spoken languages—to speak Spanish within English, for example for the purpose of making English clearer. And just as it is impossible to speak two languages simultaneously, it is not possible to sign ASL and speak English simultaneously:

> ANNE: . . . [To] be true to English. . . . That's my goal. It's not to become fluent in ASL, that would be great, but at this point, I wouldn't be using it in my classroom anyway with all the kids. Because with the population [students with different degrees of hearing loss] and it wouldn't be comfortable and I don't think accepted. But if there was to be a program of steps or something, that would be the next one for me. How to talk to the kids and tell stories to the kids using English but adding the ASL components that make the English . . . clear.

> MAL: The English meaning, written English clear?

> ANNE: Written English and spoken.

Although Anne recognized a place in her language practices for ASL, it was not her goal to use only ASL. The students in her class were there because they have a hearing loss, but, because some students could make some use of their hearing, she felt that using ASL all the time would be cheating some students out of an opportunity to be exposed to English. What language practices are beneficial for all students in her class? On one level, a mix seems to make sense for all students, but when we examined the mix in the last section, it appeared largely inadequate for learning complex ideas. The mix may not work, but Anne felt at the present time that it was the most realistic for hearing teachers:

> [A mix of signed English and ASL] doesn't work. I'm not fighting for signed English. Because I'm doing signed English in the classroom does not mean that's what I believe in. And I don't have a set belief yet. I think that that's why I'm a good teacher because I'm open to whatever . . . people are doing with [and] talking about ASL . . . but I guess it's what's in place right now. It seems to be the most realistic for the, not for the kids, but for the people who are doing it. The adults, the teachers, the parents.

Anne acknowledged that in the end, the students lose because what they receive as language input is only what their teacher is willing to provide. The students in Anne's class who do better in reading have the most hearing. The students who have to depend solely on teachers' signs do not read as well. In response to the students who do not read well, Anne reasons that they need to be exposed to English in order to learn it. Thus, circular logic takes hold in the kinds of decisions Anne makes about teaching reading or any other subject.

For example, Anne believes students' different learning styles are a product of their hearing levels. I asked, "The way they learn is different, or is what they need different?" She responded:

> I think the way they learn. I'm finding myself all the time now, whenever I talk to Beth, if I use my voice, it just does not click at all. Whatever happens when I turn off my voice and just sign with her, it just clicks. And that's what I wish I could do with her all the time. But then I feel like I would be cheating Terry and Sarah and Mary out of, well, they can get this [from me speaking]. . . . This is raising so many tough questions.

Anne described a common dilemma for teachers in deaf education. She sees students grouped according to which language is most accessible to them: students with a lot of hearing would benefit from English supplemented with a signed vocabulary.[12] Students who cannot make use of their hearing would benefit by having ASL as the language of instruction. Even if Anne knew ASL well, she was not sure she would use it because it was not used widely, if at all, in her school. The mix of ASL and English, in theory, was a compromise for everyone. The students who need signs to learn, get signs. The students who can make use of some hearing, get to hear.

Anne was well aware of the implications of this compromise: "It's neither doing signed English nor ASL. It's not doing either one well. It's a compromise." As a result, her tendency was to concentrate on the spoken language and ways in which students with more hearing benefit from her language input.

Ideal Form: To Sign Like Deaf Teachers

It made sense to Anne, in her efforts to help the students develop and learn the structure of English as well as the structure of stories, that she

12. The more generic problem of teaching heterogeneous groups is present in classrooms with deaf students as it is in regular classrooms. How can teachers meet the needs of all students who differ in levels of ability, learning styles, and language proficiency? In deaf education, the issue is complicated by the teachers' ability to communicate with their students.

use the very language that she is trying to teach: English. Therefore, she used spoken English and exposed students to written English as a kind of language template. She then added signs and ASL features to the template in order to fill in the gaps left because the students could not make sense of the template in the first place.

In Anne's view, using a mix of ASL components and spoken English with signs in English word order was supported by the way deaf teachers often sign. Anne's goal was to improve her use of this mix. She recalled a time when she and a deaf teacher both recited a poem to their students. Anne signed in the mix (signed English with some ASL features), and a deaf teacher signed the same poem in ASL:

> I read it in signed English but with ASL-like features, and then she did it in ASL . . . at first [the students] were all watching me. And then by the end, they were all watching her . . . and [we] asked them what they liked . . . and they said, "watching that" [ASL] . . . They said it was funnier. . . . so the humor came over more . . . it was more expressive . . . easier to understand. . . . that bugs me because there's something to that. That's the way kids are saying that they want to be taught, learn best, and are most interested in.

Anne realized that students seem to understand, enjoy, and learn best from deaf teachers who sign ASL or use a mix of ASL and English.

Not Ready for This Form: ASL

Throughout our interviews, Anne discussed ways in which ASL could be borrowed from in order to enhance the signed portion of her communication. She respected ASL as a language among deaf people and as a valued part of the deaf community. Anne began a deaf awareness group that brought together teachers and members of the deaf community. She encouraged deaf leaders to come and speak to the staff, and she valued the social, intellectual, and emotional interaction between deaf adults and deaf children. However, Anne did not know how ASL can be incorporated more fully into the classroom:

> I was around deaf people, and I have that gut instinct that ASL has a place [in the classroom], but everything works in a balance. I know that, but I don't know the linguistic part of it, so I would need to know that. And I would need for someone to help me understand [that] if I

did use ASL, how will it match to reading and writing? Or not even match, but how will it help promote reading and writing better than what's going on right now?

Anne realized at a "gut level" that ASL and deaf students' positive interaction among deaf people play an essential role in the education of deaf children.

Anne believes that she communicates well with her deaf friends, and she associates with members of the deaf community using ASL-like signing[13] and has advocated for more deaf awareness among her hearing colleagues at school. Anne's use of more English-like signing (using her voice while she signs) has its roots in her educational and academic background. She would need to know more ASL and would need help and support in order to integrate ASL into her teaching:

> I wouldn't want to be the only one to [use ASL in the classroom]. . . . I wouldn't want to carry it or explain it, try to convince other people, or feel funny in the classroom about doing it . . . and [have] people checking out to see if [I'm doing what I'm supposed to]. I would want it to be a group decision with other teachers and supervisors and to know that it's an experiment.

Anne wanted to make an informed decision, guided by people whom she trusts and who give her the opportunity to implement the changes in a way that is natural to her. She spoke to the importance of professional support in making any changes or decisions that affect her students.

Anne's conflict about the language choices she makes was present on a daily level. Here is an example of what Anne faced when she made the decision to sign a story to her students:

> I don't know how to do it. "Issunboshi was very excited when the river finally brought him to. . . . " Do you go ahead and sign the whole thing? Or do you sign that part and add ASL to show VERY EXCITED? In ASL it would be that [ASL sign]. You wouldn't need the "very" [in ASL], but you could still do the [English sign for] very and then still do the ASL for emphasis.

Her emphasis and struggle came with trying to do two languages at

---

13. I define ASL-like signing as not using voice, but including signs and some ASL grammar in rough English syntax.

once—an impossible task. But when I asked her if she would ever just simply "do ASL," she responded, first, that she doesn't know ASL well enough to teach using only ASL, and second, "[ASL] would not be accepted in the classroom. It's just not a way you do it."

Even if she knew ASL and it were accepted in the school, Anne still has trouble imagining using ASL as the language of instruction: "I would definitely [use ASL], but . . . English still has to be gotten to because that's a big reason why kids are in school." There is no doubt that deaf children need to be taught English, but Anne was not sure how using ASL as a language of instruction could eventually teach English. Yet, she admits that the present system of signing to students is helping the students acquire English: "But if you do [signed English] exactly, then you can add ASL. It's not putting ASL up as this language to be acquired. It's using it."

This poses an interesting logical problem. How can you use a language if you have not acquired it? It seems easier to think it is possible to combine two languages—ASL and spoken English—than to separate out the languages and teach and use them separately. When used within English, ASL provides meaning that is lost with only spoken, or strictly signed, English. But using ASL alone is somehow perceived as undermining the acquisition of English: "I see the benefits of ASL . . . being a more natural form of communication, and kids would probably be much happier, and they'd be able to express more things, and deeper things, than they can right now than in the English that they have. But then, back to the print. I need to see how it gets kids to learn English."

The benefit of ASL in the classroom is that it gives meaning to English. The sacrifice is that "the meaning is only part of what we're after. But the other part, too, is. . . . if I could do the story in ASL, [would] the kids come back to the story . . . and be able to read it?" This is a complicated question. Introducing ASL into a middle school classroom with deaf students who are not native signers will not automatically make the students good readers. As with any teacher who uses language well, the message in ASL at least would be clear and would eliminate the problem of using a language as the form of instruction. Anne, for example, has her own anecdotal evidence that when ASL is introduced at an early age in deaf families, those children "would pick up the English because they have a strong language base at home." I asked, "Pick up written language, written English?" Anne answered, "Written and signed. The same structure . . . in English."

Anne's assumption was that signs and print are the same thing, assuming a false parallel between speech and text as being the same thing. So, if you sign each word and morpheme exactly as it appears on the page, the students will "get" the language of stories. But they won't understand the meaning of the story. If you sign the story using ASL, then the students understand the story, but, Anne says, "You can't match that kind of signing with print; how can we expect kids to do it?" Anne's question was, "How can ASL be used to teach written English if it doesn't look anything like the print?"

The empirical answer to this question is subject for another paper. Theoretically, however, research on bilingualism in spoken languages indicates that bilingual students attain higher achievement levels when allowed to begin literacy instruction in their primary language before transferring to English literacy (Collier 1989; Cummins 1979, 1981; Fishman 1987; Hakuta 1986; Krashen and Biber 1988; McCollum and Walker 1990; Reyes 1987; Skutnab-Kangas 1981 cited in Reyes 1992). Jim Cummins (1979, 1981) suggests that students who learn academic concepts and literacy skills in their native language can more readily and quickly transfer those skills to a second language because knowledge is grounded in the language and schema they comprehend.

Research in deaf education provides compelling evidence that natural, early acquisition of ASL provides deaf children with age-appropriate world knowledge necessary in the stages of early literacy (Johnson and Erting 1989); initial exposure to the culture of literacy (Maxwell 1984); and access to English phonological organization (Hanson and Fowler 1987; Hanson 1989). Anne knew from anecdotal evidence that it is possible, as indicated from her knowledge that many deaf children of deaf parents do well in school:

> They come to school, and they're going to acquire English. I just believe that. And I think that there's research . . . [to support that] . . . because they already have one language intact, and you can build on that. . . . You just have an understanding of the framework of the language. So that's easier than coming from a hearing family where you have the pieces of [language].

Even so, Anne was bound to the reality that most deaf children of hearing families are not exposed to a language from birth and will not be exposed to ASL: "But it, it's not even proof of how it can, it's more the reality. How are you going to get kids to that point of acquiring ASL and at the same time [teach] reading?"

Anne and most teachers of the deaf were willing to try to teach English at the same time they instruct subject content in English. But it seems unrealistic to do it in ASL. Anne may very well be right, but I asked her how it would be if preschools for deaf children approximated the language environment of deaf families who use ASL, rather than trying to approximate hearing families who use English only. "I would love that. The only thing is the mix with home." The mix at home refers to parents who do not know ASL. Anne remembered her work in parent guidance: "I look at it more realistically. . . . [signed English] is not really successful at all, but in a home, it would be more realistic for parents to sign exact English, more natural for them, in some ways, than to use ASL for hearing parents. I just always go back to that."

The belief in deaf education seems to be that language practice needs to be more natural or easier for teachers to do, not what is most natural or easier for deaf children to acquire. The appeal of a signed English with ASL features is so powerful that, in light of all our conversations about its usefulness or futility, Anne was committed to making it work.

Preserving Current Form

How is it possible to preserve current practices in the face of counterevidence and knowledge? Within language practices are beliefs and values about language and deaf people. Counterevidence and new knowledge are not the only factors that influence change. James Gee (1990) claims that people construct their own social theory based on their own thought, reflection, study, and reading and arrive at their own theory of what is right or accurate. If counterevidence and new knowledge do not enter into a person's own theory, it is not likely that change will take hold. Theories like Anne's, built on similar broad-based theories in deaf education about language and deafness, are grounded in a logic that sustains it and can be stated as follows:

1. Expose deaf students to spoken and written English so they can acquire it;
2. If the student does not understand, change the input to include ASL;

3. Since the child's understanding does not come from English, expose the child to more English;
4. Some deaf children learn English better than other deaf children, either because of the degree of their hearing loss or because they are from deaf families.

If this is the theory, these conclusions follow:

1. Since deaf children are not learning English very well (generally they do not speak, read, or write it well), teachers need to try harder to expose deaf children to English;
2. Deaf children do not learn English well because they are not exposed to the right models or because of a lack of sufficient intellectual or linguistic abilities;
3. Teachers (and parents) need to be better models.

I have attempted to demonstrate how beliefs about language and literacy, manifested in Anne's practice and supported by her school and the wider field of deaf education, actually help create the problems deaf children face in school. In order for a change in language practice to occur, there must be a rethinking of the kinds of information about language and literacy teachers have access to; a change in the perception of ASL; and finally, a change in the overall academic expectations of deaf students.

SUMMARY AND CONCLUSION

Hopeless it is in educational practice to rely only on the conscious efforts of a child when they run counter to his principle interests and habits.—L. S. Vygotsky

In this study, I asked Anne questions she felt challenged her professional self: Can your students read? Why did you choose to present the story in this way? What do you think your students are learning in this lesson? What language are the students learning? What language are they exposed to? These particular questions evoked conflicting feelings in Anne—seeing herself sign in a way that she thought was effective on a communicative level, yet is not a full language, was bound to stir uncomfortable feelings. She believed that all students have the right to be exposed to a full language, yet she did not know the language they could understand. The students expressed what they like to see, but it is not what many hearing teachers or parents feel they are either ready to learn or what students are entitled to learn. These questions and realizations pushed Anne to consider that she believed about deaf education, sign language, and the relationship between English and American Sign Language.

I have described the literature environment, language practices, and paradoxes within which Anne teaches. Anne, a well-intentioned teacher, is open-minded with regard to new curricular approaches that seek to improve teaching and learning. Even so, Anne works within an institution that places emphasis first on speaking to deaf children and second on signing. In order to be a conscientious teacher, Anne also places primary emphasis on her spoken language, despite her own contradictory beliefs about the importance of presenting a clear, understandable language to her students.

Findings from the microanalysis revealed that Anne's effort to teach reading and literature was at great cost to the text and story, to her students, and to herself as a teacher. She worked hard to motivate and encourage the students to read, yet was reduced to simplifying even basic written texts. She spent most of her time talking *about* the text: interpreting, repeating, elaborating, and illustrating key phrases that reinforce the connections between events in the narrative. She incorporated some linguistic features of ASL to aid in clarity and understanding. However, her serious efforts at teaching deaf children to read are continually undermined as she faces the linguistic obstacles posed by speaking and signing simultaneously. At the same time, the students' energy was spent trying to interpret a communication system of signs with no grammar, no rules, and no foundation in the elements of language.

Anne was working within a philosophy of education that fundamentally believes that if teachers speak to deaf children, deaf children will hear. The efforts of creating a sign system that matches spoken language point to the assumption that deaf people can hear. Teachers are trained in signed English, schools encourage signed English, and so teachers end up speaking and signing to deaf children. Just as I did in my early years of teaching young deaf children, Anne accepted and perpetuated a rationale for speaking to the deaf.

The rationale that supports current practices is circular, based upon the pretense that children who cannot hear *can* hear. Even so, Anne found it difficult to go against the philosophy of the school, to be alone in the struggle to make radical changes in the school's language practices. And reform is not merely a matter of making conscious changes in language practice. These changes include altering people's beliefs and attitudes about deaf people. Pretending that deaf people can hear makes them more like hearing people. In this paper, I challenged this belief by identifying practices that support it.

I have examined the context within which Anne worked, her linguistic form, and her rationale for using specific language practices. Further study from the perspective of students would be fascinating. As students watch teachers sign English, what exactly are they perceiving? How is it different when they watch teachers sign ASL? What are they learning? What do they understand? What don't they understand? How do they perceive their schooling compared with their hearing friends? What is their perception of English, and how do those perceptions influence the way they experience both school and ASL? What do they expect of themselves and their teachers? Addressing these questions from the student's perspective could inform the content of teacher education programs as well as current teaching practice.

Until we in deaf education come to terms with the fact that deaf people cannot hear and begin to make changes on the level of language use and choice based on this fact, deaf education will likely remain as it has since the late 1800s, a system that serves the hearing people within its walls, not the deaf children it proposes to serve.

It is difficult to convince people to share a vision that contradicts their existing worldviews, customs, traditions, history, and culture. I believe that Anne is a visionary. She looks to improve her own practice by learning more about using ASL in the classroom. But for her, it is difficult to be a visionary when those around her do not see the need for new visions. In the case of deaf education, as with any social context, the known is always culturally preferable to the unknown that might be better but could be worse.

REFERENCES

Allen, T.E. 1986. Patterns of academic achievement among hearing-impaired students: 1974 and 1983. In *Deaf children in America,* ed. A. N. Schildroth and M. Karchmer, 161–206. San Diego: Calif: College Hill Press.

Allen, T. E., and M. A. Karchmer. 1990. Communication in classrooms for deaf students: Student, teacher, and program characteristics. In *Manual communication: Implications for education,* ed. H. Bornstein, 45–66. Washington, D.C.: Gallaudet University Press.

Chomsky, C. 1972. Write now, read later. *Childhood Education* 47:296–299.

Collier, V. 1989. How long? A synthesis of research on academic achievement in a second language. *TESOL Quarterly* 23:509–531.

Collins, A., and E.E. Smith. 1982. Teaching the process of reading comprehension. In *How and how much can intelligence be increased?* ed. D.K. Detterman and P.F. Sternberg, 175–185. Norwood, NJ: Ablex.

Cummins, J. 1979. Linguistic interdependence and the educational development of bilingual children. *Review of Educational Research* 49:222–251.

———. 1981. The role of primary language development in promoting educational success for language minority students. In *Schooling and language minority students: A theoretical framework,* ed. California State Department of Education, 3–49. Los Angeles: National Evaluation, Dissemination, and Assessment Center, California State University.

Evans, L. 1982. *Total communication: Structure and strategy.* Washington, D.C.: Gallaudet College Press.

Fishman, J. 1987. English only: Its ghosts, myths. and dangers. Keynote address at the Conference of the California Association for Bilingual Education, January, Anaheim.

Gee, James. 1990. *Sociolinguistics and literacies.* London: The Falmer Press.

Geertz, C. 1973. *The interpretation of cultures.* New York: Basic Books.

Gordon, Christine, J. 1989. Teaching narrative text structure: A process approach to reading and writing. In *Children's comprehension of text,* Newark, Del: ed. K. D. Muth, 70–102. International Reading Association.

Hakuta, K. 1986. *Mirror of language: The debate on bilingualism.* New York: Basic Books.

Hanson, V.L. 1989. Phonology and reading: Evidence from profoundly deaf readers. In *Phonology and reading disability: Solving the reading puzzle,* ed. D. Shankweiler and I.Y. Liberman, 69–89. Ann Arbor: University of Michigan Press.

Hanson, V.L., and C.A. Fowler, 1987. Phonological coding in word reading: Evidence from hearing and deaf readers. *Memory and Cognition* 15(3):199–207.

Hyde, M.B., and D.J. Power. 1991. Teachers' use of simultaneous communication: Effects on the signed and spoken components. *American Annals of the Deaf* 136(5):381–387.

Johnson, R.E., and C. Erting. 1989. Ethnicity and socialization in a classroom for deaf children. In *The sociolinguistics of the Deaf community,* ed. C. Lucas, 41–84. San Diego: Academic Press.

Johnson, R.E., S. Liddell, and C. Erting. 1989. Unlocking the curriculum:

Principles for achieving access in deaf education. Gallaudet Research Institute Working Paper No. 89–3. Washington, D.C.: Gallaudet University.

Kluwin, T. 1981. The grammaticality of manual representations of English. *American Annals of the Deaf.* 126:417–421.

Krashen, S., and D. Biber. 1988. *On course. Bilingual education's success in California.* Sacramento: California Association for Bilingual Education.

Luetke-Stahlman, B., and J. Luckner. 1991. *Effectively educating students with hearing impairments.* White Plains, N.Y.: Longman.

McCollum, P.A., and C.L. Walker. 1992. Minorities in American 2000. *Education and Urban Society* 24:178–195.

McDermott, R.P. 1976. Kids make sense: An ethnographic account of the interactional management of success and failure in one first grade classroom. Ph.D. diss., Stanford University.

MacWhinney, B. 1990. The CHILDES project: Computational tools for analyzing talk, version 93. Department of Psychology, Carnegie Mellon University.

Marmor, G., and L. Petitto. 1979. Simultaneous communication in the classroom: How well is English grammar represented? Sign Language Studies 23:99–136.

Maxwell, M. 1984. A deaf child's natural development of literacy. *Sign Language Studies* 44:191–224.

Moores, D.F. 1987. *Educating the deaf: Psychology, principles, and practices.* 3d ed. Boston: Houghton Mifflin.

Morimoto, J. 1986. *The inch boy.* New York: Viking Penguin.

Reyes, M. de la Luz. 1987. Comprehension of content area passages: A study of Spanish/English readers in third and fourth grade. In *Becoming literate in English as a second language,* ed. S.R. Goldman and H.T. Trueba, 107–126. Norwood, N.J.: Ablex.

Reyes, M. de la Luz. 1992. Challenging venerable assumptions: Literacy instruction for linguistically different students. *Harvard Educational Review* 62:427:446.

Skutnab-Kangas, T. 1981. *Bilingualism or not: The education of minorities.* Clevedon, Eng.: Multilingual matters.

Strong, M., E.S. Charlson, and R. Gold. 1987. Integration and segregation in mainstreaming programs for children and adolescents with hearing impairments. *The Exceptional Child* 34(3):181–195.

Swisher, M. V. 1984. Signed input of hearing mothers to deaf children. *Language Learning* 34:69–86.

Story Structure for Written, Spoken, and Signed Portions of *The Inch Boy* with Story Structure Labels, Temporal Markers, Tense, and Text.

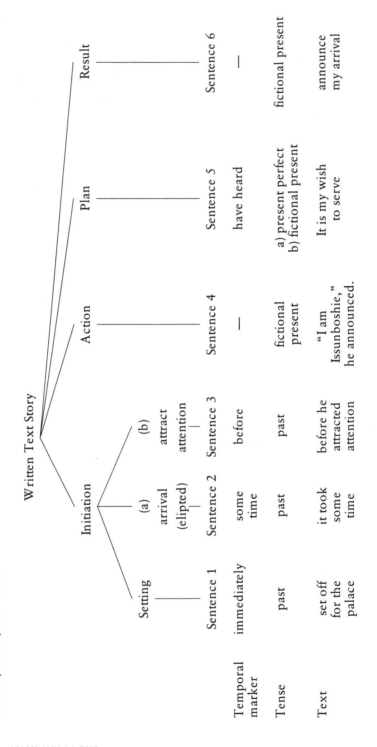

Written Text Story

	Setting	Initiation (a) arrival (elipted)	Initiation (b) attract attention	Action	Plan	Result
	Sentence 1	Sentence 2	Sentence 3	Sentence 4	Sentence 5	Sentence 6
Temporal marker	immediately	some time	before	—	have heard	—
Tense	past	past	past	fictional present	a) present perfect b) fictional present	fictional present
Text	set off for the palace	it took some time	before he attracted attention	"I am Issunboshie," he announced.	It is my wish to serve	announce my arrival

Story Structure for Written, Spoken, and Signed Portions of *The Inch Boy* with Story Structure Labels, Temporal Markers, Tense, and Text.

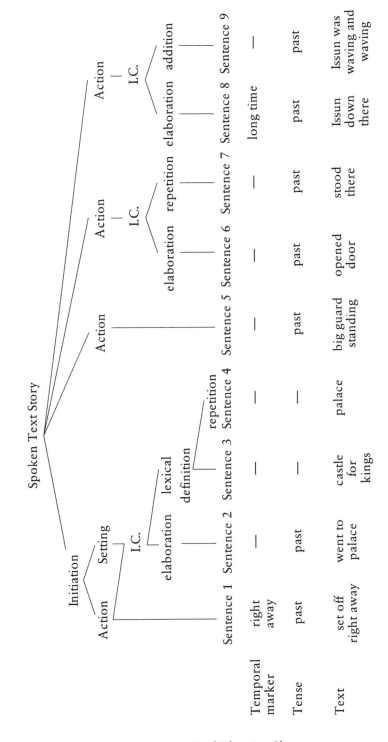

Story Structure for Written, Spoken, and Signed Portions of _The Inch Boy_ with Story Structure Labels, Temporal Markers, Tense, and Text.

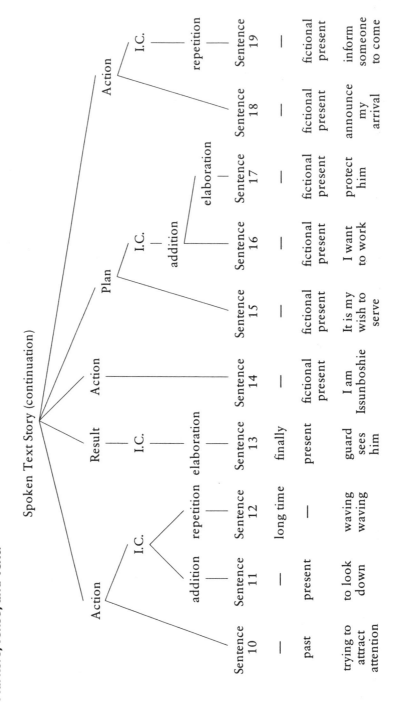

Spoken Text Story (continuation)

	Sentence 10	Sentence 11	Sentence 12	Sentence 13	Sentence 14	Sentence 15	Sentence 16	Sentence 17	Sentence 18	Sentence 19
	—	—	long time	finally	—	—	—	—	—	—
	past	present	—	present	fictional present	fictional present	fictional present	fictional present	fictional present	fictional present
	trying to attract attention	to look down	waving waving	guard sees him	I am Issunboshie	It is my wish to serve	I want to work	protect him	announce my arrival	inform someone to come

Signed Text with ASL Fingerspelling, Initialized Signs, and English Glosses.

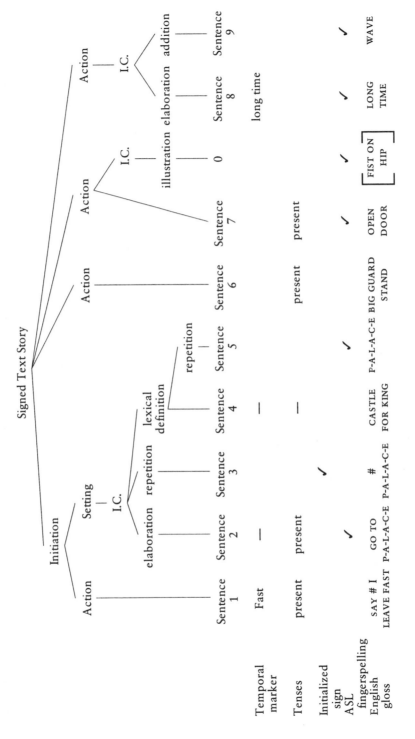

Signed Text Story

	Sentence 1	Sentence 2	Sentence 3	Sentence 4	Sentence 5	Sentence 6	Sentence 7	0	Sentence 8	Sentence 9
Temporal marker	Fast	—		—						
Tenses	present	present		—		present	present			
Initialized sign		✓	✓		✓		✓	✓	✓	✓
ASL fingerspelling										
English gloss	SAY # I LEAVE FAST	GO TO P-A-L-A-C-E	# P-A-L-A-C-E	CASTLE FOR KING	P-A-L-A-C-E	BIG GUARD STAND	OPEN DOOR	FIST ON HIP	LONG TIME	WAVE

Signed Text with ASL Fingerspelling, Initialized Signs, and English Glosses.

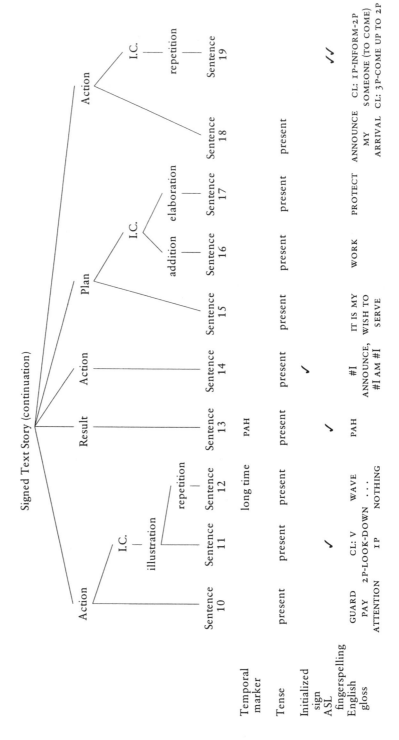

Transcription Conventions

American Sign Language [ASL] signs, or signs that the teacher uses with her students, are represented by English glosses in upper case letters. These glosses are not translations, but labels for signs. I have applied some conventions from CHAT, a computer-based transcription system, to my transcripts (MacWhinney 1990).

Main tiers, in uppercase letters, appear in this order for comparison purposes:

Text Tier   = (TXT)
Speaker Tier   = (ANN)
Signed Tier   = (SGN)

Dependent tiers, in lowercase letters, indicate simultaneous actions (act) or role play (rle) that occur with the spoken and signed message.

K-Y-O-T-O =   Uppercase letters separated by hyphens indicate fingerspelling.

    # =   Initialized sign

   [ ] =   Brackets around spoken and signed words indicate when speech and sign occurred simultaneously.

  [o] =   A zero indicates when a word, suffix, prefix, or tense is present in one modality (speech) but absent in the other modality (sign).

 +. . . =   Indicates that the sentence continues to the next line.

(112) =   The numbers in parentheses refer to the sample sentences used in the analysis.

CL:V 1P-LOOK-DOWN-2P = An ASL directional verb, first person looks down at second person.

Example:
(118) TXT: **The guard was so surprised.**

(119) ANN: [The] [guard] [was] [so] [surprise]ed [o   ] +. . .
(120) SGN: [THE] [#GUARD] [WAS] [S-O] [SURPRISE]o   [SHOCK]

(121) TXT: o.

(122) ANN: [when he saw   ] [Issunboshi] +...
(123) SGN: [CL: 1P-LOOK-DOWN-2P] [#I   ]

Communication and Language Use in

Spanish-Speaking Families with Deaf Children

Barbara Gerner de García

Deaf children entering school are typically described as having little or no fluency in any language (Johnson, Liddell, and Erting 1989; Maxwell 1985). The communication situation in hearing families with a deaf[1] child is complex, and much more so in homes where languages other than English are used. The deaf child is part of a family that is culturally and linguistically different, a family negotiating a path between the dominant Anglo culture and its language, English, and their own culture and language, a family in a trilingual situation. The children of these families—deaf and hearing—will be gaining literacy in English—a language in which the parents may have limited skills.

Although the literature notes the potential value of a home communication study with Hispanic deaf children (Bennett 1987; Maxwell 1986), none had been previously undertaken. This study provides insights into the complexity of the language situation for deaf children from Spanish-speaking homes with implications for assessment and educational programming to better meet their needs. These families are in a trilingual situation that may not be recognized by most schools for the deaf. Ideas about the bilingual/bicultural nature of the Deaf community are influencing deaf education, whereas the trilingual/multicultural situation of many linguistically diverse families with deaf children is rarely addressed.

Communication is the prerequisite for meaningful interaction between any deaf child and his or her family. Family, parental, and Hispanic community influences may be stronger for Hispanic deaf children than for their non-Hispanic deaf peers. Hispanic children are more likely to be

---

1. *Deaf* with a capital *D* is used in this chapter to indicate those who consider themselves both linguistically and culturally members of the Deaf community. In this study, the term "deaf" is used to refer to all those children usually identified as "hearing impaired," regardless of the severity of their hearing loss.

enrolled in day school programs for the deaf than in residential school programs (Cohen, Fischgrund, and Redding 1990). In day school programs, deaf children spend as few as six hours a day in the school environment, where they are exposed primarily to hearing and/or White cultural role models.[2] As a result, they have less exposure to the Deaf community and to American Sign Language (ASL) and spend more time in the cultural and linguistic community of their families.

There is a growing awareness that the number of children in the United States from families that are racially, ethnically, and linguistically diverse is rapidly increasing.[3] This growing diversity is also found in schools and programs for the deaf.[4] The 1992–93 Annual Survey of Hearing-Impaired Children and Youth indicated that 39.6 percent of 47,635 children surveyed were from racial/ethnic minorities. Of these, 15.8 percent (N=7523) were Hispanic, the fastest growing group in the Annual Survey (personal communication, A. Schildroth, January 7, 1994).

These demographic changes mean that growing numbers of professionals working with the Deaf will increasingly be in contact with Hispanic deaf children and adults and their families. However, many of these professionals may be unprepared to meet the needs of these children and their families. Schools for the deaf often underestimate the complexity of the home communication environment and lack understanding of the dynamics of communication in a multilingual environment. Schools may not consider or be aware of the strategies that these deaf children may need or use to deal with their family's three languages.

Hispanic deaf children show significantly lower academic achievement than their African American and non-Hispanic Deaf peers (Allen 1986; Jensema 1975). Schools may contribute to this lack of success by failing to recognize the language (however limited it may appear to be) and un-

---

2. Current statistics indicate that 89.8 percent of teachers of the deaf surveyed in 349 schools and programs for the deaf are hearing and white, while only 10.4 percent are from minority, ethnic backgrounds. Only 11.7 percent of the minority professionals are deaf (Andrews and Jordan 1993).

3. "Linguistically diverse" refers to a person or people who use languages other than the majority language, including deaf individuals who use ASL as a first language. It is used in this study as an alternative term for the more widely used phrases "language minority," "linguistic minority," or non-English speaking.

4. In fact, the term "minority deaf" is no longer accurate (Jordan 1990). The term "multicultural deaf" may be used in its place to reflect this new reality.

derstanding of language and culture that these children bring with them to school (Simmons de García 1988). The overall lack of achievement by all deaf children may be attributed to the failure to see them as linguistically and culturally diverse (Simmons de García 1989). Simmons de García (1988) argues that because most deaf children enter school with little or no exposure to ASL, schools must "utilize, validate and expand upon whatever communicative strategies these young children use to make meaning and act upon their surroundings" (p. 48). The communicative strategies that deaf children bring with them to school will vary. For deaf and hard of hearing children from linguistically diverse homes, understanding the role of home language and culture may be even more crucial. When a school fails to see the deaf child as having something to communicate, it is ignoring the communicative strategies the deaf child has been using to act upon his or her surroundings. These strategies vary from child to child and depend on whether the parents are hearing or Deaf, use ASL or sign language[5] or not, and also depend on the ethnic, racial, and cultural community of the family.

This study is grounded in the body of research that challenges viewing differences as deficits, a view that continues to dominate educational practice in this country. A common view of deaf children from linguistically diverse homes is that exposure to multiple languages leads to cognitive confusion or overload (Dean 1984). As previously mentioned, young deaf children entering school are commonly referred to as having no language (Johnson, Liddell, and Erting 1989), but this labeling may be applied to Hispanic deaf children entering U.S. schools and programs for the deaf for the first time, regardless of age or prior educational experience (Gerner de García 1992a). Viewing Hispanic deaf children or any deaf or hard of hearing child from a linguistically diverse family as

---

5. The term "sign language" is used in this study to include a range of visual/gestural communication, including, but not limited to, some forms of signed English, Pidgin Sign English (contact signing), educational sign systems, as well as the visual/gestural language used in the subject families (which may include Puerto Rican or Dominican Sign Language). Because authors cited frequently use the term "sign" without specifying or defining what the term includes, this study uses the term "sign language" to indicate the use of visual/gestural language that may or may not be ASL. Furthermore, for the purposes of this study, the use of the term indicates that status as a language is assumed.

deficient prevents the school from meeting the children's needs as well as seeing their potential and actual abilities. This deficit view is commonly applied to children from linguistically diverse families, deaf and hearing, as in the following excerpt describing a Mexican-American community:

> Most of the studies . . . assumed that what parents may be doing in the home is insufficient to meet the school's demands in helping children achieve. . . . Inherent in this research is the failure to examine and view the family's sociocultural environment in the home and to understand it as a source of knowledge about the children which could be used in the classroom (Delgado-Gaitan 1990, 50).

This study is an attempt to better understand the sociocultural environments of Spanish-speaking homes with deaf children and, by doing so, expand our understanding of deaf children from linguistically diverse families.

METHODOLOGY

This study of communication in Spanish-speaking homes with deaf children yielded a diverse and complex picture. The study provides data about actual language use in these homes as well as insights into the complexities of communication in families that are using three languages— two spoken and one visual-gestural.

The study included three Spanish-speaking families with deaf children. The deaf children varied in age, in percentage of hearing loss, etiology, as well as educational and linguistic experiences. The children were students at a day school for the deaf in a northeastern U.S. city. Data were gathered through interviews, field notes, participant-observation, and videotaping of the families at home. Families were observed and videotaped at approximately weekly intervals by the researcher for five to six sessions. Each visit lasted two to three hours. Field notes supplemented the videotaped data.

An ethnographic approach was chosen to gather data on language use in the homes. It was important to study family communication in the home environment where the deaf child was surrounded by family members in order to provide a picture of the dynamics and complexity of a trilingual environment. The only previous study of communication in

Spanish-speaking families with deaf children gathered data by means of a questionnnaire rather than extended observation (Lerman 1984).

Bennett's study (1987, 1988) on Hispanic deaf preschool children demonstrated the value of ethnographic approaches with this population. Ethnographic studies by Erting (1981, 1985, 1988) and Maxwell (1984, 1985, 1986) with deaf children showed this approach to data gathering offers opportunities for the observation of the natural use of language by deaf children that may not occur in experimental or school settings. While the literature contains studies documenting the lack of success experienced by Hispanic deaf children (Delgado 1984), there is a shortage of research that looks at Hispanic deaf children in their home environment or in the community of their families.

Sample

The focus of the study was on families, not just on the deaf member of the family. Therefore, the sample is described as three Spanish-speaking subject families. Each deaf child presented a different profile that could provide data helpful to understanding a variety of situations that might affect Spanish-speaking families with deaf and hard of hearing children.

The selection criteria were:

1. Hearing, native Spanish-speaking parents, preferably of Puerto Rican or Dominican origin, who used Spanish as the primary language of the home.
2. The deaf child's enrollment for at least two years as a day student in a program for the deaf with a Total Communication philosophy.[6]
3. Families that included both hard of hearing and profoundly deaf children of varying ages, educational backgrounds, and etiologies.

Families of Puerto Rican and Dominican origin were sought because these two ethnic groups make up the overwheming majority of Hispanic families with deaf children in the Northeastern United States. (Cohen

6. At the time of this study, the school the deaf children attended defined itself as using Total Communication. At the same time, the school was moving towards including more and more ASL in the classrooms. Teachers were offered on-site classes in ASL, and more deaf teachers and aides were being hired.

1987), where the study was carried out, possibly allowing broader applications of the findings. Day school enrollment would indicate that the deaf children spent more time in their home environment than at school.

A Total Communication philosophy would indicate that the deaf child had (to varying degrees) access to communication in the school environment. However, it is important to note that schools for the deaf vary in their definition and application of a Total Communication philosophy. It may include the use of Pidgin Signed English (contact signing),[7] simultaneous communication,[8] spoken English, and sometimes includes the use of ASL. At the time of the study, the Total Communication approach was the dominant educational philosophy applied in the education of deaf children. However, in some schools, including the school these children attended, the use of ASL was growing and supported.

Placement in a school that used Total Communication was a factor because it would indicate that the deaf children signed at school. It might also mean that their parents were encouraged to learn sign language (visual/gestural language that may or may not be ASL). In the school that the deaf children in the subject families attended, sign language classes with a Spanish interpreter were provided for the families. Severity of hearing loss was relevant, as it is typically assumed that a profoundly deaf child would not be influenced by the oral Spanish in the home environments (Luetke-Stahlman and Weiner 1984). A hard of hearing child, however, with the appropriate use of hearing aids, could be expected to learn some of the home language, even if it differed from the language of the school (Secada 1984). A hard of hearing child might be more affected by the difference between the spoken language of the home—in this case Spanish—and the spoken language of the school—English—than a profoundly deaf child (Dean 1984). Without intervention on the part of the school, the deaf or hard of hearing child may not develop awareness that different languages are spoken at home and in school (Gerner de García 1993).

7. This term refers to varieties of sign language used by deaf and hearing people that include elements of ASL and English (Baker and Cokely 1980). The understanding of what PSE actually means has come under renewed scrutiny (Lucas and Valli 1989, 1990). Contact signing can be described as varying from person to person depending on the control of ASL and English of the person signing.

8. The practice of simultaneously signing and speaking, also known as sim-com.

There were two categories of Hispanic deaf children who were not considered for this study. One of these categories included deaf children from homes where the parents were bilingual in English and Spanish. These were parents who reported to the school that they used English with their deaf child and/or their hearing children. The other category of Hispanic deaf students not included in the sample was immigrants who had arrived in the United States with little or no prior schooling.

The deaf children included in this study were all born outside the mainland United States, and their families had immigrated here. The immigration experiences of the families provided additional opportunities to gain insights into the process of deaf and hearing family members making the transition from a monolingual environment to a trilingual environment. Deaf children who immigrate from Puerto Rico and the Dominican Republic have to learn both ASL and English when they arrive here. Deaf children who have been to school in those countries have been exposed to written and oral Spanish, often with little or no exposure to sign language in the school environment.

THE RESEARCH QUESTIONS

Two major questions were determined. These questions include subquestions.

Research Question One

What are the patterns of language choice and language use in Spanish-speaking families with deaf children?

- What kind of code-switching is done by deaf and hearing family members?
- What literacy practices are used in these trilingual families?

What preferences or patterns of language use are evident in the data? The ethographies of each of the three subject families provide a global/holistic description of language use and dynamics in these families. Analysis of language use describes which members of each family used oral Spanish, oral English, ASL, home signs, and/or foreign signs and gestures. Use of code-switching is described for deaf and hearing family members.

Another aspect of language use is literacy. Trilingual families can be literate in multiple languages. The uses of literacy are also related to school expectations regarding literacy.

Research Question Two

What affects the communication process in these families?

- To what extent is deafness accepted in the families?
- What accommodations are made by deaf and hearing members of the families to facilitate communication?
- How does language proficiency (in Spanish, English, and sign language) affect the deaf child's view of the family, the family's view of the deaf child, and the school's view of the deaf child?
- How do dyadic, triadic, and multiparty interactions affect communication in the family?

The ethnographies describe the extent to which each family accepted deafness. Acceptance of deafness is related to the accommodation of the deaf member of the family. The videotapes were analyzed for evidence that hearing family members used a variety of strategies to accommodate the deaf family member and to facilitate communication. The descriptions delineate the extent to which hearing members of the families appeared to value learning a visual/gestural language and showed adaptation to the visual channel when communicating with the deaf child.

THE FAMILIES

The Alvarez Family

The Alvarez family had immigrated from the Dominican Republic seven years previously. It was made up of mother, Berta; her second husband, Eduardo; Rubén, eleven, who has a moderate hearing loss and is categorized as hard of hearing; Cynthia, six; Vanesa, five; and Daniel, three-and-a-half. Mr. Alvarez was in the Dominican Republic at the time of the study and did not participate. The etiology of Rubén's hearing loss was unknown. He had not been diagnosed until he began kindergarten in a bilingual program. Delayed diagnosis appears to be common for many hard of hearing children from Spanish-speaking homes (Gerner de García 1993).

In his family, Rubén was doing most of the work of accommodating his family's language needs. Everyone in the family, except his stepfather, spoke only Spanish. His two sisters were in bilingual programs in a public school and were exposed to English in that environment. His mother was taking English as a Second Language classes. Rubén spoke Spanish at home with everyone in the family. Occasionally, he used some English with his sister, Cynthia, at her request, when she wanted him to teach her something.

No one in the family had learned sign language. For Mrs. Alvarez, the school's recommendation that she learn to sign didn't make sense. Her son understood and spoke Spanish, and she felt she could help him more with Spanish and that "it is better for him to speak."

The communication environment at home presented many obstacles to Rubén. His lack of fluency in Spanish was repeatedly commented on by his sister, who often laughed at his mistakes. His mother never used Rubén's hearing loss as an excuse for his lack of fluency but defended him in other ways. On one occasion when he attempted to read in Spanish to his little brother, his sister repeatedly insisted that he didn't know how to read. His reading was in fact quite halting. Mother did not disagree with her daughter. Instead she made comments including, "He's older." "He's your brother and he's showing (us)." "Don't be disobedient" and "He doesn't know how to read a lot. We have to teach him." As these comments continued on about him (and were not directed to him), Rubén quietly asserted himself saying in (ungrammatical) Spanish, "I'm learning."

In this family there were frequent and numerous multiparty conversations when several people were talking at the same time and with a lot of competition for mother's attention. Rubén's hearing loss made it almost impossible for him to participate. In multiparty conversations, turn taking was freer, making it difficult for Rubén to know who to look at for visual cues or to lipread. No one in the family acted as a facilitator for Rubén, helping him to participate in conversations by repeating, getting his attention, or addressing him directly.

Rubén lacked strategies for interjecting and joining conversations. He did not interrupt, nor did he excuse himself in order to get into conversations. In these conversations, he did not assert himself or make it known when he did not understand. However, in dyadic conversations with his mother, he would indicate when he didn't understand, usually by asking, "¿Que?" ("what?)".

Probably most crucial to Rubén's behavior was the lack of recognition of his hearing impairment at home and the lack of recognition of him as Spanish-speaking in his school environment. At home, he was an imperfect speaker of Spanish and treated as such, not as hard of hearing. His deafness was denied at home: he denied it, his mother denied it, and thus his siblings didn't acknowledge it. This denial was so deep that Rubén often assumed the role of interpreter for his mother, a job often given to the eldest child in a linguistically diverse family. He did Spanish-English interpreting for her in the clinic, at the hospital, and in other situations.

At school, the denial that he was a Spanish-speaker extended to his own behavior. He rarely used Spanish in the school setting even with Spanish-speaking staff. The denial of his other self that occurred both at school and at home forced Rubén to function in different roles in each of these settings. He had few opportunities to be recognized as a multilingual child. When he was viewed only in terms of his Spanish language ability, English ability, or ASL/sign language ability, he was viewed primarily as deficient because he was not fluent in any of these languages.

The Blanco Family

The Blanco family was made up of mother, father, and three children: Iris, nine; Elena, ten; and Wilfredo, five, who has a congenital profound hearing loss. The family had moved from Puerto Rico three years previously. Wilfredo's deafness was diagnosed after the move to the mainland and was a result of heredity. Mrs. Blanco had a deaf sister and grandfather and through genetic testing was found to be a carrier of deafness.

The Blanco family used a number of strategies to accommodate their deaf member. All family members, including the father, used sign language to communicate with Wilfredo. They consistently signed without voice, although they voiced occasionally in English for emphasis or when reprimanding Wilfredo.

Mrs. Blanco stated that she had always been able to communicate with her son since he was little. She went to sign language classes at her son's school. She said she didn't need the classes, but it was "good" to go.

This may have been her internalization of a message from the school that going to sign language classes meant one was a good parent. Her daughters also went to class with her, but Mrs. Blanco said her husband would not go.

The family was observed using a number of signs that were not ASL signs. Wilfredo appeared to adjust the sign variations in his family. Some signs were variations on ASL signs and meanings that he used with his mother. For example, they signed, I, ME to mean *mine*, and WAIT, with the palm oriented out instead of in. The family used a home sign for *playground*, and Wilfredo had a home sign to indicate a kind of Puerto Rican cracker. One of the signs he used—the sign for *birthday*—appeared to be a home sign, as this sign varied from the three signs for *birthday* in the Puerto Rican Sign Language dictionary (Matos 1990), as well as being unfamiliar to two informants (see figure 1). However, this sign was later found, in fact, to be a sign used in Puerto Rico.[9] The use of this

FIGURE 1. *BIRTHDAY/Puerto Rican sign*

9. On a trip to Puerto Rico a few months later, a deaf man used this sign in a conversation with me. This sign was later verified by another source. Minnie Mae Wilding-Díaz, of Brigham Young University, later told me that this is the sign her Puerto Rican (deaf) husband uses.

sign provided evidence of the family's use of Puerto Rican signs. Wilfredo's understanding and use of home signs and gestures, as well as his accommodation of the ASL variation used by his mother, indicated that he was code-switching at home with his family.

In this family, there was constant use of three languages: Spanish, sign language, and English (see figure 2). Wilfredo's two older sisters constantly code-switched between Spanish and English. The parents spoke only Spanish, but Mrs. Blanco often interjected remarks in Spanish into her daughters' English conversations, indicating her receptive knowledge of English.

Despite the fact that the family accepted Wilfredo's need for visual/gestural communication, there were obstacles to a total integration of the deaf experience with the Hispanic/Puerto Rican experience. Mrs. Blanco expressed deep feelings about her experience as a mother of a deaf child. She had tried to become involved at the school for the deaf but had not been successful. She had awards hanging in her living room testifying to her dedication as a member of Bilingual Parents Councils on behalf of her two daughters, yet she had not been able to assume a similar role in the school for the deaf. She stated that despite her limited

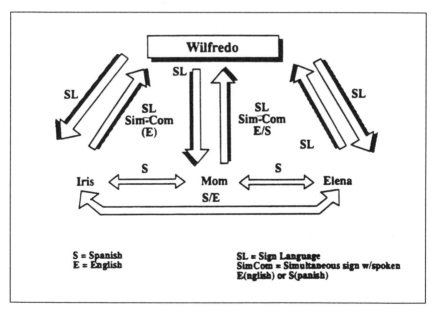

FIGURE 2. *Language use in the Blanco family.*

abilities in English, she believed that she could still do something. Perhaps she was not seen as an asset to her son's school because of the linguistic differences. She spoke Spanish, had limited English skills, and her sign language was influenced by the signs she had used with deaf family members in Puerto Rico and did not conform to the school language.

Furthermore, Mrs. Blanco had experienced prejudice as the Hispanic mother of a deaf child. She described how medical personnel or human service providers often assumed that she must have caused her child's deafness through the use of drugs or alcohol. In her own community, Mrs. Blanco stated that the prevalent view was that children were born with disabilities because their parents were sinners. Mrs. Blanco avoided visiting her husband's family in Puerto Rico because her in-laws constantly lamented the fact that their grandson was deaf and seemed to blame her.

The Castillo Family

The Castillo family was made up of mother; Alicea, fourteen; Pablo, twelve; and Jasmín, eleven, who is profoundly deaf. Mrs. Castillo, who was divorced, had moved to the United States four years before her children, leaving them in the care of their grandmother and extended family. The children had moved from the Dominican Republic to rejoin their mother two years prior to the study. Jasmín, deaf as a result of meningitis as a toddler, had begun her schooling in an oral school for the deaf in Santo Domingo. When Jasmín had come to her present school, her mother had turned down trilingual support for her, believing Spanish would confuse her. The school did not recommend otherwise, because of Jasmín's profound deafness. However, Jasmín had been in a Spanish language environment for the first eight years of her life and had been taught literacy skills in Spanish for three years, which most likely influenced her to some extent.

In this family, the oldest child, Alicea, was the primary communicator with Jasmín. Alicea and her mother had learned some sign language, but mother's ability to sign was very limited. It was observed that conversing with Jasmín was often trying. She was difficult to understand due to a lack of basic pragmatic skills. Jasmín often failed to establish topics or stick to one once it was set. Not only were there repeated episodes of this with her mother and sister, but her teachers had made the same observation. The communication situation at home couldn't improve until

Jasmín's family learned more sign language and she improved her conversational skills.

There were also episodes when Jasmín ridiculed her sister's signing, refused to show her sister how to correctly sign a word, and refused to show her mother signs. Although it is unlikely that deaf children can teach their families to sign, they can provide reinforcement for what the family is learning in sign language classes. Both her mother and sister expressed frustration with her unwillingness to help. The Castillo family needed an adequate language base in order to communicate meaningfully with Jasmín. Jasmín was frustrated as well. The family members may have been blaming each other for the difficulties that their multilingual situation posed.

Additionally, Jasmín needed help understanding more about her multilingual environments. She described her view of language use in her family: "My sister wants (to speak) English, not Spanish. She wants (to speak) English. I want (to use) English, too, not Spanish anymore. I (want to use) English. I know a lot of sign language. I don't know Spanish Sign Language."

Jasmín seemed to express an idea she had that a person had to give up their first language (in this case, Spanish) to learn another one (English). She appeared to describe this not only for herself but for her sister as well. Jasmín's repeated questions to me during observations about language in her home—what language was the TV show in (the family often watched Spanish-language television), what languages did various family members speak—possibly reflected her attempts to develop metalinguistic understanding.

Deaf children in multilingual situations have to be made aware that they are, in fact, dealing with different languages (Blackwell and Fischgrund 1984). Jasmín described her understanding of language use by her family, as well as her transition as a deaf child who arrived knowing some Spanish, to a deaf child who was now learning English and sign language in school:

> My sister (speaks) a different (language), Spanish and English. I (speak) English. My mother (speaks) Spanish and English, too, like my sister. My father (speaks) Spanish. Both of them (the reference is unclear). Not me. I sign English, English. I sign, nothing but English. I (use) English. I (know) a little bit of Spanish. I don't understand or talk

Spanish. I sign a little (Spanish), but I don't know how to speak it. When I arrived here (from Santo Domingo) I knew a lot of Spanish.

All members of the Castillo family had had to make adjustments to a new linguistic environment since moving from Santo Domingo. Jasmín was being taught through sign language for the first time. She prioritized learning ASL, while her mother and siblings had to learn English in order to survive. Providing support for learning both English and ASL could have alleviated some of the conflicts over communication that the family was experiencing.

DISCUSSION

The questions in this study centered on language use and language choice in immigrant Spanish-speaking families with deaf children. The purpose of this focus was to gain understanding of communication patterns and practices in these families. The discussion of results is organized to present (a) the perspective of families who were dealing with a deaf member, (b) the perspective of the deaf children dealing with their experience in a linguistically diverse family, and (c) the way in which schools typically attend to linguistically diverse families and their deaf children. This will help to depict the range of possible outcomes in trilingual (or multilingual) contexts involving deaf children and to make recommendations for schools to meet the needs of linguistically diverse families and their deaf children.

The Family's View of the Deaf Child

The family's view of the deaf child may be affected by the language proficiency of family members in the home language, in English and in sign language; acceptance of deafness; and willingness or ability to use strategies to accommodate the deaf child.

LANGUAGE PROFICIENCY

All three deaf children had been born outside the country. Being immigrants created additional stress on the families as they learned two new languages and cultures. Deaf and hearing family members had to learn the English language and culture of the United States. The need to learn the language and culture of the Deaf community overwhelms many hearing parents. Immigrant parents need additional support to facilitate their acquisition of ASL and awareness of Deaf culture while they are also learning English.

In addition to the use of ASL signs, communication in the three families included the use of home signs, foreign signs and gestures, and oral Spanish. In the two families that used visual/gestural communication, there was little use of simultaneous communication. When sign and speech were produced simultaneously, English, not Spanish, was used. This was despite the fact that in these children's school, linguistically diverse parents had long been advised that they could/should continue to speak their native language with their children and combine spoken Spanish with signs.

There were possible explanations for these results. In the school for the deaf that the children attended, sign language classes for parents were being taught by Deaf teachers who emphasized ASL and did not voice while signing. Additionally, the parents may not have signed and spoken Spanish simultaneously because they had no models. At school, parents saw teachers signing and speaking English. This also was what their deaf children were more accustomed to seeing. Thus, when the parents used visual/gestural communication, they used it in the ways they had seen modeled in the school environment and sign language classes. Additionally, the families may have used oral English when combining speech and signs because they realized their children knew little, if any, Spanish.

The families' knowledge of sign language was, as expected, a significant factor. In the Blanco family, the use of sign language had a positive impact on the type and quantity of interactions that Wilfredo had with family members, although it did not extend to including him in multiparty interactions. In the Alvarez family, Rubén's communication needs as a hard of hearing child were never considered—because his deafness was denied. Only one hearing member of the Castillo family, Alicea, used sign language conversationally with Jasmín. Jasmín had no one who interpreted or facilitated communication for her in the family.

The families varied in their use of English. Some family members, such as Rubén's little brother, knew no English. However, the two Blanco sisters spoke a great deal of English and constantly code-switched with one another. This added to the linguistic complexity of the home language environment. In the case of the Castillo family, a desire to be competent in English led to an emphasis on acquiring English over learning sign language.

ACCEPTANCE OF DEAFNESS

Acceptance of deafness emerged as a theme across the families. Acceptance of deafness involved more than acknowledging deafness and accommodating it. It appeared from consideration of these three families that acceptance was a process involving three stages:

1. acknowledging the child's deafness
2. accommodating the child's deafness
3. accepting the child's deafness

It appeared for these families that there was no advancement to the next stage until the family had gone through the previous stage.

The Alvarez family had not acknowledged Rubén's deafness. This prevented them from accommodating or accepting his deafness. Mrs. Alvarez never referred to Rubén's hearing loss. Her silence may have been a denial of his difference. She seemed to accept or expect less from him. Mrs. Alvarez also used Rubén as an interpreter, establishing a conflict for him. Rubén, wanting to please his mother and demonstrate his competence, interpreted for her. By assuming a responsibility often given to the eldest child in linguistically diverse families, Rubén was claiming his status as eldest and in the process participating in the denial of his deafness.

The Blanco family appeared to be in the second stage of the process. They were working to accommodate Wilfredo's deafness. Although the family accepted Wilfredo's need for visual/gestural communication, Mrs. Blanco demonstrated feelings of guilt about her son's deafness. These feelings may have interfered with acceptance of his deafness. Her in-laws reinforced her view that as a genetic carrier of deafness, she was responsible. Additionally, Mrs. Blanco faced prejudice in her experiences dealing with negative assumptions about the causes of her son's deafness.

The Castillo family acknowledged Jasmín's deafness but were not yet in the second stage of accommodating her need for visual/gestural language. They were focused on their needs as recent immigrants. In order for them to deal with these issues as well as the need to accommodate their deaf member, the family needed help. The parents' program at the school centered on teaching sign language and running parents' groups that focused on general issues such as discipline. Although the school did

TABLE 1. *Communication Strategies Used by Hearing Family Members*

| | | Family | |
Strategy	Alvarez	Blanco	Castillo
1. Uses ASL signs	—	X	X
2. Uses home/foreign signs	—	X	X
3. Uses gestures	—	X	X
4. Uses facial expression	—	X	X
5. Uses writing and/or drawing	—	—	—
6. Taps a shoulder to get the deaf child's attention before speaking/signing	—	X	—
7. Waves to get the deaf child's attention before speaking/signing	—	X	—
8. Follows the gaze of the deaf child	—	X	—
9. Places self where deaf child can see speaker when communicating	—	X	—
10. Alternates vocabulary/simplifies language when deaf child doesn't understand	—	X	—

have a parent liaison for Spanish-speaking families (who made up the majority of the school population), there were no programs designed for immigrant parents.

ACCOMMODATION WITHIN THE FAMILIES

As described in the previous section, acceptance of deafness varied across the three families. Acknowledging deafness and accommodating a deaf child's linguistic needs leads to acceptance of the child's deafness. This section compares the use of visual/gestural language and strategies—essential to accommodating the deaf child—among the families. The use of strategies among the three families is illustrated in table 1.

The Alvarez family used none of the strategies. Not only did they not use sign language, but they also failed to use some of the strategies that facilitate communication with a hard of hearing person. For example, no one in the family moved so that Rubén could see them better when talking to him (#9), nor did anyone, particularly Mrs. Alvarez, simplify language or restate things for Rubén (#10).

None of the families used writing and drawing (#5), a finding consistent with Maxwell's research on uses of literacy (1986). The Blanco family used every strategy except writing and drawing. Mrs. Blanco had used visual/gestural language growing up with deaf family members. Her communication style likely served as a model for her daughters and husband.

The Castillo family attempted to use visual/gestural language with Jasmín. However, the family members did not use any of the visual attention-getting strategies, such as tapping Jasmín or waving to get her attention. Mrs. Castillo spoke to Jasmín when her back was turned, commenting that she did so out of habit. Mrs. Castillo's failure to use more of the strategies could be due to the fact that she and Jasmín lived apart for several years.

Changing from an auditory orientation to a visual orientation is not easy for hearing people (Erting 1988). Hearing parents of deaf children have limited opportunities to interact with deaf adults, who can model appropriate visual strategies to use with deaf children. The use of accommodating strategies by hearing family members corresponded to the family's use of visual/gestural communication with the deaf child. Use of these strategies reflects a visual, rather than an auditory, orientation.

In these families, multiparty conversations occurred often but excluded the deaf children. Hearing families with deaf children often sign only when something is to be communicated or addressed specifically to the deaf child (Mounty 1986). In these families, hearing members did not sign to each other. In contrast, in a family observed in the pilot study for this research, the mother facilitated communication for her deaf daughter by clarifying and repeating parts of multiparty conversations.

In the Blanco family, Iris and Elena often interpreted English conversation into Spanish for their mother, but no one interpreted into sign language for their deaf brother, Wilfredo. They may have translated into Spanish out of respect for their mother and the home language. Neither Wilfredo nor sign language had the same status.

The Deaf Child's View

The deaf children's experiences were affected by their birth order in the family, their ability to use language choice, and their repertoire of strategies to use in communicating with hearing family members.

POSITION IN THE FAMILY

The age of the deaf child—whether older or younger than the siblings—was important in Rubén's case and Wilfredo's. Rubén assumed the role of the older brother, helping his younger siblings with literacy, both Spanish and English. He also assumed the role of interpreter for his mother. As the baby of the family, Wilfredo received a lot of special treatment and attention. Because his sisters were older, they were more able to accommodate him and learn sign language.

LANGUAGE CHOICE AND CODE-SWITCHING

As expected, hearing family members code-switched from spoken Spanish to spoken English and demonstrated language choice decisions. The deaf children also code-switched and were affected by language choice decisions. Wilfredo's and Jasmín's code-switching included the use of home signs, gestures, oral Spanish, and fingerspelling in English. They appeared to code-switch in order to facilitate communication with hearing family members.

In contrast, Rubén did not engage in any code-switching with family members. He may have had less control over language choice. His mother did not believe that it made sense for her to learn to sign because Rubén could speak and understand Spanish. It appeared that mother had made the decision to use only oral Spanish, and Rubén conformed.

STRATEGIES USED BY THE DEAF CHILDREN

The three deaf children used more strategies (see table 2) to communicate with hearing family members than their families used with them. Rubén, who used only oral Spanish, was the extreme example. None of the children used writing or drawing to communicate. Nor did they teach signs or help family members with their signing. Rather, their accommodations moved toward adopting hearing members' forms by using home signs, gestures, foreign signs, and oral Spanish.

All of the children used their voices to get the attention of hearing family members (#1). It is common for deaf children and adults to use auditory attention getters, but it is not common for hearing people to use visual attention getters. Rubén and Jasmín both tried to say words to clarify the meanings of signs. Rubén spoke Spanish, rarely signing in the home environment. Jasmín had been in an oral school that emphasized the use of speech until she was eight years old.

TABLE 2. *Strategies Used by Deaf Child with Family Members*

	Deaf Child		
Strategy	RUBÉN	WILFREDO	JASMÍN
1. Uses voice to call family members	X	X	X
2. Tries to say the word when the hearing interlocutor doesn't know the sign	X	—	X
3. Uses non-ASL signs and gestures	—	X	X
4. Uses spoken English or Spanish.	X (S)[a]	—	X (S)[b]
5. Uses written English or Spanish.	—	—	—
6. Teaches signs to family members	X[c]	—	—
7. Serves as ASL model for family	—	X	—

[a] (S) = Spanish
[b] Child said individual words when sign was not understood.
[c] This occurred only when his siblings requested it.

None of the children used written language to communicate with family members (#5). This finding may have been due to the tendency of hearing parents of deaf children to fail to use this strategy (Maxwell 1986). Wilfredo was only five and unable to use writing in this way. Jasmín and Rubén wrote only English, although their mothers' primary language was Spanish. However, their mothers did have some knowledge of English.

The deaf children differed in their willingness to teach signs to family members. Rubén, who did not use sign language at home, loved the role of teacher. When his sisters asked him to show them signs, he was always willing to do so. Wilfredo looked to his mother as the model. This was evident when he modified his signs to match hers. Jasmín was unwilling to show her family signs. She was unsatisfied with communication in the family but didn't want to become her family's teacher.

The School's View

The view that many schools and professionals have of language use in linguistically diverse families with deaf children may be limited by their lack of familiarity with theories of bilingualism. Deaf education has been slow to incorporate principles of bilingual education, ESL methodology, and multicultural education (Gerner de García 1992b; Humphries 1993).

As a result, schools and educators dealing with multicultural deaf children, particularly those from linguistically diverse families, may view their differences as something to ignore (being color-blind) or eradicate or perhaps as an additional handicap.

How Schools View Linguistic Diversity

Is the linguistic complexity of their homes an insurmountable obstacle that leads to a lack of communication within Spanish-speaking families with deaf children? Is the relatively low achievement of Hispanic deaf students a result of their multilingual situation? Bennett (1988) contended that Hispanic deaf students' lack of success should not be seen as their fault but rather must be seen as a result of the interaction between educational institutions, the Hispanic deaf students, the individual student, and society overall.

In the United States, linguistic diversity is often viewed as a deficit (Nieto 1991). Nieto states that students who speak languages that have little power socially and politically are seen as having a problem and that their fluency in another language is considered an obstacle to learning English. Skutnabb-Kangas (1988) refers to negative views of linguistic differences as *linguicism*. Such views may affect deaf individuals just as they affect hearing linguistically diverse individuals.

Schools' View of Language Use

Upon arrival in the United States, the needs of immigrant deaf children may not be addressed as they adjust to the trilingual situation they face. Rubén and Jasmín were initially educated in schools in which Spanish was the language of instruction. Rubén entered the school for the deaf at age six and Jasmín, at age eight. They did not receive any support to help their transition to the school for the deaf that used two languages—English and Sign Language—that were new for them.

Although these children came from Spanish-speaking families, the school viewed them primarily as deaf. This was not only the case for Wilfredo and Jasmín, who were profoundly deaf, but also for Rubén, who was hard of hearing. At school, Rubén was not seen as Spanish-speaking, and he rarely used Spanish at school. Rubén moved between languages and cultures without appearing to fit in the world either as deaf or as a Spanish-speaker.

Rubén was not recognized either at home or school as both trilingual and hard of hearing. He separated his home and school languages. Rubén was constantly choosing both a language and culture with which to identify. Bicultural or, in Rubén's case, multicultural individuals may have difficulty being accepted in either, or any, of their cultural groups. They experience this difficulty when they try to define themselves as one or the other. To overcome this, bicultural or multicultural individuals must see themselves as both, or all three, rather than choosing to try to function in solely one of their cultures (Grosjean 1992).

Additionally, schools' views of hard of hearing and profoundly deaf children from linguistically diverse families may be oversimplified. Schools may expect the hard of hearing child to speak the home language to some extent. In-school assessments may not reveal the extent of the child's knowledge of that language. Previous studies have indicated that deaf and hard of hearing children may in fact not demonstrate any knowledge of the home language in the school environment, where only sign language and English are used (Lerman and Vilá 1984).

Furthermore, schools may assume that a profoundly deaf child is not influenced by the home language. This assumption may be made even in the case of school-age children who have immigrated. The home language is considered to be a spoken language and thus inaccessible to a deaf child. Most often, non-ASL signing is not seen as an alternative form of visual/gestural language. Rather, the school, while acknowledging that there may be some use of home signs or gestures, will view this communication as deficient. Just as linguicism exists towards spoken languages, schools for the deaf may be guilty of linguicism in their attitudes toward different forms of visual/gestural communication or foreign sign languages.

CONCLUSIONS AND IMPLICATIONS OF THE DATA

In order to meet the needs of linguistically diverse families and their deaf children, schools must recognize these children's experience. Ignoring their trilingual reality may impede the acquisition of sign language and English by the deaf children's parents. Deaf children in linguistically diverse families may be at a disadvantage, not because they are dealing with three languages but because the schools do not accommodate the needs this creates. The families need sign language classes and communication programs that address their needs as trilingual families. Deaf children from linguistically diverse families can experience success if they and their families are given the support and respect they deserve.

Schools must also be aware of possible linguicism on their part. Assessments of deaf children from linguistically diverse families, especially children who are recent immigrants, must not assume non-ASL corresponds to having "no language." Schools and professionals should avoid such negative characterization of deaf children and adults. The professionals as well may be in a position of not knowing a language—the language these children and adults are using.

Culturally sensitive testing should include Deaf adults from the same background as the child, or Deaf adults with experience with a range of non-ASL visual/gestural language. It might be more appropriate to characterize signs as either ASL or non-ASL. Non-ASL signs cannot be assumed to be idiosyncratic home signs but may be a foreign sign language. For Deaf immigrants, and possibly also deaf children who use a different sign language at home, learning ASL may be learning a second (signed) language.

Previously it was stated that school-based assessments will likely yield limited results as deaf children are likely to suppress their knowledge of Spanish in this environment (Lerman and Vilá 1984). Findings in this study that deaf children may code-switch and use other kinds of sign language at home point to further limitations of school-based assessment. If the school is concerned about communication in the family, then a home-based assessment is necessary to yield additional insights. When in-school assessments include members of the family, it should be noted that siblings may be the most fluent communicators with the deaf child.

Although it is more likely that a hard of hearing child rather than a profoundly deaf child uses the home language, this may be an oversimplification of the possible outcomes. This view focuses on the use of a spoken language and does not consider non-ASL visual/gestural communication. It may be most appropriate to view all deaf and hard of hearing children from linguistically diverse homes as being exposed to more languages and language variations than deaf children from English-speaking homes. The assumption should be that such children may be using a variety of strategies to communicate. The school's role should be to expand and build on these children's linguistic repertoire, not deny or denigrate their versatility.

How can these families improve their deaf children's access to communication in the home? The issue of communication between deaf children and their families should begin with the premise that all parents (barring a very few) want to communicate with their deaf children. They may not use the school-sanctioned methods, including ASL or simultaneous communication, to accomplish this. They may be doing their best to create a system that works for them as a multilingual family.

What kind of classes would best serve these families? Spanish-speaking parents would benefit from trilingual classes such as described by Christensen (1985, 1986), which would use English and Spanish to teach sign language. By focusing on teaching hearing family members sign language, schools may not be doing enough. This focus may ignore the complexity of environments in which both spoken and visual/gestural languages are used. The deaf and hard of hearing child cannot gain full access to all the communication interactions that take place in the home environment.

This study demonstrated that some linguistically diverse parents attempt to do what the school asks. Mrs. Blanco went to sign language classes but felt the classes did nothing to enhance communication with her son. Her own sign language was not validated by the school.

Some parents may passively resist the school's advice, as in the case of Mrs. Alvarez. She has ignored the school's urgings to learn sign language. This advice made no sense to her because her hard of hearing son spoke Spanish. As she explained, it was likely that he was more capable in Spanish than she would ever be in sign language. However, parents with hard of hearing children would benefit from learning strategies for enhancing communication with or without using sign language.

The Castillo family as well hasn't heeded the school's advice. Learning English was a priority for this family. The school failed to recognize that learning English is a priority for many immigrant families. Parents in such families have to learn English to survive, to advocate for their deaf children, and to learn their rights as parents. Is it surprising that the expectation that they learn another minority language and culture is difficult to comply with when they have to learn English and the majority culture to survive?

RECOMMENDATIONS

Schools and/or professionals in the schools for the deaf may assume that deaf children from linguistically diverse families are at risk because of the language differences. They may view the "problem" of language diversity as something the family must overcome if the deaf child is to succeed in school. Such a view may hinder changes in the school to accommodate such families and their children through programs and approaches that embrace their diversity and work towards mutual accommodation.[10]

By failing to consider the actual language dynamics of linguistically diverse families, schools may perpetuate the lack of integration of these families into the school as well as do little to foster communication between deaf and hearing family members. The school may look at linguistically diverse parents only as needing services and may be unable to consider what they can contribute. Such a view works against the empowerment of parents and inhibits them from becoming partners in the education of their children. The school must see these linguistically diverse parents as capable of assuming an active role.

The following recommendations are based on a point of view that linguistically diverse families must be empowered and that this in turn will benefit the deaf child. To this end, the schools must:

1. Work to make all parents partners in their deaf children's education; the schools must include the input of linguistically diverse parents regarding the roles they will assume in the school.
2. Provide support for immigrant families, recognizing the needs of all family members including the deaf child, in their adjustment to new cultures and languages; and provide interpreters/translators who are readily accessible to the parents.
3. Recognize and validate what the family does in order to communicate with the deaf member and expand upon it.

10. Mutual accommodation is a term used by Díaz, Moll, and Mehan (1986) to describe a two-way process in which school programs and individual teachers adapt the school environment, curriculum, and methodology in response to their multicultural students. Nieto (1992) describes mutual accommodation as including the use of the languages and cultures of the students in teaching, and the students' use of the school's language and culture in learning.

4. Provide parents opportunities to interact with Deaf adult models, for example through workshops run by Deaf adults who share the ethnic, linguistic and/or cultural experiences of the diverse populations of the school (e.g., Black Deaf, Hispanic Deaf, Asian Deaf).

5. Consider the whole family as a system, including extended family, in any attempts to get information about the deaf child's language and behavior at home; recognize the needs of hearing siblings who may be trilingual.

6. Recognize the importance of English literacy for deaf and hearing family members. Families should be encouraged to view closed-captioned television to improve the English literacy of everyone in the family.[11]

7. Provide sign language classes in Spanish and consider innovative approaches for other linguistically diverse families.

8. Encourage parents to organize their own groups based on shared linguistic and cultural experiences, for example, an Asian parents' group, a Spanish-speaking parents' group.

Few schools for the deaf engage in mutual accommodation with their multicultural deaf students or their families. Humphries (1993) states that a society that is reluctant to see Deaf individuals as bicultural is probably not prepared to consider that some Deaf people are multicultural. Furthermore, the growing multicultural education movement in education for hearing children has had little influence on the education of the deaf. Humphries attributes this to a tendency to view students in schools for the deaf as having a lack of hearing in common, while ignoring their ethnic, cultural, and linguistic differences.

In order to address the needs of deaf children from racially, ethnically, culturally, and linguistically diverse homes, schools for the deaf should:

1. View all deaf children as coming to school with something, rather than viewing them as having "no language." Recognize and validate the home languages of the children in the school environment.

11. Research has demonstrated the value of closed captioning for children and adults who are learning English as a Second Language (The National Captioning Institute 1990). As of July 1, 1993, all televisions larger than thirteen inches must have a built-in closed-captioning decoder, making this technology virtually universally available.

2. Provide support for incoming immigrant students to enable them to bridge the cultures and languages they live with, addressing the needs of those children who are learning American Sign Language (and may or may not know another sign language).

3. View home language as an issue for profoundly deaf children as well as for hard of hearing children; understand home language diversity to include non-ASL visual/gestural language; consider the best way to meet the needs of hard of hearing children from linguistically diverse homes.

4. Provide for naturalistic assessment of deaf children in and out of school, especially multicultural deaf children. Assessments in school should include the participation of Deaf adults who share the cultural and linguistic backgrounds of the children. Out-of-school assessments should include a home visit to observe the child with the family.

5. Promote awareness of the multiculturalism and multilingualism of deaf children from diverse homes through inclusionary curriculum throughout the school.

6. Provide multicultural deaf children with diverse staff, including hearing and Deaf adults from their own communities.

7. Provide school-based programs for Hispanic deaf children that address their linguistic and cultural heritage. Reinforce knowledge of the home language for those children who have a base. Teach Spanish to those children who have little or no knowledge of their families' language.[12]

8. Provide training for school staff on issues that affect multicultural deaf children, including bilingual theory, bilingual methodologies, methods of teaching English to Speakers of Other Languages (ESOL), and multicultural issues in deaf education.

In order to help families, and particularly parents, deal with the complexity of multiple languages, professionals need training. Professionals in deaf education have to become familiar with theories in areas such as second-language acquisition, bilingual and multicultural education, and cross-cultural issues. They must learn to identify resources that can be accessed outside the field of deaf education. In order to take advantage

12. In Sweden, under the Bilingual Act, all children, including deaf children, must receive in-school instruction in the home language (Madebrink 1990).

of resources, educators of the deaf must consider that the deaf children they are teaching and their families come from communities that the teachers themselves may not know well. Developing new skills and expanding professional knowledge will enable teachers to improve the educational experiences of multicultural deaf children.

LIMITATIONS OF THE STUDY

This study involved three families with three different profiles. Therefore, it should not be used to overgeneralize about Hispanic deaf children and their families. Furthermore, as the families were of Dominican and Puerto Rican origin, their home cultures not only vary individually but would be expected to vary from other Hispanic subgroups such as Mexican.

Despite these limitations, it is possible to suggest broader applications. The recommendations apply not only to Spanish-speaking families but also to other linguistically diverse families regardless of the languages they speak. The failure of many schools to adequately address the needs and concerns of Hispanic deaf children and their families applies to other nonmainstream families with deaf children. Finally, recommendations for naturalistic assessment should be applied to all deaf children, including those from Deaf families.

REFERENCES

Allen, T.E. 1986. Patterns of academic achievement among hearing impaired students: 1974–1983. In *Deaf children in America,* ed. A.N. Schildroth and M.A. Karchmer, 161–206. San Diego: College Hill Press.

Andrews, J.F., and D.L. Jordan. 1993. Minority and minority-deaf professionals: How many and where are they? *American Annals of the Deaf* 138(5):388–396

Baker, C., and D. Cokely. 1980. *American Sign Language: A teacher's resource text on grammar and culture.* Silver Spring, Md.: National Association of the Deaf.

Bennett, A. T. 1987. *Schooling the different: Ethnographic case studies of Hispanic deaf children's initiation into formal schooling.* Final report to the Office of Special Education and Rehabilitation, U.S. Department of Education.

———. 1988. Gateways to powerlessness: Incorporating Hispanic deaf children and their families into formal schooling. *Disability and Society* 3(2):19–51.

Blackwell, P.M., and J. E. Fischgrund. 1984. Issues in the development of culturally responsive programs for deaf students from non-English-speaking homes. In *The Hispanic deaf,* ed. G. L. Delgado. 154–166. Washington, D.C.: Gallaudet College Press.

Christensen, K.M. 1985. Conceptual sign language as a bridge between English and Spanish. *American Annals of the Deaf* 130(2):244–249.

———. 1986. Conceptual sign language acquisition by Spanish-speaking parents of hearing-impaired children. *American Annals of the Deaf* 131(3):285–287.

Cohen, O.P. 1987. Current and future needs of minority hearing impaired children and youth. Testimony before the Commission on Education of the Deaf on behalf of the Conference of Educational Administrators Serving the Deaf, 19 March.

Cohen, O.P., J.E. Fischgrund, and R. Redding. 1990. Deaf children from ethnic, linguistic and racial minority backgrounds: An overview. *American Annals of the Deaf* 135(2):67–73.

Dean, C.C. 1984. The hearing-impaired Hispanic child: Sociolinguistic considerations. In *The Hispanic deaf,* ed. G.L. Delgado, 58–68. Washington, D.C.: Gallaudet College Press.

Delgado, G. L. 1984. *The Hispanic deaf: Issues and challenges for bilingual special education.* Washington, D.C.: Gallaudet College Press.

Delgado-Gaitan, C. 1990. *Literacy for empowerment: The role of parents in children's education.* Philadelphia: Falmer Press.

Díaz, S., L.C. Moll, and H. Mehan. 1986. Sociocultural resources in instruction: A context-specific approach. In *Beyond language: Social and cultural factors in schooling language minority students,* ed. C. Cortes, 187–238. Los Angeles: Office of Bilingual Education, California State Department of Education, Evaluation, Dissemination and Assessment Center.

Erting, C. 1981. An anthropological approach to the study of the communicative competence of Deaf children. *Sign Language Studies* 3(2):221–238.

———.1985. Sociocultural dimensions of Deaf education: Belief systems and communicative interaction. *Sign Language Studies* 4(7):111–125.

———. 1988. Acquiring linguistic and social identity. In *Language, learning and deafness,* ed. M. Strong. New York: Cambridge University Press.

Fischgrund, J.E. 1984. Language intervention for hearing-impaired children from linguistically and culturally diverse backgrounds. In *The Hispanic deaf,* ed. G.L. Delgado, 94–105. Washington, D.C.: Gallaudet College Press.

Gerner de García, B.A. 1992a. Non-discriminatory assessment for Hispanic deaf students. Paper presented at The Hispanic Deaf Experience, 12–14 November, San Antonio, Tex.

———. 1992b. Diversity in deaf education: What can we learn from bilingual and ESL education? *Proceedings of the First International Symposium of Teacher Education in Deafness,* vol. 2, 126–139. Washington, D.C.: Gallaudet University.

———. 1993. Addressing the needs of Hispanic deaf children. In *Multicultural issues in deafness,* ed. K.M. Christensen and G.L. Delgado, 66–90. White Plains, N.Y.: Longman.

Goldin-Meadow, S. 1982. The resilience of recursion: A study of a communication system developed without a conventional language model. In *Language acquisition: The state of the art,* ed. L. Gleitman and E. Wanner, 51–77. New York: Cambridge University Press.

Grosjean, F. 1982. *Life with two languages: An introduction to bilingualism.* Cambridge, Mass.: Harvard University Press.

———. 1992. Another view of bilingualism. In *Cognitive processes in bilinguals,* ed. R.J. Harris. Amsterdam: Elsevier.

Humphries, T. 1993. Deaf culture and cultures. In *Multicultural issues in deafness,* ed. K. M. Christensen and G.L. Delgado, 3–15. White Plains, N.Y.: Longman.

Jensema, C. 1975. *The relationship between academic achievement and the demographic characteristics of hearing impaired youth.* Washington, D.C.: Gallaudet College Office of Demographic Studies.

Johnson, R.E., S.K. Liddell, and C. Erting. 1989. *Unlocking the curriculum: Principles for achieving access in deaf education.* Gallaudet Research Institute Working Paper 89(3). Washington, D.C.: Gallaudet University.

Jordan, I.K. 1990. Preconference lecture. American Society for Deaf Children, June, Vancouver, B.C.

Lerman, A. 1984. Survey of Hispanic hearing-impaired students and their families. In *The Hispanic deaf,* ed. G. Delgado, 38–56. Washington, D.C.: Gallaudet College Press.

Lerman, A., and C. Vilá. 1984. A model for school services to Hispanic hearing-impaired children. In *The Hispanic deaf,* ed. G.L. Delgado, 167–179. Washington, D.C.: Gallaudet College Press.

Lucas, C., and C. Valli. 1989. Language contact in the American Deaf community. In *Sociolinguistics of the Deaf community,* ed. C. Lucas, 11–40. San Diego: Academic Press.

———. 1990. ASL, English and contact signing. In *Sign language research: Theoretical issues* ed. C. Lucas, 288–307. Washington, D.C.: Gallaudet University Press.

Luetke-Stahlman, B., and F. Weiner. 1984. Language and/or system assessment for Spanish deaf preschoolers. In *The Hispanic deaf*, ed. G.L. Delgado, 106–121. Washington, D.C.: Gallaudet College Press.

Madebrink, R. 1990. How to support immigrant deaf children. Paper presented at the Seventeenth International Congress on Education of the Deaf, 29 July–3 August, Rochester, N.Y.

Matos, A.L. 1990. *Aprende Señas Conmigo: Lenguaje de Señas en Español-Inglés*. San Juan, P.R.: Editorial Raices.

Maxwell, M. 1984. A Deaf child's natural development of literacy. *Sign Language Studies* 44: 191–224.

———. 1985. Ethnography and education of Deaf children. *Sign Language Studies*, 47:97–108.

———. 1986. Some functions and uses of literacy in the deaf community. *Language and Society*. 14:205–221.

Mounty, J. 1986. Nativization and input in the language development of two deaf children of hearing parents. Ed.D. diss. Boston University.

National Captioning Institute. 1990. Using captioned television to improve the reading proficiency of language minority students. Falls Church, Va: National Captioning Institute.

Nieto, S. 1991. We speak in many tongues: Language diversity and multicultural education. In *Multicultural education in the twenty-first century*, ed. C.F. Díaz. Washington, D.C.: National Education Association.

———. 1992. *Affirming diversity. The sociopolitical context of multicultural education*. White Plains, N.Y.: Longman.

Orum, L. 1992. *The education of Hispanics: Status and implications*. Washington, D.C.: National Council of la Raza.

Secada, W.G. 1984. The language of instruction for hearing-impaired students from non-English speaking homes: A framework for considering alternatives. In *The Hispanic deaf*, ed. G.L. Delgado, 80–93. Washington, D.C.: Gallaudet College Press.

Simmons de García, J. 1988. The linguistic and cultural diversity of deaf children: Implications for language and literacy development. Unpublished paper, Graduate School of Education, Harvard University.

———. 1989. Language arts curriculum in programs for deaf children. Paper presented at the Deaf Way Conference, 9–14 July, Washington, D.C.

Skutnabb-Kangas, T. 1988. Multilingualism and the education of minority children. In *Minority education: From shame to struggle*, ed. T. Skutnabb-Kangas and J. Cummins, 9–44. Philadelphia: Multilingual Matters.

Trueba, H. 1987. *Success or failure: Learning and the language minority student*. Cambridge, Mass.: Newbury House.

———. 1989. Raising silent voices: Educating the linguistic minorities for the twenty-first century. Cambridge, Mass.: Newbury House.

Part 5 **Discourse Analysis**

Constructed Dialogue and Constructed

Action in American Sign Language

Melanie Metzger

Fifty years ago, the sign language used by Deaf people in the United States was thought to be little more than a primitive form of gesturing used by a group of people who had no real language. However, William Stokoe (1960) began a systematic investigation of these signs based on linguistic principles and discovered, on the basis of the linguistic description of spoken languages, that these signs comprised a phonology, morphology, and syntax in a visual/spatial medium. Over the past thirty years, valuable research has addressed the linguistic structures and grammatical processes of American Sign Language (ASL). In addition, sociolinguistic researchers have examined such topics as variation and conversational regulators in ASL. In recent years, researchers have started to examine discourse strategies in ASL. This paper will address a discourse construction in ASL that has often been termed *role playing, role shifting,* or *taking on the role of a character* in narrative discourse.

Role playing or role shifting in ASL has been referred to by numerous researchers as conveying a character's thoughts, words, emotions, and/or actions. Lentz (1986) describes one- and two-character role shifts that can describe the incidents in which a character is involved. The signer assumes the role of the character and can demonstrate the character's manner or expression while describing his or her appearance. Liddell (1980), Padden (1986, 1990), Meier (1990), Engberg-Pedersen (1992), and Lillo-Martin (1992) discuss role shifts used for direct quotation. The

I would like to thank Heidi Hamilton and Elif Rosenfeld for their guidance and encouragement, Scott Liddell and Betsy Winston for their insightful feedback, and Byron Bridges, Eric Shapiro, and Tina Neumann for their comments and assistance.

Deaf with a capital *D* is used here to indicate those who consider themselves both culturally Deaf and members of the Deaf community.

use of classifiers to describe events is addressed by Padden (1990), Meier (1990), and Liddell (1980). Liddell also describes the use of pantomime to demonstrate actions or events. Padden (1986) discusses the body shifts, changes in facial configuration, and eye gaze that contrast two characters. These features are also addressed by Lillo-Martin and Klima (1990) and Lillo-Martin (1992), who discuss the change in signing style as another aspect of indicating a change in frame-of-reference or point-of-view. Body shifts, as well as turning the head to the left or right, are also addressed by Meier (1990) and Liddell (1980). Although different features are discussed by different researchers, there seems to be general agreement that signers use their body, head, and eye gaze to report the actions, thoughts, words, and expressions of characters within the discourse.

REPORTED EVENTS VERSUS CONSTRUCTED EVENTS

Traditionally, linguists have addressed the notion of direct quotations in discourse as a form of *reported speech*. However, Tannen (1986) suggests a replacement for this terminology, based on the knowledge that reported speech is often not really a verbatim report of the words as they were spoken originally. Tannen (1989) observes that reported speech has been removed from the original context and is a function of the new reporting context. Thus, "in the deepest sense, the words have ceased to be those of the speaker to whom they are attributed, having been appropriated by the speaker who is repeating them" (Tannen 1989, 101). Tannen describes the "reporting" of dialogue as being as creative a process as the dialogue constructed in a novel. Thus, Tannen refers to this phenomenon as *constructed dialogue*.

The existence of constructed dialogue in ASL has been alluded to in the discussion of "direct quotation" and "reported speech" in previous literature. Specifically, evidence of constructed dialogue in ASL is discussed by Roy (1989) in the analysis of an ASL lecture in which the signer constructs the comments and thoughts of a fish that, clearly, never actually uttered anything. However, reference to reported speech in the ASL literature also coincides with descriptions of reported actions, behaviors, and emotions of narrated characters.

Reported *actions* in ASL seem to be similar to the notion of reported *speech* in that the events of one context are reported in another. Liddell (in press) observes that signers will interact with imaginary or surrogate people who are treated as though they were in the environment of the signer. The signer will interact with the surrogate's height, looking up to a taller person and down to a shorter individual. Liddell (in press) also refers to imagining surrogates as being on the floor or a ladder (Liddell, 14), and, thus, the signer appears to be discussing events as they occur within a specific environment. If the events of one context are reported in another in ASL, it seems likely that these actions are as affected by the reporting context as reported dialogue is; thus, it seems likely that signers creatively construct both events and dialogue in ASL discourse.

Winston (1991, 1992) describes constructed action and constructed dialogue in ASL as being parallel strategies. Constructed action in ASL is described as what was once referred to as "role playing," in which the signer assumes the posture and actions of a character "and imitat(es) them, either as mime, or while signing about that character" (Winston 1992, 98–99). Winston terms this *action performatives* and describes the dynamic interaction of constructed action and dialogue in an ASL lecture as discourse strategies used to more actively involve the audience.

The construction of dialogue in ASL seems to be very similar to the construction of events. In this paper, based on Tannen's (1989) examples of dialogue constructions, these two phenomena will be examined in ASL narrative discourse.

METHODOLOGY

The data were collected via a series of videotaped sociolinguistic interviews. In these interviews, Deaf informants were videotaped while conversing with one another. All informants were native Deaf ASL signers, having either grown up with a Deaf family or in a residential school. The data were transcribed using English glosses and following conventions for transcription of nonmanual signals, such as body posture, head placement, mouth, cheek, eyebrow movements, and eye gaze, as applicable (see Appendix A). In order to examine the occurrence of constructed dialogue and action in ASL, a variety of data ranging from personal experience narratives to describing comics strips were used. Based on Tannen's (1989) examples of dialogue constructions, equivalent categories were designed to look for parallel constructions of action performatives. Tannen's examples of dialogue constructions include: representing what was not said ("You can't say, 'Daddy, I didn't HEAR you'" p. 111); dialogue as instantiation (capturing a general phenomenon, as in, "The minute the kids get old enough . . . " p. 111); summarizing dialogue ("and this man is essentially saying, 'We shouldn't be here' . . . " p. 113); choral dialogue ("And then all the Americans said, 'Oh in that case, go ahead.'" p. 113); dialogue as inner speech ("and I thought, 'Oh, God'" p. 114); the inner speech of others ("And the bus driver was like, 'Oh, my Go::d!'" p. 115); dialogue constructed by a listener (Daisy: And the minute the kids are old enough to do it themselves, that's when— Mary: "You do it yourself" p. 116); dialogue fading from indirect to direct (And it was like he was telling everybody to, "have your wisdom teeth taken out" p. 117); dialogue including vague referents ("Go get this and it looks like this and the other" p. 118); and dialogue cast in the persona of a nonhuman speaker (in speaking for a cat, "She says, 'I see a beautiful world just waiting for me'" p. 118) (Tannen 1989, 110–118). The data were examined for examples of each of these ten categories for constructed dialogue and the eight applicable categories of constructed action. In addition, two narratives were examined for frequency of occurrences of constructed action, constructed dialogue, and combinations of the two.

FINDINGS

Analysis of the data indicates that ASL does make use of the same categories of constructions identified by Tannen (1989). In fact, evidence suggests that in ASL, constructed dialogue is a form of constructed action. In addition, constructed actions seem to sometimes co-occur with classifiers, suggesting the possibility that action performatives in ASL are represented by a variety of forms.

Taxonomy of Constructions

In order to verify whether or not Tannen's ten categories of dialogue constructions apply to ASL, several data sources were analyzed for samples appropriate to each category. In addition, these categories were applied to the notion of constructed action, yielding the following par-

Categories of Constructed Dialogue	Examples[a]		Categories of Constructed Action
	Dialogue	Action	
representing what was not said	0	G	representing what was not done
dialogue as instantiation	0	H	action as instantiation
summarizing dialogue	A	I	summarizing action
choral dialogue	B	J	choral action
dialogue as inner speech	C	?	actions as inner action?
inner speech of others	D	?	inner actions of others?
dialogue constructed by a listener	0	0	action constructed by a listener
fadein, fadeout (direct/indirect quote)	E	K	fadein, fadeout (direct/indirect action)
vague referents	0	L	vague 'action'
nonhuman speaker	F	M	nonhuman's actions

FIGURE 1. *Action performatives.*
[a]See Appendix B for examples from the data
[b]0=no occurrence

allel constructions for ASL (see Appendix B for examples): representing what was not done (example G); actions as instantiation (example H); summarizing action (example I); choral action (example J); action constructed by a listener; action fading from indirect to direct (example K); action including vague referents (example L); and actions cast in the persona of a nonhuman actor (example M). Two of the original dialogue constructions do not appear to be applicable to constructed actions. Although ASL seems to incorporate examples of "inner speech" as a form of constructed dialogue, the parallel construction would seem to be "inner action," and it is not clear what an inner action would entail.

Thus, the seemingly parallel constructions, "actions as inner actions, inner actions of others" were not included in the list of potential action constructions, yielding a total of eight categories of potential constructed actions.

Of the ten dialogue constructions, the data included examples of six (see figure 1). Those constructions found in the data provide cross-linguistic evidence for Tannen's analysis and support the notion that ASL discourse strategies involve dialogue constructions similar in form to those used in English. Analysis regarding those constructions not found in the data is inconclusive, since these data may have been unlikely to elicit such constructions on the basis of topic, setting, or other factors. One suggestion for future research in this area is to examine a larger data pool in order to determine whether these constructions occur in ASL.

Of the eight parallel action constructions, the data included examples of seven. The only construction not included in the data was "action constructed by a listener." This is likely due to the fact that most of the data comprise narrative discourse with relatively few occurrences of turn-taking. Analysis of ASL conversational discourse is an area that warrants further study. Despite the fact that examples of every construction are not included in these data, enough examples of both constructed dialogue and constructed action warranted analysis of the relative frequency of these forms in ASL.

Relative Frequency of Constructed Dialogue and Constructed Action

In order to conduct a preliminary comparison of constructed dialogue and constructed action in ASL, two ASL narratives are analyzed. Occurrences of constructed dialogue and constructed action within the two narratives are tallied in order to determine the frequency of occurrences. Single occurrences of constructed dialogue are measured as the span between the beginning and end of a constructed "commentary." In other words, a single character might construct commentary, to be followed by narration, and then additional commentary. This type of sequence was tallied as two occurrences of constructed dialogue. Similarly, if one character signs and another character responds, this is also considered to be two separate occurrences of constructed dialogue.

	Constructed Action	Constructed Dialogue
Narrative 1	11	6
Narrative 2	14	9
TOTAL	25	15

FIGURE 2. *Relative frequency of occurrences of constructed dialogue and constructed action.*

The same measurement holds true for constructed action. From the time a character begins an action or series of actions to the end of that uninterrupted sequence is considered to be one occurrence of constructed action. Moreover, when the action shifts from one character to another, this is considered to be two occurrences of constructed action.

Within the two narratives, the total number of occurrences of constructed dialogue and constructed action reveal two interesting results (see figure 2). First, the total occurrences of constructed action is twenty-five (eleven in the first narrative and fourteen in the second), whereas the total number of occurrences of constructed dialogue is fifteen (six in the first narrative and nine in the second). This suggests that constructed action may be more common in ASL than constructed dialogue. This is an area that warrants further research with a larger corpus of data.

Second, in analysis of occurrences of constructed dialogue and constructed action in the narratives, it became obvious that the two may co-occur. In one narrative, the overlap is very clear. The constructed action involves the signer directly portraying a man who is seated at a table with cards in hand, looking up at a stranger who has just asked for a guy named Baker. In the constructed dialogue, this same character responds to the request:

EXAMPLE I

to addressee	gaze forward to up left	lower lip extended/head tilt/gaze up left

MAN CARDS-IN-HAND LOOK-UP, "THAT (raise hand) THAT PRO.I"
So one of the guys at the table says, "Yeah, I'm Baker, that's me."

As the signer constructs the actions of the character, these actions seem to include three separate parts: first, holding cards in one hand; second, looking up and to the left at the stranger; and finally, signing to the stranger. This implies that in ASL, constructed dialogue is actually one form of constructed action. Thus, it may be inappropriate to say that constructed action occurs more frequently than constructed dialogue. Rather, constructed actions of various types seem to be occurring within the discourse, and constructed dialogue is simply one type. Examination of other types of constructed action in ASL is an area for further research.

Linguistic Forms of Constructed Action

In tabulating the occurrences of constructed action within the narratives, it became clear that constructed action can be represented in more than one way. Constructed action involves the use of all parts of the signer's body that are involved in the event. Thus, in the previous example of the man playing cards, the hand and arm are involved because the signer is choosing to construct the event in a direct manner. Similarly, the head and eyes are involved because the signer chooses to construct the event in such a way that the man is looking at the stranger. Perhaps the only tool, or the best tool, that the signer has for constructing events is his or her body, head, limbs, eyes, and so forth. However, it is also possible for a signer to add a form of narration along with the action constructions as an indirect description of events. Thus, these data include three forms of constructed action: direct action, in which the actions are constructed by body, face, and so forth, with limited use of lexical signs or classifiers; simultaneous direct and indirect action, in which the body, face, and so on co-occur with limited signed narration; and indirect action, in which the narrator is primarily describing events with limited co-occurrence of body involvement.

DIRECT ACTION

Direct action as a way to reconstruct events in ASL is relatively simple. As described above, the signer makes use of the body, head, limbs, face, and eyes as necessary to construct the actions and events. In one narrative, the signer relays a fight in which a man standing next to a card table reaches down to grab one of the card players and punch him in the face:

EXAMPLE 2

gaze down	gaze to addressee		gaze left	head shifts left to right
GRAB-HIT	AWFUL MAN		FIST-HIT-CHIN	FALL-DOWN-FROM-CHAIR

And the guy hauls off and hits him, it was terrible. Knocked the guy
right out of his chair!

The signer uses direct action to indicate the stranger punching the man. The signer's eyes are gazing down because the stranger is standing, but the man to be hit is seated. The signer uses his left hand to grab and hold onto the "man" and uses his right hand to punch the area above the hand, presumably where the man's face is located. After this, the signer makes eye contact with the addressee, commenting on the situation, "It was terrible." Next, the signer constructs the action from the man's perspective, eyes gaze left toward the stranger while the signer's right fist constructs the stranger's punch as it hits the chin of the signer. Although it appears that the signer is punching himself, this is clearly not the meaning being conveyed by the constructed action. The fist hitting the chin is another example of direct constructed action.

Direct action seems to be a relatively straightforward construction in ASL. However, though often labeled as mimelike, this type of construction is not generally easily mastered by second language learners, as one might expect since mimelike gesturing is a genre accessible to all linguistic communities. Examination of examples such as FIST-HIT-CHIN, in which the signer's fist constructs the actions of one character while the signer's head represents the actions of another character suggest that direct action is a complex construction in ASL. This is a rich area for further study.

SIMULTANEOUS DIRECT AND INDIRECT ACTION

When constructing action, the use of direct action can be supported by minimal narration. For instance, the body can be used to construct events in just the manner described in the previous section. In addition, the signer can add a minimal comment that supports or describes the action taking place. An example of this can be found in example 1, repeated here for convenience:

EXAMPLE 1

to addressee	gaze forward to up left	lower lip extended/head tilt/gaze up left
MAN CARDS-IN-HAND LOOK-UP,	"THAT (raise hand) THAT PRO.1"	

So one of the guys at the table says, "Yeah, I'm Baker, that's me."

In the initial segment, the signer looks up and to the left toward the stranger, who just asked for the man named Baker. However, in addition to this constructed action, the signer also signs LOOK-UP. This sign indicates the upward and left direction that the signer has already constructed with his body. This sign is understood not to be a comment by the character whose actions are being constructed. Rather, while constructing this character's actions, the signer is adding an indirect description, simultaneously, with his free hand.

Simultaneous direct and indirect action also occur in the following example:

EXAMPLE 3

| gaze forward, | |
| frown, bite lower lip | body forward, head tilted up, eyes wide |

CL:CC (lift to TV), ARMS-FLAIL AWKWARD ARMS-FLAIL PUSH TV BUTTONS
Garfield picks him up and holds him out to the TV,
and he changes the channel

The constructed action begins when the signer constructs Garfield's action, reaching beside himself to lift the owner and hold him forward in the direction of the TV. There is a shift to the construction of the owners' actions, in which the signer holds his arms out forward, flailing around, and signs AWKWARD, then repeats the flailing motion before pushing the TV buttons with his right hand. In this case, the flailing movement of the arms is the construction of awkward movement, yet the signer adds the comment AWKWARD. Again, this comment does not appear to the viewer to be the words or thoughts of the character, but rather a narrated comment designed to reinforce the actions being constructed by the signer's body movements, head tilt, eye gaze, and so forth.

Simultaneous direct and indirect action seem to be quite similar to direct constructions, with a brief supportive description inserted by the narrator. The form and length of these narrations is not clear from this study. Research with a larger corpus of ASL data would be useful in addressing this question.

INDIRECT CONSTRUCTED ACTION

When the signer narrates an event, or part of one, but still involves the body minimally, this type of constructed action can be referred to as indirect constructed action. It is distinguishable from simultaneous direct and indirect action on the basis of a greater amount of narration and less body involvement (see example 4).

EXAMPLE 4

<u>gaze left/eyes close</u>   <u>gaze and head move right/head shakes</u>

PUNCH-NOSE (left hand) CL:V (fall-back) CL:5 (head-hit-wall)
*and, **bam**, he's got a fist in his face. Knocked him right out
of his chair and into the wall*

At the end of example 4, the signer uses classifiers to describe the action of the man falling out of his chair. It is perhaps understandable that the signer does not use his body to construct this portion of the narrative. Nevertheless, what is interesting is that when signing HEAD-HIT-WALL, the signer uses his own head to construct the head-shaking response one would expect to see from the man at that point in the narrative. The head movement is relatively minimal, yet it is there and supports the narrator's description of events.

The use of indirect constructed action emphasizes the narration but includes minimal body constructions to support the narration. It is also possible for a signer to narrate without any body constructions involved. In the previous example, the signer describes the man falling out of his chair, FALL-BACK, without any body involvement. It is questionable whether this would be considered constructed action. It seems likely that this is simply an example of narrative discourse that does not make use of the type of constructions being discussed here.

There are clearly three forms of constructed action represented in these data: direct, simultaneous direct and indirect, and indirect constructed action. These constructions appear to fall on a continuum ranging from fully constructed direct action to partial narration to heavily narrated discourse. Clearly, signers make choices as to which form of construction will be used at any point in a narrative. Examination of the use of these forms in various genres is another area for future research.

CONCLUSION

For many years, researchers have recognized that signers using ASL convey the actions, words, thoughts, and mannerisms of narrated characters. The use of both pantomime and signs such as classifiers have been linked to the description of events. The reporting of the words and thoughts of characters in ASL appears to be similar to the same phenomenon in spoken languages. Thus, it is not surprising that Tannen's (1986, 1989) identification of reported speech as a creative construction of dialogue in spoken languages appears to apply to ASL. Moreover, as suggested by Winston (1992), signers appear to use a parallel discourse strategy—constructed actions—to convey the actions and mannerisms of narrated characters.

Often referred to as role playing, constructed action is the creative construction of an event described by a signer in ASL discourse. Examination of constructed actions on the basis of Tannen's (1989) examples of dialogue constructions indicates that in two ASL narratives, constructed action occurs more frequently than constructed dialogue. Moreover, since communicating is a form of human behavior, it seems possible that in ASL constructed dialogue is one type of constructed action. The data include three forms of constructed action, which fall on a continuum ranging from full constructions with no narration to almost full narrations. In direct action constructions, the signer makes use of the body, head, facial expressions, and eye gaze to construct a narrated character's action. Simultaneous direct and indirect action is very similar to direct constructions, only with co-occurrence of some minimal signed narration. When the signed narration increases and is minimally supported by the use of the body, limbs, face, eye gaze, and so forth, this is indirect constructed action.

The use of constructed action and constructed dialogue in ASL discourse is a rich area for future research. Suggested areas for further examination include constructed dialogue and constructed action based on Tannen's examples of constructions, analysis of the three forms of constructed action, and a more detailed examination of these discourse strategies as they occur in ASL narrative and conversational discourse. In addition, an examination of the occurrence of constructed action in spoken language data could provide a basis for comparison of this narrative discourse strategy between spoken and signed languages.

REFERENCES

Engberg-Pedersen, E. 1992. Speech reports, reported thoughts, and other kinds of reports. Paper presented at Theoretical Issues in Sign Language Research IV, 5–8 August, San Diego.

Fischer, S. and P. Siple, eds. 1990. *Theoretical issues in sign language research, Vol. 1: Linguistics.* Chicago: University of Chicago Press.

Lentz, E. M. 1986. Teaching role shifting. In *Proceedings of the fourth national symposium on sign language research and teaching*, ed. C.A. Padden, 58–59. Silver Spring, Md.: National Association of the Deaf.

Liddell, S. K. 1980. *American Sign Language syntax.* The Hague: Mouton.

———. In press. Real, surrogate, and token space: Grammatical consequences in ASL. In *Language, gesture and space*, ed. K. Emmorey and J. Reilly. Hillsdale, N.J.: Lawrence Erlbaum Associates.

———. In press. Tokens and surrogates. In *Proceedings of the fifth international conference on sign language research*, ed. I. Ahlgren, B. Bergman, and M. Brennan. Salamanca, Spain.

Lillo-Martin, D. 1992. The point of view predicate in American Sign Language. Paper presented at Theoretical Issues in Sign Language Research IV, 5–8 August, San Diego.

———, and E. Klima. 1990. Pointing out differences: ASL pronouns in syntactic theory. In *Theoretical issues in sign language research, Vol. 1: Linguistics*, ed. S. Fischer and P. Siple, 191–210. Chicago: University of Chicago Press.

Lucas, C., ed. 1990. *Sign language research: Theoretical issues.* Washington, D.C.: Gallaudet University Press.

Mather, S. 1989. Visually oriented teaching strategies. In *The sociolinguistics of the deaf community*, ed. C. Lucas, 165–187. San Diego: Academic Press.

Meier, R. 1990. Person deixis in American Sign Language. In *Theoretical issues in sign language research, Vol. 1: Linguistics*, ed. S. Fischer and P. Siple, 175–190. Chicago: University of Chicago Press.

Padden, C. 1986. Verbs and role-shifting in American Sign Language. In *Proceedings of the fourth international symposium on sign language research and teaching*, ed. C.A. Padden, 44–57. Silver Spring, Md.: National Association of the Deaf.

———, ed. 1986. *Proceedings of the fourth international symposium on sign language research and teaching.* Silver Spring, Md.: National Association of the Deaf.

———. 1990. The relation between space and grammar in ASL verb morphology. In *Sign language research: Theoretical issues*, ed. C. Lucas, 118–132. Washington, D.C.: Gallaudet University Press.

Roy, C.B. 1989. Features of discourse in an American Sign Language lecture. In *The sociolinguistics of the Deaf community*, ed. C. Lucas, 231–251. San Diego: Academic Press.

Stokoe, W. 1960. Sign language structure: An outline of the visual communication system of the American deaf. In *Studies in linguistics: Occasional papers 8*. New York: University of Buffalo.

Tannen, D. 1986. Introducing constructed dialogue in Greek and American conversational and literacy narratives. In *Reported speech across languages*, ed. F. Coulmas, 311–332. The Hague: Mouton.

———. 1989. *Talking voices: Repetition, dialogue, and imagery in conversational discourse*. Cambridge: Cambridge University Press.

Winston, E. 1991. Spatial referencing and cohesion in an American Sign Language text. *Sign Language Studies* 73:397–410.

———. 1992. Space and involvement in an American Sign Language lecture. In *Expanding horizons: Proceedings of the twelfth national convention of the registry of interpreters for the Deaf*, ed. J. Plant-Moeller, 93–105. Silver Spring, Md.: RID Publications.

———. 1993. Spatial mapping in comparative discourse frames in an American Sign Language lecture. Ph.D. diss., Georgetown University.

Transcription Symbols

Symbol	Example	Use
Capital letters	ME	English gloss for a specific manual sign
Hyphen	LOOK-AT	Used when more than one English word is required to represent the ASL sign; also used to represent an ASL compound
CL: with # or letter	CL:I	Used to represent a classifier predicate, the number or letter represents the handshape, as in the fist with index finger extended, represented by the 1 in this example
Words in parentheses	CL:V (walk-up)	Used to explain the meaning of a classifier within a given utterance; occasionally used here to clarify which hand is articulating a specific sign
Line and description above glosses	*gaze right* DON'T-WANT	Used to transcribe nonmanual features within the discourse
PRO.#	PRO.I	Indicates pronoun and person
++	CRY++	Represents repetition of sign

Examples of Constructions
Based on Tannen (1989)

Example A: (from SF narrative)
> 9   LOOK-UP MUMBLE NAME SPELL-TO B-A-K-E-R WHERE B-A-K-E-R
> *I looked up at him and he said, "Uh, is there a guy here named Baker?"*

Example B: (from Mather 1989, 185)
> (mouthing "meow") (The cats) CRY ++
> *"Meeow, meeow, meeow"*

Example C: (from SF narrative)
> 26   (looks down) WHO? MUST BACK BUT AWFUL CHAOS . . .
> *I was like, "Who is this guy?" Course, we had to put everything back together, it was an awful mess . . .*

Example D: (from Garfield narrative)
> 7   CAT LOOK-UP "SHOOT" REMOTE-CONTROL
> *And Garfield just looks up at him with the remote control in his hand, and he's like, "Aw, shoot!"*

Example E: (from SF narrative)
> 9   LOOK-UP MUMBLE NAME SPELL-TO B-A-K-E-R WHERE B-A-K-E-R
> *I looked up at him and he said, "Uh, is there a guy here," and he spelled his name, "named Baker?"*

Example F: (from Garfield narrative)
> 9   CAT (remote in hand) FLIP-FINGER WHY CL: CC (grab owner, hold to TV)
> *And Garfield's like, "Why you . . ." and he picks the guy up and holds him out to the television . . .*

Example G: (from Garfield narrative)
> 8   KNOW-THAT YOU MUST CL: V (walk-to) TOUCH-TV-BUTTONS
> *Y'know, now you've got to get up, walk over there, and change the channel by hand*

Example H: (from Brawl narrative)

13 ME WHAT-DO ME PUSH ME WRONG HIT/FIGHT FINALLY

And so y'know what I did? I pushed him. And he took a swing at him, and they finally fought it out.

Example I: (from SF narrative)

12 CL: TABLE-OVER FIGHT ME CARDS-FLY-FROM-HANDS CONFUSED

The table went over and they were smashing each other. My cards flew out of my hands, I was really dazed.

Example J: (from Brawl narrative)

<u>eyebrows up, eyes narrow, mouth puckered</u>

12 . . . MAN 2 CL:1 (left and right, bend/unbend)

These two guys are circling each other, ready to strike...

Example K: (from SF narrative)

24 PUNCH-NOSE (left hand) FALL-BACK HEAD-HIT-flat vertical object

and, bam, he's got a fist in his face. Knocked him right out of his chair and into the wall

25 FIGHT/MESS TABLE-FLIP-OVER MY ___?___ CONFUSE

and they were fighting and the table flipped over, and my (—?—), I didn't know what was going on.

Example L: (from SF narrative)

24 PUNCH-NOSE (left hand) FALL-BACK HEAD-HIT-flat vertical object

and, bam, he's got a fist in his face. Knocked him right out of his chair and into the (wall)

Example M: (from Garfield narrative)

9 CAT (remote in hand) FLIP-FINGER WHY CL: CC (grab owner, hold to TV)

And Garfield's like, "Why you . . . " and he picks the guy up and holds him out to the television . . ,

Turn-taking and Eye Gaze in Sign

Conversations Between Deaf Filipinos

Liza B. Martinez

Recent studies of discourse analysis by Thibeault (1993) and Martinez (1993) on a sign conversation between two deaf Filipinos reported some interesting findings. Thibeault's (1993) data revealed a high number of turns with overlap. He described the conversation as having a high-involvement style, and he attributed this in his analysis to familiarity of topic and shared knowledge between the interlocutors. He also discussed the different functions of overlap in the conversation (e.g., requesting and giving verification, choral repetition, and cooperative overlap). Thibeault's observation of high overlap is interesting in that it appears to be distinct from anecdotal evidence for the generally nonoverlapping turns in sign discourse (Valli and Lucas 1992, 311–313). In other words, generally only one person signs at a time during a conversation.

The analysis by Martinez (1993) revealed a number of patterns as well. Gaze aversion (-GZ) of a signer was shown to be characteristic at the beginning of an utterance, whereas eye contact (+GZ) was found toward the end, patterns that have also been observed in spoken English discourse. In terms of similarity to ASL discourse, there was also a strong tendency in both interlocutors for +GZ when they were the addressee. Martinez also noted some gender differences in that the female informant never averted gaze when she was not signing. During their utterances, the female informant was also more inclined to maintain eye contact than the male.

The study by Martinez also included some unusual results. There were a few instances of -GZ preceding and at times continuing on to the start of an utterance; -GZ toward the end of an utterance; and mutual -GZ. Her data on directions of eye gaze were also intriguing. She reported a

The author is grateful to Ceil Lucas for her comments on the manuscript and to Rosalinda Macaraig and Julius Andrada for their contribution to the research.

tendency for the informants to avert gaze to the side or downward when signing. Furthermore, for side-directed -GZ, she noted a strong preference for looking to the side of greater "free space."

Despite the intriguing findings in these studies by Thibeault (1993) and Martinez (1993), it is possible that these were merely features of that particular conversation, or dyad. However, it is equally possible that these may be unique characteristics of the discourse between deaf Filipinos. This study was undertaken to gather more data in order to determine the existence and consistency of such patterns in other conversations.

BACKGROUND

Philippines

The Republic of the Philippines is an archipelago of more than 7,100 islands lying off the coast of Southeast Asia. Its spoken languages belong to the Austronesian family. The major languages are Cebuano, Tagalog, Ilocano, Hiligaynon, Bicol, Waray, Kapampangan, and Pangasinan, spoken by about 90 percent of the population, and none of which are mutually intelligible. Depending on how *language* is defined, the number of minor languages ranges from seventy to two hundred (Gonzalez 1981, 48–51). Pilipino (based on Tagalog)[1] and English are the official languages, while Filipino (though yet to be developed) is the national language. Knowledge of Spanish and Arabic is significant among certain groups (Crystal 1987, 339; Bright 1992, 143).

The nation is now in the midst of a debate between the "Filipino First" proponents and the bilingualists. The issue is whether to develop an in-

---

1. The terms Pilipino and Filipino are not used consistently in popular usage. Historically, the official and national language from the time of the provisional Biak-na-Bato constitution in 1897 was Tagalog (used in the capital, Manila). In the postwar years, the nomenclature adopted was that of "Pilipino," which was based on Tagalog. Later on, "Pilipino" was replaced with "national language" in view of resistance from non-Tagalog speakers. The 1987 constitution fueled the controversy by referring to the national language as "Filipino". The current debate going on in academic circles is whether "Filipino" is truly a new language that has evolved from the Philippine languages and from contact with foreign languages, or, whether it is still just liberalized Tagalog-based Pilipino.

digenous language or to encourage bilingualism between Filipino and English (Cristobal 1987, 26–27; Gonzales 1981, 48–59; Scott 1989, 44–45; San Juan 1991, 69–88; Nerney 1991, 212–14). The nature of Filipino is itself still nebulous since it is taken to be equivalent to Tagalog, yet this has been strongly resisted by ethnic groups who speak the other seventy to two hundred native languages. The issues confront a country struggling to come of age—a country that has emerged from three centuries of Spanish rule and now with a growing restlessness wishes to disengage itself from relations with the United States (see Martinez 1992).

Sign Language in the Philippines

There are no official statistics on the number of deaf individuals in the Philippines (much less the number of sign language users). Shaneyfelt (1987, 96) and Bright (1992, 143) estimate the number of deaf people at about 100,000. A coordinator of a statistical research center at the De La Salle University, Manila, says that 300,000 is the oft-quoted number. However, he estimates the figure to be somewhere between 30,000 and 600,000, thus placing the incidence at 5 out of 1,000 (L. Moortgat, interview with the author, 1993).

Published material about the sign language in the Philippines has taken the form mainly of vocabulary lists (MacFadden et al. 1977; Sandager 1986; Shaneyfelt 1985; Department of Education, Culture, and Sports n. d.; Gamez-Saulo n. d.). Two of these are included in Carmel's checklist of national sign languages (Carmel 1991, 1992): the MacFadden et al. (1977) and Shaneyfelt (1985) references. They are authored by Americans, and both acknowledge the incorporation of American Sign Language (ASL) and English signs. The Department of Education, Culture, and Sports (DECS) and Gamez-Saulo publications are written by Filipinos and also incorporate ASL and English signs. A prayer book in sign language has also been developed by the Catholic Organization of the Deaf newsletter, 1975. An American missionary working with the Deaf Evangelistic Alliance of the Deaf is preparing a dictionary of signs to be used with her students (A. Coryell, interview with the author, 1993). A videodisc of over 760 signs is being prepared at the National Technical Institute for the Deaf (NTID) in New York in cooperation with the Philippine School for the Deaf. The vocabulary list was generated by interpreters from the Philippine Registry of Interpreters for the Deaf and was initially put on videotape at NTID utilizing a Filipino interpreter as the talent (G. Silver, interview with the author, 1992).

Views of the nature of the sign language used in the Filipino deaf community are quite mixed. Most of the foreign publications refer to it as "Philippine Sign Language" (Sandager 1986; Shaneyfelt 1987; Bright 1992). Shaneyfelt (1985) in his description of more than a thousand signs "in English and Pilipino" refers to some signs as "traditional" signs.[2] MacFadden et al. (1977) introduce their publication of signs by writing:

> "We wish to apologize for this book not being PILIPINO IN SIGNS. There are not yet enough Pilipino signs for Pilipino words to enable one to sign in grammatically correct Pilipino. In the meantime, rather than deny one the acquisition of linguistic proficiency in a language and, subsequently an education, while waiting for the repertory of Pilipino signs to be expanded, we have presented these English signs."

The DECS publication includes sections on both Filipino and English signs and states that most of the signs are from ASL and SEE. In Gamez-Saulo (n. d.), the sign language is referred to as Filipino Sign Language. In her section on Historical Notes, she describes sign language in the Philippines as having its roots in ASL. She relates this to the establishment of the Philippine School for the Deaf by an American missionary, Delight Rice. She writes that deaf Filipinos assimilated "about 80% of Amesian, and incorporated local signs to constitute Filslan . . . ." She further relates

2. Sandager (1986, PHI 1–32) included a collection of 119 signs for the Philippines. He showed the manual alphabet for Pilipino and listed the signs according to Tagalog vocabulary. There appear to be a number of inconsistencies, for example, the Tagalog translations, the handshapes for the letters *t* and *ng*.

On the other hand, W. Shaneyfelt's book (1985) includes over a thousand signs "in English and Pilipino." He presents the manual alphabet from ASL, and although he provides the Tagalog equivalents alongside the signs, they are actually listed according to an English vocabulary. A number of signs and idiomatic expressions presented in the book seem to be quite incongruous with Filipino culture.

Comparing these two publications brings up an interesting point. Of Sandager's 119 signs, 101 are clearly borrowed ASL signs. The remaining 18 are either somewhat or completely different from the corresponding ASL signs. It is interesting to note that of these 18, 14 are found in Shaneyfelt's book, and furthermore, 12 of these Shaneyfelt labels as "traditional" signs. These 12 signs may be examples of indigenous Filipino signs.

that American deaf educators and missionaries developed the sign language in the country. Curiously, Garcia (1976, 50–52), in her brief history of the sign language, describes instead the history of ASL. Schools appear to view the sign language as equivalent to Signed English (SAID Model School 1975, 3; Kasayahan 1976). Martinez (1992) initially referred to the sign language as "Philippine Sign Language" but changed to the name "Filipino Sign Language" (Martinez 1993) after receiving some feedback from members of the deaf community. Rosalinda Macaraig (interview with the author, 1993), Director of the CAP College School for the Deaf, believes there is a bona fide sign language but that it probably is more easily observable outside of the classroom.

Thus, it appears that language contact between the Filipino deaf community and deaf/hearing Americans has played quite a role in the history of the sign language. This has taken place primarily through missionary organizations (Argila 1970, 1971; TPBP Newsletter 1973; Shaneyfelt 1985), the Peace Corps (Bonoan 1976); MacFadden et al. 1977; Olson 1989; *Newsweek* 1990; Parsons 1991) and linkages to academic institutions such as Gallaudet University (R. Mobley, interview with the author, 1992) and NTID (G. Silver, interview with the author, 1992).

DISCOURSE RESEARCH

Spoken Language Discourse

TURN-TAKING

The classical view of turn-taking is found in the Sacks et al. model published in 1974. These authors believe there exists an ideal organization for turn-taking. A basic set of rules allocate for the next turn and coordinate transfer of turns so that gap and overlap are minimized (Sacks et al. 1974). Since that time, numerous ideas have emerged from research, and some of these ideas contest this initial proposal. For instance, Searle has presented two controversial theses: that conversation does not have any intrinsic structure upon which a theory can be formed, and that conversation is not subject to rules (Searle 1992, 7–30; Parret and Verschueren 1992, 1–6). This opposing view has spawned numerous discussions on the concept of conversation itself (Searle et al. 1992).

O'Connell et al. (1990) give a critical analysis of all the research on turn-taking after this traditional model and conclude that our current view of turn-taking needs to be more dynamic than what was initially proposed by Sacks et al. (1974). They propose that the concepts of turn, back-channeling, overlap, and interruption be redefined and standardized across various research projects. Furthermore, they advocate that anecdotal evidence be replaced by instrumental and statistical measurement of the turn-taking corpora. They propose a context-sensitive approach in the analysis of data and the view that conversation be defined as a "shared finality involving shared means" (O'Connell et al. 1990, 369). They suggest that speaking and listening be viewed as involving active participation and that "turns not be conceived as the key elements of conversation, but rather as part of the overall dynamic of the social interaction of interlocutors engaged in purposeful activity . . . turn taking must be considered as part of the overall finality of conversations rather than an end in itself." (O'Connell et al. 1990, 370).

They support the case for the "contractual" element of conversation, which at its broadest would include culture-specific patterns. Examples are interruptions or unsmooth turn-taking in Indian-English colloquial conversations as a gesture of cooperative talk and acceptable behavior (Ervin-Tripp 1979); the American Indian conversational style of an absence of an immediate response (Philips 1976); or the distinctive interruptions in an Italian conversation (Eco 1986). In the light of this evidence from other research, O'Connell et al. (1990, 367–8) view the simplest systematics of Sacks et al. (1974) as in need of modification.

Tannen views conversation as "joint production," listening and speaking as both active and passive roles (1989, 9–35). She emphasizes the interactive nature of conversation and the style and strategies that are utilized in achieving coherence and involvement goals (Tannen 1984, 7–23).

Current trends in turn-taking research for spoken languages have branched into various directions: for example, acquisition of skills in children (Hecht et al. 1993; Self 1993; Sherwood 1991), repair mechanisms (Larrue and Trognon 1993), gender differences (Nordenstom 1992; Craig and Evans 1991), and turn-taking cues (Stephens 1991), to name a few.

EYE GAZE

The classical view of the role of gaze in social interactions is found in the early studies of Kendon (1967, 22–63). He observed that a speaker tends to look away at the beginning of the utterance (and often, even before it), then looks back at the addressee as he approaches the end of it; and that the speaker tends to look less at the addressee while he is speaking than when he is listening. He suggested that gaze aversion at the beginning of an utterance could signal an intention to hold the turn and preclude interruptions as well as enable the speaker to organize his utterance. Brief eye contact at phrase endings and longer gaze at the end of utterances may serve to monitor feedback as well as signal turn-yielding. Kendon thus proposed three basic functions of eye shifts for speakers: monitoring (to gather information about addressee), signalling (to inform addressee of intentions and expectations), and expressive (to emphasize feelings and attitudes). Argyle and Cook (1976) postulated similar functions for eye gaze: as a signal for grammatical junctures and speaker-select, as a channel for obtaining feedback, and gaze aversion as it relates to a "cognitive overload hypothesis." Two recent comprehensive reviews on the role of eye gaze in social interaction and cognitive processing are those of Rutter (1984) and Kleinke (1986). Both include extensive discussions of these three basic functions of eye gaze as originally proposed by Kendon (1967). The regulatory function includes signalling at the beginning and ending of utterances and the synchrony of turn-taking.

Sign Language Discourse

Turn-Taking

Baker (1977) proposed a system of "multichannel behaviors" through which initiation, continuation, shift, or termination regulators could shape ASL discourse. These included various manual as well as nonmanual signals such as signing speed, hand "rests," head tilt, eye gaze, and so on. Some recent research on turn-taking examines early acquisition of conversation skills in deaf children (Caissie 1993; Christie 1992).

Eye Gaze

There are a number of studies on nonmanual signals in general for ASL (e.g., Baker 1976a; Liddell 1980; Baker-Shenk 1983). However, there are only a few papers that focus on the role of gaze and only one of which investigates eye gaze in discourse. Baker (1976b, 1–13) summarized the various functions of eye shift in ASL grammar. She proposed the symbol "+GAZE" to signify eye contact and "-GAZE" to mean averted gaze. These various functions were discussed more extensively by Baker and Padden (1978, 27–57) and are categorized as follows:

Regulatory
  Speaker   -GAZE to control interruptions, for turn maintenance
             +GAZE to signal turn-yielding
  Addressee +GAZE to signal turn initiation or maintenance
             -GAZE to signal a possible interruption
Linguistic
  I.   Gaze direction
         Lexically determined
         Noun modifier
         Pronominal reference
         Direct quotation
         At constituent boundaries
  II. Lengthy eye closure (for emphasis)
  III. Blinking (for marking constituent boundaries)

Baker's study (1976b, 1–13) concluded that signers also tended to look away from the addressee while initiating a turn and then look back to check the addressee's decoding. She also emphasized the importance of considering the context of interaction and individual discourse styles in analyzing data. She recognized the difficulty of such investigations because eye gaze patterns could be a combined outcome of discourse, lexical, and grammatical factors. A later study by Baker (1977) proposed four kinds of turn-taking regulators (initiation, continuation, shift, and termination) that frequently utilized eye gaze.

Mather (1987) examined eye gaze in classroom communication. She distinguished between I-GAZE (individual gaze) and G-GAZE (group gaze). She concluded that turn exchanges proceeded a lot more smoothly with teachers who were native signers and made effective and appropriate use of gaze signals.

A recent study on Norwegian Sign Language examined eye gaze in interrogatives (Vogt-Svendsen 1990). It emphasized the importance of the context of speech acts in understanding the associated gaze patterns for this speech type.

Philippine Language Discourse

The current linguistic situation in the Philippines is complex—a result of history, linguistic and cultural diversity, and bilingualism issues in education (Martinez 1992). Recent studies on discourse analysis are not extensive. Filipino has received attention due to the attempt to re-late discourse to its "intellectualization" as the national language (Carreon 1992). The use of gesture and some discourse markers at turn-transition points for Ilocano, another major language, was discussed by Streeck and Hartge (1992, 135–57).

Filipino Sign Language Discourse

The most recent linguistic studies on Filipino Sign Language are those of Thibeault (1993) and Martinez (1993) on discourse analysis. Both noted some striking patterns in turn-taking (Thibeault) and eye gaze (Martinez) that seem to be different from those of American Sign Language and/or spoken English. The term Filipino Sign Language, or FSL, is adopted in the following section according to its use by Martinez (1993). This is solely for the purpose of discussion. Current research is being undertaken to determine the actual usage and acceptability of this term in the deaf community in the Philippines. Now, the sign Filipino is executed using an F handshape with small, repeated circular or straight movements by the nose. It is often accompanied by mouthing of the word "Filipino."

METHODOLOGY

Data were collected in January, 1993, at three deaf schools: the Cap College of the Deaf (dyads 1 through 3) and the Philippine Association of the Deaf (dyad 4), both in Manila, and the Deaf Evangelistic Alliance Foundation (dyads 5 and 6) in Laguna. Informal conversations between two deaf students were videotaped. Dyads 1–3 were made up of a male and female; dyads 4 and 6, both females; and dyad 5, males. They ranged in age from their teens to early twenties. Members of each dyad were previously acquainted with each other. The investigator seated them approximately two feet from each other at about a 45° angle. They started their own conversations, all of which involved their personal experiences, mostly relating to their education. In dyads 1–3, the videotaping proceeded with only the two informants present. In dyads 4 through 6, a third deaf person was present: a co-student in dyad 4 and a teacher in dyads 5 and 6. One- to two-minute segments of the conversations were then glossed, and nonmanual signals were included in the transcript.

Several assumptions were made prior to the data analysis. An utterance was defined to be any signed (manual) segment of the conversation. Following this definition, isolated nonmanual signals without accompanying manual parameters (e.g., head nod) were not counted as utterances. Pauses and gaps were counted together and deemed "short" if less than a single count. Turn transitions without overlap included both gapped and gapless shifts. Unsuccessful attempts to take a turn were grouped with other "simultaneous talk (sign) events" (Fasold 1990, 71–3) such as back-channelling, choral repetition, verification, and so forth.

Line diagrams were made for each conversation following the scheme used by Martinez (1993), that is, utterances and eye shifts were represented by lines drawn against an axis of numbers (from VCR counter). After conversion of the data into line diagrams, the structure of the conversations was described: length and frequency of utterances, and turn exchanges. Then, eye shift patterns were described: eye shifts in general, eye shifts during signing, directions of eye shift, and position of eye shift in relation to an utterance. For the directions of eye shift, "side" meant a nonmedial direction on the horizontal plane at eye level. "Up" or "down" included points on the median vertical plane. All other directed-gaze outside of these two places (except toward the signer's hand) were classified under "combination."

RESULTS

Turn-Taking

Figure 1 shows a graph of the number of utterances of both informants in all the dyads. Dyads 4–6 show an almost equal number of utterances between informants, as different from the first three dyads. Figure 2 shows percentages of the number of long (>5 counts) and short utterances by informants in each dyad. Short utterances were characteristic of nine of the informants. There does not seem to be any relationship between the length of utterance and gender, school, or observer influence.

Figure 3 shows the percentage of time that the informants in dyads 1–3 signed. Informant A (the male informant) signed more in each conversation than B. The same-gender dyads (4–6) did not reveal any striking patterns in terms of percentage time of signing (data not shown).

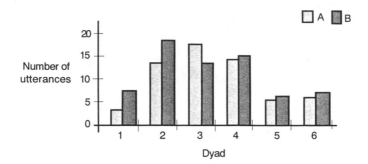

FIGURE 1. *Total number of utterances for informants A and B in dyads 1–6.*

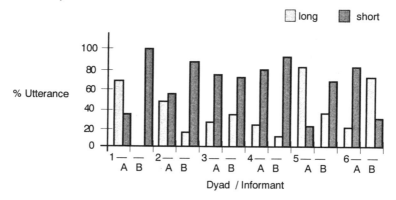

FIGURE 2. *Percentage number of long and short utterances of informants A and B in dyads 1–6.*

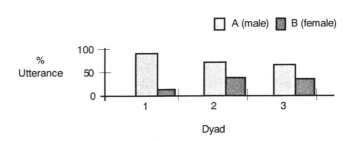

FIGURE 3. *Percentage utterance (by time) of informants A (male) and B (female) in dyads 1–3.*

| Dyad | Number of Turn Exchanges | | | |
| | With overlap | | Without overlap | Total |
	by A	by B		
1	1	0	1	2
2	2	6	10	18
3	6	6	9	21
4	3	4	17	24
5	3	2	6	11
6	1	4	7	12

The number of turn exchanges with or without overlap in each dyad is shown in table 1. Dyad 1 is different from the rest in that it has a very small number of turn shifts, and informant B was the only one in all the dyads who did not attempt any overlap during turn-taking. Dyad 3 shows an equal number of overlaps between interlocutors. Figure 4 combines the number of overlapping exchanges for both informants and shows all these data in percentages. Dyads 2, 4, 5, and 6 all show more turn shifts without overlap than with overlap. Dyad 4, in particular, shows a very high number of nonoverlapping turns.

Turn exchanges initiated by overlap were observed in all the dyads. The majority of these involved an overlap of only one sign. For instance, in the following excerpt, FIVE signed by A is overlapped by the same sign by B:

```
                                       blink__
A: ... ——— FIVE YEAR │ FIVE │        YEAR FIVE...
                     │      │   q
B: YOU WORK          │ FIVE │ YEAR                [Dyad 2]
```

Occasionally, two or three signs overlapped. For example, in the following, informant A signs "Pro-1 WORK ++ HARD++," which overlaps with informant B signing " . . . BEFORE HARD++ WHAT":

```
                             blink
A:        │ Pro-1 WORK++    HARD++  │ NOT LOOK-FOR...
          │                hnds dwn │
B: Pro-1  │ BEFORE HARD++    WHAT   │              [Dyad 2]
          │                hnds dwn │
```

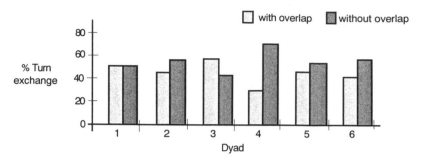

FIGURE 4. *Percentage number of turn exchanges with or without overlap in dyads 1–6.*

In another excerpt shown below, B signs "Pro-1 NOT BORN DEAF," Pro-1 overlapping with the sign BORN by informant A, and BORN DEAF (by B) overlapping with HEARING BORN (by A):

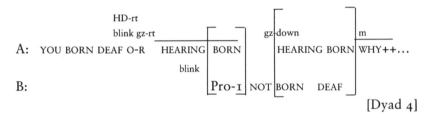

[Dyad 4]

Table 2 shows the data for the number of pauses and gaps in each conversation. Dyad 4 had the highest number, while dyad 6 had a 12–count discontinuity, probably more appropriately referred to as a lapse according to a definition of the term by Fasold (1990, 70).

The number of simultaneous signing events and the number of turn exchanges with overlap for all the dyads are shown in table 3. Simultaneous sign events that seemed to be distinct from each other were observed in the dyads. A number of these appeared to have some kind of back-channel function. They frequently occurred with the sign YES and occasionally with OH-I-SEE and FINE. This example shows simultaneous signing of YES by informant B during A's utterance:

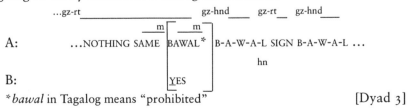

bawal in Tagalog means "prohibited"

[Dyad 3]

TABLE 2. *Number of Pauses/Gaps during Conversation for Each Dyad*

Dyad	Number of Pauses / Gaps	
	Short (<1)	Long
1	2	0
2	1	0
3	2	4
4	6	5
5	2	1
6	1	4

In this example, A signs OH-I-SEE without interrupting B's utterance:

<pre>
                               ┌ hn gz-rt____   ┐
A: ... YOU   │ OH-I-SEE   │
     gz-lft _____   │   m   │
B: Pro-1   THINK STUDY │ C-A-P COLLEGE │ FINISH Pro-1...
</pre>

[Dyad 4]

Another kind of simultaneous sign event showed a repetition of a portion of the turn-holder's utterance. It was either exactly simultaneous, or the repetition was just slightly ahead of the current signer, indicating shared knowledge of the topic. For instance, the name of the high school is signed almost simultaneously by the informants in this excerpt:

<pre>
        gz-rt gz-rt____ blink   ┌   ┐
A: ... THEN GO LOOK-FOR D-H-S D-H-S │ (name of high school)... │
                                  │   │
B: │ (name of high school) │
                                  └   ┘
</pre>

[Dyad 2]

A third kind of simultaneous sign event also showed some repetitions but involved several signs in a different order (here, involving the signs YOU, DESCRIBE, and YOUR):

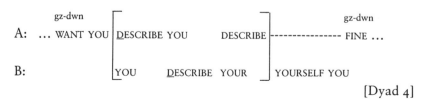

<pre>
        gz-dwn   ┌   ┐   gz-dwn
A: ... WANT YOU │ DESCRIBE YOU   DESCRIBE │-------------- FINE ...
                  │   │
B: │ YOU   DESCRIBE YOUR   │ YOURSELF YOU
                  └   ┘
</pre>

[Dyad 4]

TABLE 3. *Number of Simultaneous Sign Events and Turn Exchanges with Overlap by Informants A and B in Each Dyad*

Dyad	Simultaneous Sign Events by Informant		Turn Exchanges with Overlap by Informant	
	A	B	A	B
1	0	5	1	0
2	1	8	2	6
3	2	4	6	6
4	2	3	3	4
5	0	0	3	2
6	0	0	1	4

It was interesting to note how synchrony was evident in one dyad, even without some of the manual signals, and occurred simply by mouthing Tagalog words (i.e., TAPON ["throw"], BASURA ["garbage"]):

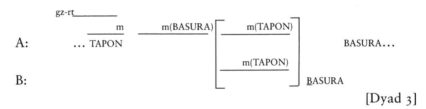

[Dyad 3]

In several instances, simultaneous signing appeared to be part of verification or correction. The following excerpt shows clarification of the name of a city (i.e., P-A-S-A-Y) that was mispelled by Informant A (P-S-A-Y):

<pre>
        gz-hnd_ ┌─────────┐   gz-hnd_ gz-hnd_ gz-hnd
A: ... P-S-A-Y │ C-I-T-Y │   P-S-A-Y P-S-A-Y C-I-T-Y...
                │   │
B: │ P-A-S-A-Y │ HOW FINGERSPELL YOU PAST WHAT   P-A-S-A-Y
                └─────────┘
</pre>

[Dyad 2]

The last kind of simultaneous signing event was deemed to be an unsuccessful interruption, as seen in the next example (informant B begins with "Pro-1," but A continues with CLEAN+++, until B is able to take the turn successfully with "SWEEP ... "):

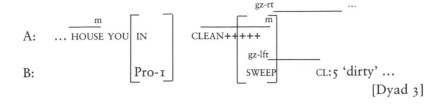

[Dyad 3]

Eye Gaze

The graph in figure 5 shows the percentage data of eye shifts (based on time) by both informants in each dyad when they are signing. Eight of the twelve informants showed greater +GZ than -GZ during signing. Of the four that did not show this pattern, Informant A in dyad 1 was strikingly different in that his -GZ was extremely high. Both informants of dyad 3 had slightly higher -GZ than +GZ, and the same was true of Informant B in dyad 6.

The percentage data of eye shifts (based on time) by both informants in each dyad when not signing is shown in figure 6. All informants in all dyads exhibited significantly higher +GZ than -GZ when they were the addressee. Four informants had 100 percent +GZ, and all the other informants had +GZ ranging from 82 percent–>99 percent. Conversely, this meant that those four informants never averted gaze when they were the addressee. The others averted gaze <1 percent–18 percent of the time. It is also interesting to note that in dyads 2 and 3, Informant B (the female informant) showed higher +GZ than A (the male informant). (In dyad 1, both male and female informants had 100 percent +GZ.)

Figure 7 summarizes the data on direction of -GZ of informants A and B while they are signing. For all informants in all the dyads, the highest -GZ was to the side direction (this is combined for left and right). Furthermore, two of the informants (1B and 3B) showed all of their -GZ solely in the side direction.

Looking more closely at the side-directed -GZ, the right-seated informants of each dyad (informants A) displayed a tendency to gaze toward the right (figure 8). Similarly, the left-seated informants of each dyad (informants B) showed a preferential side gaze to the left (figure 9). For seven of the twelve informants, this predisposition was manifested 100 percent of the time. In other words, if these informants directed their gaze toward the side while signing, it would be consistently only to the right

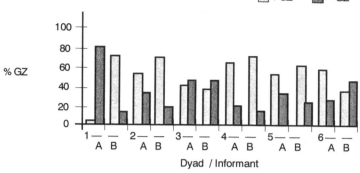

FIGURE 5. *Percentage +GZ and -GZ (based on time) of informants A and B in dyads 1–6 when signing.*

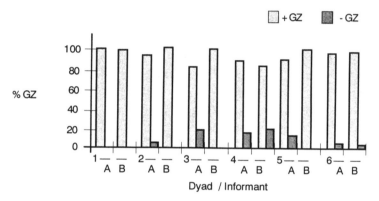

FIGURE 6. *Percentage +GZ and -GZ (based on time) of informants A and B in dyads 1–6 when not signing.*

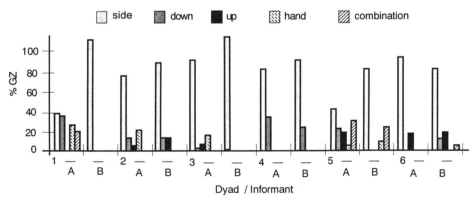

FIGURE 7. *Percentage frequency of -GZ direction by informants A and B in dyads 1–6 while signing.*

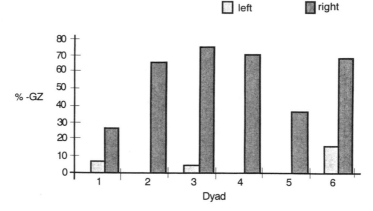

FIGURE 8. *Percent frequency of -GZ to the left or right by right-seated informants (informants A) in dyads 1–6 when signing.*

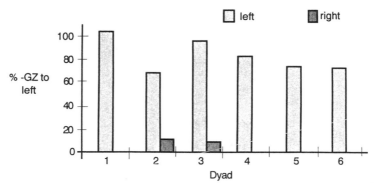

FIGURE 9. *Percent frequency of -GZ to the left or right by left-seated informants (informants B) in dyads 1–6 when signing.*

if they were seated at the right (figure 8) or only to the left if they were seated at the left (figure 9).

Table 4 lists the percentage frequency data on the occurrence of major eye gaze patterns in relation to the signer's utterance. Data on the signer's gaze aversion during his or her utterances were varied for all the informants. However, two extremes are seen in informant 4B, who did not avert gaze at all during her utterances, and informant 6A, who averted gaze all the time when she signed. Four informants (1A, 2A, 5B, and 6B) also showed high -GZ (ranging from 92 to 96 percent) during their utterances. Results for -GZ at the beginning of the signer's utterance were also varied. Extremes were seen for three informants, 1B and dyad 6,

Dyad	Informant	-GZ during Utterance (%)	+GZ toward End (%)	-GZ at Beginning (%)
1	A	96	100	67
	B	50	100	0
2	A	92	92	17
	B	67	94	6
3	A	88	88	24
	B	53	77	31
4	A	43	93	50
	B	0	87	27
5	A	81	100	67
	B	93	100	17
6	A	100	100	0
	B	94	100	0

who had no -GZ. This meant that all the beginnings of their utterances were accompanied by +GZ.

A strongly consistent pattern found for all informants in all dyads was the tendency for +GZ toward the end of their utterances. Half of the dyads showed this pattern 100 percent of the time. The rest also showed high occurrences of this pattern (table 4, figure 10).

Several instances of mutual gaze aversion were noted similar to what Martinez (1993) had previously reported. The following is an example

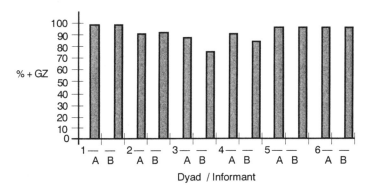

FIGURE 10. *Percentage frequency of +GZ toward the end of the signer's utterance for informants A and B in dyads 1–6.*

showing exactly coinciding gaze aversion during a gap. The gap occurs at counter #14–15+, after A's utterance and before B's utterance: A averts gaze to the right while B looks to the left. Both then synchronously resume eye contact when B begins to sign [(1) is the line diagram for the gloss excerpt in (2)]:

(1)

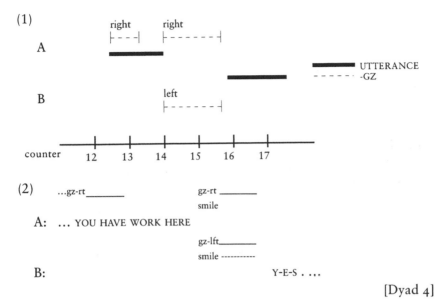

(2)   ...gz-rt_____   gz-rt _____
                                 smile

A: ... YOU HAVE WORK HERE

                                 gz-lft_____
                                 smile ----------

B: Y-E-S . ...

[Dyad 4]

Other observations of mutual gaze aversion were not completely simultaneous, as shown in the following examples. In (3), informant A looks to the right (#52–55+) in between his utterances. Informant B begins to avert gaze to the left (at #53) and returns to +GZ, at the exact time that A resumes eye contact and begins signing [(4) is the gloss excerpt for the line diagram in (3)]:

(3)

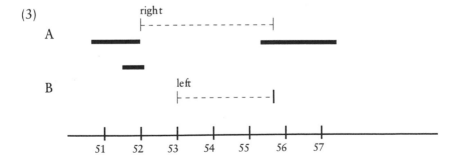

(4)

```
                              gz-rt_____
                        hn                        m
A:   REALLY COLLEGE C-A-P              HOW LONG ...
                                   gz-lft____
B:                          Y-E-S ++
```

[Dyad 4]

In the third example, B begins to look down (prior to #18) after A finishes his utterance and continues to look down until A begins signing again at #21. At #24, B looks left and looks back at A when A shifts gaze to the right. Informant A is signing from #18 onwards but appears to go through "false starts" from #18 to 21. For most of these false starts, A gazes downward, looks at B briefly (about #20–21), then looks back down again when B starts to return gaze. Informant A shifts gaze (down to right) at the exact time that B returns gaze (at about #26.5) [(5) is the line diagram for the gloss excerpt in (6)]:

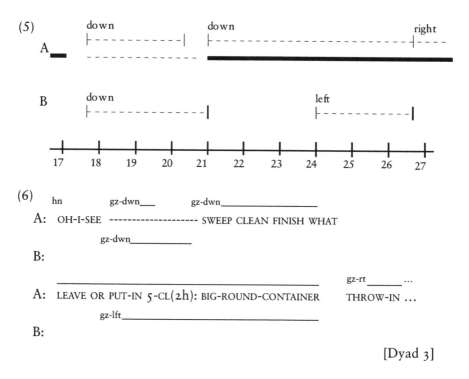

(5)

(6)

```
    hn          gz-dwn__      gz-dwn_____
A:  OH-I-SEE -------------------- SWEEP CLEAN FINISH WHAT
                gz-dwn_____
B:

    _____      gz-rt_____  ...
A:  LEAVE OR PUT-IN 5-CL(2h): BIG-ROUND-CONTAINER   THROW-IN ...
            gz-lft_____
B:
```

[Dyad 3]

DISCUSSION

Turn-Taking

The overall structures of the conversations in each dyad appear to be comparable to each other except dyad 1. It is different from all the other dyads in that only one informant (A) did virtually all of the signing (figure 3); there was a very small number of turn shifts (table 1); there were only a few pauses/gaps, all of which were short (table 2); and one informant (B) made no attempt to take an overlapping turn, despite initiating a number of simultaneous sign events (tables 1 and 3). Aside from dyad 1, the long lapse in dyad 6 is also striking.

Despite these divergent features in dyads 1 and 6, there are two patterns that split the data into two sets: dyads 1 to 3, and dyads 4 to 6. First, dyads 4–6 showed very close numbers of utterances between both informants, whereas dyads 1–3 showed more variability (figure 1). Second, in dyads 1–3, which had both genders, informant A (the male informant) signed more (i.e., percent length of time) than B (the female informant) (figure 3). This was despite the fact that informant A in dyads 1 and 2 actually had a smaller number of utterances than B (figure 1). Naturally this meant that informant B in these first three dyads was an addressee for a greater part of the conversation than A. Again, this was despite the fact that informant B in dyads 1 and 2 actually signed a greater number of utterances than A.

A likely reason for the split in the data seems to be the gender difference. Data from dyads 4 to 6 (same-sex dyads) revealed that one interlocutor signed almost as frequently as the other. Dyads 1 to 3 (cross-gender dyads), on the other hand, showed that the male interlocutor (informants A) signed more at length throughout the conversation than the female (informants B).

Nowell (1989, 273–88) in research on white deaf adults concluded that there were no significant gender differences in her data in terms of total amount of talk, number/kind of questions, and manual back-channels. However, she did observe that women signed more than men in the off-task (interviewer absent) portion of her study. Her first observation may have been different from this study in that she was utilizing an interview format (with a deaf or hearing interviewer) for participants unacquainted with each other. Also, she analyzed solely total amount of

talk and did not include the frequency and length of the individual utterances during the conversation.

In spoken languages, Fasold (1990, 116) discusses the "female register," or linguistic features that women tend to use, and its relation to
cross-sex conversation. He states that "men use various interactional
means to seize and maintain control over the progress of conversations."
He describes women, on the other hand, as employing strategies that are
more supportive of the male's agenda and that also ensure that her contributions will be attended to. This generalization seems to apply to this
study as well and could be the explanation for the split in the data. However, the data on frequency and length of utterances is not in exact agreement, so some interaction may be occurring between the two. Also, it is
possible that other factors may be at work. The study of Craig and Evans
(1991) shows that this gender difference of males being more assertive
conversationally than females is observed in children as young as eight
years of age. In their review of the literature, they point out that women
tend to use more question forms, thus facilitating conversation, and that
men tend to interrupt women more (Craig and Evans 1991, 866).

If gender differences were the primary factor that shaped the discourse
structure of the conversations, then one could ask further if this was a
result of or an interaction with a broader cultural context. O'Connell et
al. call for a culture-sensitive approach (1990, 367–8) to research on turn-
taking, which may be appropriate to this study's discourse situation. Also,
dyads 1 to 3 are not only cross-sex dyads, they all also include informants from the same school and same college level (CAP is located at
the very center of the business district of Manila). Dyads 4 to 6 are from
two other schools (the PAD is also in Manila, but the Laguna school is
in a very isolated rural community), and although the ages of the interlocutors are comparable to those of dyads 1 to 3, they are closer to high
school level. One other possible factor could be observer influence. Dyads 1 to 3 were videotaped by themselves, whereas dyads 4 to 6 had a
third deaf person watching. This may have directly or indirectly influenced the structure of the conversation.

Comparison with Thibeault's study (1993) warrants discussion. At first
glance, the data almost seem contradictory. Thibeault reported extensive
overlap in the conversation he analyzed. Figure 4 of this study, however,
shows that only one dyad had a greater percentage of turn exchanges
with overlap than without. However, a closer look at Thibeault's discus-

sion of the possible functions of overlap shows an inclusion of cooperative overlap, verification, and choral repetition. Thus, it seems that he was actually grouping these simultaneous sign events with the overlapping turn exchanges. Thibeault does not explain his reason for this approach, but in this study, an examination of the simultaneous sign events, in comparison to overlaps during turn shifts, shows some connections that appear to justify considering them together.

There has been virtually no study on the syntax of Filipino Sign Language, but there have been preliminary observations that seem to disclose grammatical distinctions from ASL (Rosalinda Macaraig, interview with author, 1993, 1994). However, because of this dearth of information, it was frequently difficult to determine clause boundaries in the data of this study. Categorizing the simultaneous sign events as to whether they were back-channeling signals, cooperative attempts to construct or finish a sentence, or requests for verification, and so forth, was not always straightforward. At times, a single simultaneous sign event would appear initially to be a back-channelling signal and then proceed to be an attempt to take a turn. Because of this, issues of method arise, such as the precision of transcription and the judgment of where a sign begins and ends. Lining up the sign glosses in the transcript to indicate coinciding utterances may not be precise enough to impart the subtle differences in the simultaneity of sign production. A superficial view of the utterances may clearly depict overlap and simultaneous signing by both interlocutors, but whether the individual signs coincide exactly or whether a sign of an interlocutor is nested (slightly or completely) in between the signs of the other interlocutor may not be accurately depicted in the transcription. Furthermore, a second issue arises: the boundaries of an individual sign during discourse are not always distinct. With two manual articulators, it is not uncommon for the hands to be engaged in two different signs at one time during the conversation. For example, perseveration of one or both hands during the flow of discourse was observed a number of times. This feature appears to be unique to sign languages that utilize two physically distinct articulators as opposed to spoken languages that use only one.

Except for dyad 4, the ratio of turn exchanges with or without overlap in all the other dyads is approximately 1:1 (figure 4). This means that half of the time, the beginning of a signer's turn overlaps with the end of the other interlocutor's utterance. One may ask if this is typical for deaf Filipinos—if this degree of overlap is mandatory or perhaps appropriate or acceptable for informal conversation only. At this point, it is difficult to say whether such a degree of overlap is resisted, tolerated, or expected in a conversation between two deaf Filipinos. Dyad 4 may not be truly consonant with the other dyads in this aspect because it not only shows the greatest percentage of nonoverlapping turn exchanges (figure 4) but it also has the highest number of pauses and gaps (table 2). Clearly, some factor(s) was (were) causing discontinuities in the dyad's individual utterances and in the flow of discourse.

It is noteworthy that in dyads 1–3 (the cross-sex dyads) the female informants (Informants B) were the ones who initiated a greater number of the simultaneous signing events (table 3). However, it seems to bear no relationship to overlap during turn shifts. Dyads 5 and 6 showed no simultaneous sign events at all by either informant. One may speculate if this was due to the factor of school/location, as the data from these two dyads were collected from a rural setting. Interestingly enough, despite this absence of simultaneous sign events, the proportion of turn exchanges with overlap was comparable to that of the other dyads. The case of dyad 1 is intriguing for a different reason: Informant B initiated all the simultaneous sign events during the conversation but never overlapped with the other interlocutor when taking her turn. Informant A, on the other hand, never initiated any simultaneous sign events but did overlap half of the time when he began his turn.

The implications of the preceding observations may extend not only to discourse but also to visual perception and processing. When two signers are signing at the same time, how much of the concomitant signing of one interlocutor is actually perceived by the other? Does it affect cognitive processing and, consequently, sign production if a signer is simultaneously encoding and decoding signals? Is this feature of discourse acquired specific to a certain cultural setting? Perhaps there is some parallel to spoken language discourse, for example, comparing the characteristically interruptive nature of Italian conversation (Eco 1986) to the smoother nonoverlapping turn shifts in English (O'Connell et al. 1990, 367–8). Further investigation of overlap during turn exchanges and of simultaneous sign events is clearly needed.

Eye Gaze

The results of this study confirm a number of the findings of Martinez (1993). The informants showed a tendency to +GZ when they were the addressee. In the cross-sex dyads, the female informants also tended to maintain more eye contact when they were the addressee. This may again be related to the female register described by Fasold (1990, 116). Argyle and Ingham (1972), in their study of male and female dyads, considered two possibilities for this greater propensity for eye contact in women. Women may be socialized to have more of an affiliative orientation that is expressed through greater eye contact or, because of having such an orientation, they may be more sensitive to social cues and thus tend to engage in more eye contact.

The previous claim of Martinez (1993) with regard to preferential -GZ toward the side and particularly toward the side of greater free space is very strongly supported by the data in this study. In terms of the position of eye shift patterns to an utterance, +GZ toward the end of an utterance was clearly evident in this data set.

In the case of the observations of mutual gaze aversion, it is interesting to note that the majority of these occurred in dyad 4. One may speculate that this is coincidental to that dyad having the highest percentage of nonoverlapping turn exchanges as well as the greatest number of pauses/gaps. Excerpt (1)/(2) (see Results) shows mutual -GZ in synchrony. Informant A appears to be signalling clause and utterance boundary, while B seems to be acknowledging this. It is curious that B has anticipated this accurately, so that her gaze aversion as well as accompanying smile coincide with that of A. They not only both direct their gaze to the side but also to the side of greater free space.

It would seem useful to employ more sensitive techniques or equipment for future studies to determine if there are subtle differences in the relative timing of these eye shifts. It is possible that one interlocutor may avert or shift gaze back slightly before or after the other interlocutor, thus providing coordinated signals. For instance, in the example (1)/(2), one may hypothesize that Informant A may have started to avert gaze following his utterance, fractions of a second ahead of Informant B; B then picked up the signal and mimicked the eye shift behavior. Similarly, B may have started back toward eye contact just slightly before A to communicate her attempt to take a turn. Informant A then probably picked up the cue and responded with +GZ as B began her utterance.

Excerpt (3)/(4) is somewhat different in that informant A breaks eye contact earlier than B (following her utterance and B's simultaneous sign), although they return to eye contact at the same time. The side-directed gaze pattern in (3) similar to (1) is again observed here, that is, the left-seated informant averts gaze to the right, while the right-seated informant averts gaze to the left (to both, their side of greater free space). Excerpt (5) shows mutual gaze aversion directed downward (is the identical direction coincidental?). Again, more precise monitoring of the eye shifts may give insights as to whether the eye movements of one interlocutor influence or are coordinated with the other informant. Our current view of the role of eye gaze in discourse is focused on its regulatory and monitoring functions. However, perhaps there exists a more dynamic relationship not only between the utterances of the signer himself and his eye gaze patterns but also those of the other interlocutor as well. Especially in a visual language where eye contact and gaze aversion are virtually switching, signalling "on" and "off," such eye shifts may be crucial to the discourse process. A sign conversation, because of its visual modality and gaze mechanisms, may be a great deal more dynamic and highly fine-tuned than the way it is viewed now. Clearly, this is an area to probe further, not only for Filipino Sign Language but for other sign languages as well.

The other data in this study that did not seem to have discernible patterns (greater +GZ when signing; -GZ at the beginning of, and during, utterances) may be due to different reasons. The variation in the results could be explained by the co-occurring discourse and nondiscourse functions of eye gaze. Throughout a conversation, eye gaze may be constantly shifting in its roles as a regulatory, referential, or syntactic signal; a channel for feedback; and an outcome influenced by cognitive processing. It may help to delineate these functions by examining the contexts of the speech acts themselves. However, even this may not be an easy job since, for example, even though eye shifts may be related to some nonmanual syntactic markers, this is not always an obligatory occurrence. Deictic or anaphoric functions of gaze are complex in that they accompany a gestural component in establishing the location of referents in the infinite points of the signing space. Overlying this, too, would be the influence from cognitive processing and social interaction dynamics among deaf signers.

Considering, then, how numerous and complex the factors are that could influence eye gaze in a conversation between two deaf people, it is remarkable that any pattern would surface in the analysis. But this study does reveal a few patterns, and they are quite striking generalizations. The patterns observed in the data that match those previously documented in English and ASL discourse are (1) the strong tendency to maintain eye contact in the role of addressee and (2) the shift back to eye contract with the other interlocutor as a signer approaches the end of his utterance. Of the new findings in this study that support the previous claims of Martinez, significant issues are brought to fore. Some of the patterns observed here again appear to be strongly related to gender. Similarly, how many of these are determined by a broader cultural context? Studies have shows that the Black community (Asante and Davis 1989, 374–391) and a northwest Amazon community display relatively less sustained eye contact than the White community (Goodwin 1981, 55–94). Pascasio (1981), in her comparison of Filipino to American dyads, concludes that cultural values such as *utang-na-loob* (debt or sense of gratitude), *hiya* (shame or sense of social propriety), *pakikisama* (sense of camaraderie), and so on, in Filipino culture, are strongly linked to language use. Baker (1977, 222) states that "it is socially rude in ASL discourse for an addressee not to maintain eye gaze on the speaker's face . . . ." In contrast, the data in this study for deaf Filipinos show that one-third of the informants spent 10–20 percent of the time not watching the person who was signing. Is this simply negligible variability, or is there something more to this? These issues appear to underscore the need for a gender- and culture-sensitive approach in data collection and analysis of sign discourse.

The need for this awareness is even more acute in relation to the finding on preferential direction for side gaze. It appears that this investigator unknowingly established a physical setting for data collection that resulted in the predisposition for -GZ to the side of larger free space. How profound is the effect of seating arrangement and distance on sign discourse? Two possibilities exist: the preferential side gaze could be a compensatory mechanism for such a physical setting and actually be beneficial to discourse, or it could be a constrained outcome of a hampered flow of discourse. Intuitively, the latter seems more acceptable. It is easy to conjecture that visual signalling and monitoring of feedback for two signers would be optimal if they were seated directly opposite each other rather than at a 45° angle. Seating them at an angle may constrain the signing space (as well as the surrounding space), causing it to shift or decrease. To two speakers, this would not constitute a problem since the auditory signals would be unimpeded. But to two signers whose signing space is part of the articulatory and grammatical space, the effect could be quite profound. Perhaps an analogy for spoken language discourse can be drawn between the hands as the articulators in the signing space and the tongue in the oral cavity. Confining the signing space may be similar to obstructing the oral cavity. Thus, videotaping two signers in such a seating arrangement that constrains/shifts the signing space may be like trying to record a spoken conversation from informants "who have their mouths full" (C. Lucas, conversation with author, 1994). Another effect of such physical arrangement and proximity could be on cognitive functions. One of the proposed functions of gaze aversion is that of the "cognitive overload hypothesis" (Argyle and Cook 1976): a speaker will look away to avoid distraction in an attempt to focus on what he is going to say. If you limit the space to which a signer can direct his gaze, are you influencing his cognitive processing and, consequently, his signing and role in discourse?

It is interesting to note that the presence of the videocamera did not appear to influence these observations on preferential side gaze. Furthermore, this tendency remained unaffected in dyads 4–6, where there was a third deaf person. They may have been far enough away that they did not influence the conversation. Or, because these persons were really just spectators during the conversation, their presence was irrelevant to the discourse situation.

These arguments can perhaps be carried further to apply not only to eye gaze and discourse but to the production and reception of manual signals as well. This may be supported by the research on morpheme structure constraints on locations of signs. Despite the existence of infinite locations for signs in the signing space, there are systematic restrictions on many of these locations. This is because the optimal visual signal needs to be easily and clearly perceptible at areas of high visual acuity. Thus, signs develop with these systematic restrictions based on the dynamics of the manual articulators and principles of visual perception (Battison 1978).

These principles of perception are intuitively followed among deaf signers. Groups of signers will invariably sit or stand in a circle when conversing to maximize their fields of view. Two signers chatting in a relatively open space will not sit/stand next to each other as speakers might but will position themselves perhaps two or three times farther apart, directly opposite each other. If it so happens that the sitting or standing arrangements are fixed, for example, sitting alongside each other in a bus or an auditorium, the signers will probably try to adjust by positioning themselves to face the other person more squarely or switching to the more distant hand to fingerspell, for instance. If one of the hands is occupied or unable to sign, adjustments are made on the free hand or with nonmanual signals and perhaps even by mouthing.

The research of Muirhead and Goldman (1979) showed that pairs of hearing people seated opposite each other had significantly more mutual eye contact than pairs seated adjacent to each other. In addition, the two variables—seating position and distance—may interact with each other. So conceivably, a seating arrangement at a 45° angle for two signers would probably not be consequential if they were seated so far apart that they had free space virtually all around them. Similarly, if they were facing each other but were only a foot apart, their proximity to each other would probably affect the conversation. A classical equilibrium model for social interaction has proposed that nonverbal behaviors such as eye contact and interpersonal distance are inversely related (Argyle 1967).

SUMMARY

Turn-Taking

These data on turn-taking show a split of the dyads into two groups with contrasting patterns. The cross-sex dyads showed that the male informant always signed more lengthily than the female informant; in other words, the female informant tended to be the addressee for the greater part of the conversation. On the other hand, the same-gender dyads demonstrated an almost equal number of utterances from both interlocutors. Although gender differences seem to be the most likely explanation for these patterns, they may also be explained by the influence of school, educational level, and/or observer presence.

The gender differences observed here appear to concur with what has been documented in spoken language discourse. This not only is significant for the pioneering research on Filipino Sign Language, but it also points to the importance of considering gender differences in the data collection and analysis of sign discourse.

In contrast to Thibeault's findings (1993), overlap during turn exchanges did not appear to be the norm in the dyads studied here. However, simultaneous sign events appeared to constitute a stronger pattern. These two would be areas ripe for future research.

Eye Gaze

The data on eye gaze in this study clearly support the following findings in the previous study of Martinez (1993):

1. Sustained eye contact (+GZ) when the informant (especially the female informant) is the addressee;
2. +GZ toward the end of utterances; and
3. Preferential -GZ to the side and particularly to the side of greater free space.

The first two findings demonstrate the data's similarities to ASL and English discourse. The third pattern is a new finding and an issue that needs to be considered carefully in data collection for sign language discourse. This is also an impetus to probe the phenomenon further. Manipulation of the variables of seating arrangement and distance may reveal novel insights into not only discourse but also cognitive processing and the use of space in signing. Mutual gaze aversion in the data was also noted, although the importance of the synchrony is still unclear.

The absence of other patterns in the remainder of the data is attributed to the combined effect of the discourse and nondiscourse functions of eye gaze. It is evident that more innovative methods are necessary to isolate these distinct functions. Similarly, deviations from predicted patterns may again underscore the need for more gender- and culture-sensitive approaches to discourse analysis of sign.

REFERENCES

Argila, C. 1970. Land of the morning, child of the sun returning. *Deaf American* (December):5–7.
Argila, C. 1971. Land of the morning, child of the sun returning—A sequel. *Deaf American* (December):9–12.

Argyle, M. 1967. The psychology of interpersonal behavior. Cited in N.F. Russo, Eye contact, interpersonal distance and the equilibrium theory. *Journal of Personality and Social Psychology* 31 (1975):497–502.

———, and M. Cook. 1976. Gaze and mutual gaze. Cited in G. Beattie, Sequential temporal patterns of speech and gaze in dialogue. *Semiotica* 23(1978):29–52.

———, and R. Ingham. 1972. Gaze, mutual gaze and proximity. Cited in N.F. Russo, Eye contact, interpersonal distance and the equilibrium theory, *Journal of Personality and Social Psychology* 31 (1972):497–502.

Asante, M.K., and A. Davis. 1989. Encounters in the interracial workplace. In *Handbook of international and intercultural communication,* ed. M.K. Asante and W.B. Gudykunst. Newbury Park, Calif.: Sage Publications.

Baker, C. 1976a. Eye-openers in ASL. In *Proceedings of the sixth California linguistics association.* Manuscript.

———. 1976b. What's not on the other hand in ASL. Twelfth regional meeting of the Chicago Linguistics Society. Manuscript.

Baker, C. 1977. Regulators and turn-taking in American Sign Language discourse. In *On the other hand: New Perspectives on American Sign Language,* ed. L.A. Friedman. New York: Academic Press.

Baker, C., and C.A. Padden. 1978. Focusing on the non-manual components of American Sign Language. In *Understanding language through sign language research,* ed. P. Siple. New York: Academic Press.

Baker-Shenk, C. 1983. Non-manual behaviors: Some methodological concerns and some research findings. Paper presented at Third International Symposium on Sign Language Research, Rome.

Battison, R. 1978. *Lexical borrowing in American Sign Language.* Silver Spring, Md.: Linstok Press.

Bonoan, R. 1976. Said: A Growing center for Deaf education. Kasayahan '76: Souvenir program, Southeast Asian Institute for the Deaf.

Bright, W., ed. 1992. *International encyclopedia of linguistics.* Oxford: Oxford University Press.

Gonzales, A. 1981. Language policy and language-in-education policy in the Philippines. In *Annual review of applied linguistics,* ed. R. Kaplan, 48–59. Rowley, Mass.: Newbury House.

Goodwin, C. 1981. *Conversational organization: Interaction between speakers and hearers.* New York: Academic Press.

Hecht, B.F., H. Levine, and A.B. Mastergeorge. 1993. Conversational roles of children with developmental delays and their mothers in natural and semi-structured situations. *Linguistics and Language Behavior Abstracts* 27(2):817.

Kendon, A. 1967. Some functions of gaze-direction in social interaction. *Acta Psychologica* 26:22–63.

Keinke, C.L. 1986. Gaze and eye-contact: A research review. *Psychological Bulletin* 100:78–100.

Larrue, J., and A. Trognon. 1993. Organizations of turn-taking and mechanisms for turn-taking repairs in a chaired meeting. *Linguistics and Language Behavior Abstracts* 27(2):724.

Liddell, S.K. 1980. *American Sign Language syntax*. The Hague: Mouton.

MacFadden, J., D. Slagle, P. Spanbauer, and G. Vollmar. 1977. *Sign as you speak*. Quezan City: SAID. ix-xi.

Martinez, L.B. 1992. Setting the stage for research on Philippine Sign Language: Language issues in the Philippines. Unpublished manuscript, Department of Linguistics and Interpreting. Gallaudet University, Washington, D.C.

———. 1993. Eye-gaze as an element in Filipino Sign Language discourse. Paper presented at Communication Forum 1992–93, Gallaudet University, Washington, D.C.

Mather, S.A. 1987. Eye gaze and communication in a deaf classroom. *Sign Language Studies* 54:11–30.

Muirhead R.D., and M. Goldman. 1979. Mutual eye contact as affected by seating position, sex, and age. *Journal of Social Psychology* 109:201–206.

Nerney, P. 1991. Review of *The role of English and its maintenance in the Philippines*. *Journal of Southeast Asian Studies* 22:212–214

Nordenstom, K. 1992. Male and female conversation style. *Linguistics and Language Behavior Abstracts* 26(4):1830.

Nowell, E. 1989. Conversational features and gender in ASL. In *The sociolinguistics of the Deaf community*, ed. C. Lucas. San Diego: Academic Press.

O'Connell, D.C., S. Kowal, and E. Kaltenbacher. 1990. Turn-taking: A critical analysis of the research tradition. *Journal of Psycholinguistic Research* 19(6):345–373.

Olson, J. 1989. Project IDEA: International Deaf Education Association. *American Annals of the Deaf* (December):338–340.

Parret, H., and J. Verschueren. 1992. Introduction to *(On) Searle on conversation*, by J. Searle, H. Parret, and J. Verscheren, 1–6. Amsterdam: John Benjamins.

Parsons, F. 1991. Deaf Peace Corp volunteers. *The NAD Broadcaster* 23 (December).

Pascasio, E. 1981. How value orientations affect social relationships through language use. In *Linguistics across continents*, ed. A. Gonzalez and D. Thomas, 80–96. *LSP Monograph*. Manila: Summer Institute of Linguistics and Linguistic Society of the Philippines. Series 11.

Philips, S.U. 1976. Some sources of cultural variability in the regulation of talk. Cited in D.C. O'Connell, S. Kowal, and E. Kaltenbacher, Turn-taking: A critical analysis of the research tradition, *Journal of Psycholinguistic Research* 19(6)(1990):368.

Pulling out of the Peace Corps. 1990. *Newsweek*, 9 July, 41.

Rutter, D.R. 1984. *Looking and seeing: The role of visual communication in social interaction*. New York: John Wiley.

Sacks, H., E. Schegloff, and G. Jefferson. 1974. A simplest systematics for the organization of turn-taking for conversation. *Language* 50:696–735.

SAID Model School. 1975. Deaf Filipino Newsletter. Vol. 1, special issue #1:3.

San Juan, E., Jr. 1991. Philippine writing in English: Postcolonial syncretism versus a textual practice of national liberation. ARIEL 22(4):69–88.

Sandager, O.K. 1986. *Sign languages around the world*. Hollywood: OK Publishing.

Schegloff, E. 1992. To Searle on conversation: A note in return. In *(On) Searle on conversation*, ed. J. Searle, H. Parret, and J. Verschueren, 113–128. Amsterdam: John Benjamins.

Scott, M. 1989. Confusion of tongues. *Far Eastern Economic Review* 145:44–45.

Searle, J. 1992. Conversation. In *(On) Searle on conversation*, ed., J. Searle, H. Parret, and J. Vershcueren, 7–30. Amsterdam: John Benjamins.

Searle, J., H. Parret, and J. Vershcueren. 1992. *(On) Searle on conversation*. Amsterdam: John Benjamins.

Self, P.L. 1993. "Verbal turn-taking behaviors of early education teachers and students. *Dissertation Abstracts International A: Humanities and Social Sciences* 53(3):715A.

Shaneyfelt, W. 1985. *Love signs*. Manila: D and M Print.

———. 1987. Philippine Sign Language. In *Gallaudet encyclopedia of deafness and deaf people*, ed. J. V. Van Cleve. New York: McGraw-Hill.

Sherwood, V. 1991. Regulation of turn-taking in children's verbal interactions. *Dissertation Abstracts International B: Science and Engineering* 52(4):2326B.

Stephens, J.F. 1991. Toward a model of turn-taking in conversation. *Dissertation Abstracts International* 51(9):4643B.

Streeck, J., and U. Hartge. 1992. Previews: Gestures at the transition place. In *The contextualization of language*, ed. P. Auer and A. DiLuzio. Amsterdam: John Benjamins.

Tannen, D. 1984. *Conversational style: Analyzing talk among friends*. Norwood, N.J.: Ablex.

Tannen, D. 1989. *Talking voices: Repetition, dialogue, and imagery in conversational discourse*. Cambridge: Cambridge University Press.

Thibeault, A. 1993. Overlap in Filipino Sign Language discourse. Paper presented at Communication Forum 1992–93, Gallaudet University, Washington, D.C.

TPBP. 1973. Newsletter. Mabuhay and Pilipinong Bingi. 1(1):1–3.

Valli, C., and C. Lucas. 1992. *Linguistics of American Sign Language: A resource text for ASL users*. Washington, D.C.: Gallaudet University Press.

Vogt-Svendsen, M. 1990. Eye gaze in Norwegian sign language interrogatives. In *SLR '87: Papers from the Fourth International Symposium on Sign Language Research*, ed. W.H. Edmondson and F. Karlsson, 153–162. Hamburg: Signum Press.

Sign Language Studies 5:20–30.

Woodward, J., and T. Allen. 1987. Classroom use of ASL by teachers. *Sign Language Studies* 54:1–10.

Empowerment from Within: The Deaf

Social Movement Providing a Framework

for a Multicultural Society

Kathy Jankowski

Although the study of social movements by rhetorical scholars is still a relatively new area of study, the tendency has been to treat social movements as marginalized groups trying to establish access to the dominant society. Such an approach is basically an integrationist theory of appeal. Social movements are thus studied from the framework of the marginal trying to access the dominant society by persuading the dominant to allow them to do so, rather than the framework of converting society into accepting diversity. As this study of the Deaf[1] social movement will illustrate, studying social movements from a framework of empowerment[2] brings out a new dimension of social movements. Such a treatment posits social movements as a powerful force challenging the dominant society to create change by accommodating marginalized peoples.

This approach to studying movements brings on an understanding of how the process of empowerment not only creates the impetus for a so-

This essay is from the author's dissertation. The author thanks James F. Klumpp, her advisor, for his guidance throughout the dissertation process.

1. Recent custom has been to distinguish between audiologically and culturally deaf people by respectively using the lowercase "d" and the capital "D." This study adopts that convention as well.

2. The term *empowerment* is so widely used that it is often given a variety of interpretations; it thus merits explanation. Definitions for empowerment have included upward mobility, self-assertion, and political activity. Bookman and Morgen (1988) explain that "empowerment begins when they [marginalized members] change their ideas about the causes of their powerlessness, when they recognize the systematic forces that oppress them, and when they act to change the

cial movement but also allows us, for example, to appreciate the efforts of the movement to build an internal community. In this vein, the integrationist approach to the study of movements is restrictive in that a narrow frame of access to the dominant society overshadows the research; thus, significant strategies for empowerment may be overlooked. This suggests that studies of social movements would benefit from a theory of empowerment to escape from integrationist inclinations.

Using Foucault's (1977) depiction of the normalizing process to study movements fits in well with a theory of empowerment. For one thing, a Foucaultian approach helps us to understand the position of social movements as they challenge the normalizing pattern so ingrained in the dominant society. Beyond that, the rhetorical construct of normality helps us reach an understanding of how movements become marginalized by rhetorical studies in the assumption that movements seek access to society. The perception of the dominant society as "normal" has inadvertently created a parallel expectation that movements, in representing the "deviant," seek access to the normal. So implicit is this practice that rhetorical scholars have accepted this integrationist approach as the norm. By using a Foucaultian approach, this tendency becomes clear and thus becomes a useful guide in preventing such tendencies.

This study of the contemporary Deaf social movement is a continuing rhetorical narrative of the American Deaf movement. This study, which examines the rhetoric of the Deaf movement in the aftermath of the ground-breaking "Deaf President Now" protest at Gallaudet University in 1988, continues the analysis of the earlier American Deaf social movement with its beginnings in 1880. The inception of the American Deaf social movement came about in response to "normalizing" practices by the dominant society at the historical 1880 conference of educators of the deaf at Milan, Italy. At this international conference, it was formally declared that sign language—the primary means of communication for Deaf people—would no longer be tolerated and that speech

---

condition of their lives" (p. 4). Bookman and Morgen conclude that "fundamentally, then, empowerment is a *process* [original emphasis] aimed at consolidating, maintaining, or changing the nature and distribution of power in a particular cultural context" (p. 4). This process, however, includes much resistance and consent along the way as the sources of power come into conflict. This study, accordingly, treats empowerment as a process through which a marginalized group alters the distribution of power between itself and the dominant culture.

and lipreading,[3] the "superior" mode, would be enforced as the only acceptable form of communication for Deaf people. The Deaf social movement has since then resisted these and other efforts to "normalize" them. The most effective undertaking conducted by the Deaf movement, however, was the "Deaf President Now" protest at Gallaudet University. The protest symbolized a dramatic achievement in "ownership" for the Deaf community when the board of trustees' original choice (a hearing person) was replaced with a Deaf president for the first time in the university's 124–year existence, and a mandate to have a deaf majority on the board was established.

This study of the more recent movement follows the Gallaudet University uprising. Although the contemporary Deaf social movement has not solidified to the point where it can be studied as a fully accomplished rhetorical phenomenon, the strategies that mark this stage thus far indicate an emerging rhetorical form. The American Deaf social movement after Gallaudet has capitalized on the move by African-Americans, Native-Americans, Hispanic-Americans, and others to create community through promotion of cultural diversity.

The rhetorical trends of these cultural diversity movements exemplify three necessary attributes for community building within a multicultural ideology: creation of a sense of self-worth, establishment of an internal foundation for community building, and participation in public life. This newer ideology stipulates that these attributes promote the preservation of each culture not only to enable marginalized peoples to take pride in their cultural identity but also to foster greater multicultural tolerance and acceptance in the dominant society. Therefore, striving for a greater amount of ownership within a marginalized community corresponds to a greater demand for participation in public life and ultimately contributes to a more pluralistic society.

BALANCING INTEGRATION AND SEPARATISM

The post-1960 multicultural movements balance separatism and assimilation. As Lisa Jones, daughter of African American poet Amiri

3. The use of primarily spoken speech and lipreading to communicate is called *oralism*. Oralism was created out of both the belief that deaf people needed to master the spoken word to achieve communication and also the practice of that belief in the education of deaf people.

Baraka, puts it, diversity movements seek "to fuse self-help and the fight against racism together into one" (cited in Harrington 1991, 25). These movements have made inroads in creating women's and African American studies at many universities and curricula that reflect the diversity of cultures in America. The cultural diversity movements have also been embraced by more members of the dominant society than was, for instance, the Black Power movement.

The cultural diversity strategy has, however, adopted many of the goals of the earlier separatist movements, such as creating a sense of pride in cultural groups and establishing the power to make decisions that affect the lives of members. For example, Black Power presented the 1960s with a growing militancy that threatened many members of the dominant society. Many integrationists, fearing a backlash of Civil Rights efforts, painted the dominant sentiment of Black Power as symbolic of "anti-white power" (Wilkins 1966, 14), in other words, a hatred for white people and for America. Because many people also believed Black Power proponents preached violence, it was feared that this "hatred" would be transformed into violence.

However, critics have noted the prevalent societal misinterpretations of the phrase. Scott and Brockriede (1969) explain that to people such as Stokely Carmichael, Black Power symbolized "personal pride in being black, responsibility to other blacks, and power as a group to deal with outsiders" (p. 5). Inherent in Black Power rhetoric was the struggle for the right of marginalized peoples to define and identify themselves (Scott and Brockriede 1969; Campbell 1971).

Scott and Brockriede (1969) also point out that, contrary to rejecting access to the public sphere, Black Power was a statement in support of *institutionalized* integration rather than *individualized* integration; in other words, integration as promoted in the Civil Rights legislation benefitted only the most "qualified" African Americans, rather than the entire group. Further, Campbell (1971) argues that the violent threats in Black Power were symbolic "because it threatens, because it is frightening, assures him [sic] of his equality, dignity, and manhood. When so assured, it becomes possible for the Black man to confront the White man as an equal, with pride, self-respect, and dignity" (p. 159).

The cultural diversity strategy is an expanded descendant of the Black Power symbolism. However, rather than using the rhetoric of "power," which is seen as threatening by the dominant society, the movements adopt words such as "cultural diversity" and "multiculturalism." These terms succeed where Black Power struggled, since they play on the democratic idealism of America. Cultural diversity sends the message that America, the home of freedom and opportunity to numerous immigrants, would be mean-spirited to begrudge marginalized groups that same right, especially if her strength comes from that diversity. Where Black Power demands group integration, cultural diversity extends an invitation to society to celebrate along with marginalized groups their culture and identity as a solution to institutional integration. Further, Black Power speaks for African Americans, whereas cultural diversity presents a spirit of coalition for all dispossessed groups.

In effect, cultural diversity has transformed Black Power rhetoric into a position of respectability. Additionally, cultural diversity presents a solution to integrationists in the form of access to the dominant society. By legitimizing the preservation of unique groups within the dominant society, cultural diversity becomes a strategy to ensure full participation in public life.

THE DEAF MOVEMENT ADOPTS THE MULTICULTURAL IDEOLOGY

The rhetorical trends of the Deaf social movement since the Gallaudet protest indicate this direction as well. To illustrate the movement toward seeking a diversified America, I will briefly discuss strategies through which the Deaf social movement balances separatism and assimilation within a multicultural framework. Through these strategies the movement develops a sense of self-worth, builds a strengthened internal foundation of the community, and commands greater participation in the public sphere.

Creating a Sense of Self-Worth

One function of social movements is to develop a sense of self-worth in the membership. At Gallaudet this was achieved through the many confrontations with the board of trustees. But in the post-Gallaudet protest atmosphere, the movement has sought to provide an ongoing rhetoric that establishes the self-worth in more pervasive ways and, in turn, serves as a basis for acceptance of the Deaf community within a framework of diversity. Legitimizing the group identity as "the good" serves to instill pride and creates a buffer against dominant characterizations of the group as "the bad" or the "deviant." The sense of self-worth that emerges is a crucial element if social movements are to succeed in establishing communities within a dominant society.

The aftermath of the Gallaudet protest has produced within the Deaf social movement a new rhetoric of assertion that provides a sense of self-worth. Perhaps the comparison of an old and a more recent Deaf joke illustrates this. The age-old joke takes on varieties of this form:

> There was once a Deaf man who was driving until he came to some train tracks. However, he was not able to drive through because the crossing signal gates were blocking his way. After waiting for a very long time, the Deaf man got out of the car and walked to where the gate controller was stationed. While the gate controller was talking on the phone, the Deaf man wrote on a piece of paper, "please but." The gate controller couldn't figure out what the Deaf man was trying to get across.

This joke does not make sense to nonsigners because it is based on a sign play. The written word "but" is a reference to a sign in American Sign Language (ASL)[4] that means "to open the gate," which is also the sign for the word "but."

The more recent joke takes on this form:

> A Deaf person was riding on a train and met a Cuban and a Russian. After smoking only half a cigar, the Cuban throws the remainder out the window. The Deaf person asks, "Why did you throw that out?" "Oh," says the Cuban, "we have plenty of cigars in Cuba." Later, the Russian too throws out a half-empty bottle of vodka. "We have plenty of vodka in Russia," says the Russian. The Deaf person contemplates all this. Then, as a hearing man walks by, the Deaf person picks him up and throws him out the window. "We have plenty of hearing people in this world" is the explanation.

Douglas (1968) explains that jokes reveal the marginalized group's vi-

---

4. American Sign Language is a rule-governed language with its own grammatical structure, morphology, and syntax (Klima and Bellugi 1979; Stokoe 1960; and Woodward 1973, 1974). These characteristics mark ASL as a complete language, just as English, French, and German are.

sion of the inequalities in society, and this one articulates a vision of a strong Deaf person challenging an inferior status.

The "but" joke establishes the gatekeeper in a symbolic role of the hearing person, who is frequently in control of the Deaf person's destiny, and pokes fun at Deaf people's struggles with English. Anthropologist Susan Rutherford (1989) explains that this joke is "a picture of lack of control, lack of self-determination, negation of identity, stifled development, blocked communication, external control characterized by benevolent paternalism and authoritarianism" (p. 76).

In contrast to the older joke, the newer joke illuminates a sense of power and control, depicts self-determination, and is a positive enactment of the Deaf identity. However, hearing people often express distaste for this joke. Such a response could be expected because there is a rhetoric of confrontation—even a threat—in the joke. If expressive of a mood of many Deaf people in more recent times, it sounds a challenge.

Nevertheless, the transformation of consciousness evident in the two jokes exemplifies the newer sense of self-worth. The older joke that mocks the Deaf person as the deviant reinforces societal perceptions. The newer joke rejects the negative depiction and symbolically substitutes the bad for the good.

Oppressed groups often use humor as a coping strategy against prejudice and discrimination from the dominant culture. Humor enables an oppressed group to symbolically condemn its unequal status, which manifests the transformation of its "misery by poking fun at oppressors" (Fine 1983, 173). By attacking the dominant culture, a symbolic release from oppression is transformed into pride and self-worth in marginalized peoples, thus creating a strengthened framework for cultural diversity (Martineau 1972).

Another example of such humor, perhaps less pointed but still confrontational, appeared in the treatment of the hearing aid in the comic strip "Oxford," created by Bruce Hanson, featuring a Deaf monkey.[5] The Deaf monkey is shown snatching a hearing aid from a nurse who is handing it to him; he then proceeds to swallow the hearing aid and comments that it needs more ketchup. This comic strip takes a current manifestation of the dominant pathologizing strategies and attacks it in a way that

5. Hearing aids are assistive devices that help people with much residual hearing and word discrimination understand speech to some extent. However, for a majority of Deaf people, hearing aids serve little or no use.

promotes self-worth. In doing so, it brings humor to a more general strategy to build self-worth by attacking the pathological dominance.

The hearing aid and, more recently, the cochlear implant, symbolize age-old dominant practices to convert Deaf people into hearing people.[6] Where Deaf people previously sought to ward off pathological discourses by promoting Deaf identity, current strategies essentially reverse the earlier by directly attacking symbols of pathology to promote identity. By celebrating the Deaf identity, the current strategies of confrontation blatantly denigrate the high value placed on the ability to hear by dominant discourses.

Past internalization of such dominant discourses reinforced the status of Deaf people by stressing inabilities rather than abilities. Such reinforcement maligned their self-worth. The direct assault on these symbols of pathology, on the other hand, performs a rhetoric of self-worth within a culture of diversity. To embody this rhetoric of self-worth, practices such as the ceremonial destruction of hearing aids have been carried out by Deaf people at an international symposium in France ("The Future," 1990). National Association of the Deaf (NAD) former president Roz Rosen (1991) has also concluded that ears have usefulness as a resting place for her glasses. Such declarations assert the wholeness of the Deaf being.

The symbolism of the cochlear implant has provoked an especially intense reaction. In 1990, the Food and Drug Administration approved the marketing of cochlear implants for children aged two to seventeen. The NAD has established a task force and developed a position paper condemning this "experimentation" on children as "ethically offensive" (Cochlear Implants 1991, 1). Slogans have materialized—"stop the cochlear madness" or "if it's not broken, don't fix it"—to denounce the spread of cochlear implants.

The cochlear implant embodies the prevailing painful and torturous medical strategies that so many Deaf people have experienced, especially in childhood, to convert them into hearing, speaking people.[7] The co-

6. Cochlear implants are a fairly recent medical development. They are used in an attempt to restore or augment at least some residual hearing. The cochlear implant requires major surgery, during which a hole is drilled in the skull to transplant the device.

7. Medical strategies include hearing aids, listening devices (including gigan-

chlear implant is perceived as an especially agonizing process because, unlike hearing aids that can be taken off on a whim, cochlear implants are surgically implanted.[8] Deaf adults, after going through, in many cases, a difficult process to accept themselves as Deaf, perceive the cochlear implant as an affront to their self-worth. Further, it is deemed offensive to their experiences, which indicate that the cochlear implant is simply an extension of the hearing aid and not likely to be of much help to most Deaf people. The central theme captured in the movement's response to the cochlear implant is that the hard-won battle for self-worth has become so precious that given a choice, many Deaf people would rather remain Deaf. As a Gallaudet student has avowed, "if there was a medication that could be given to deaf people to make them hear, I wouldn't take it. Never. Never til [sic] I die" (cited in Karlen 1989, 134).

Not only has the Deaf social movement assaulted the rhetoric of pathology to reinforce the self-worth of the Deaf community, some discourse even turns the tables of pathology back onto the dominant society. Deaf people label members of the dominant society much the same way that Deaf people have been labelled. Stratiy (1989), for instance, created a chart evaluating the skills of hearing people just learning to sign, assigning them such characteristics as "signing impaired," "hard-of-finger-spelling," "dexterity disabled," and other such labels. These labels have often been attributed to Deaf people by dominant discourses. By creating a reversal in the rhetoric of pathology, such discourses by Deaf people illustrate a conscious refusal to be categorized according to dominant standards. By doing so, the sense of self-worth is legitimized.

The strategies to perform a rhetoric of self-worth illuminate discourses of assertion, even confrontation, to attack prevailing discourses of pathology. Such a strategy, even though confrontational, validates the self-worth of the Deaf community. With this validation, the movement creates a discourse of difference, a rejection of the norm, and thus a celebration of diversity. Strategies of confrontation are more reminiscent of Black

---

tic earphones) worn by Deaf students while the teacher wears a microphone, and other similar devices to thrust the development of speech and listening faculties on Deaf children.

8. The cochlear implant is especially condemned by many Deaf people because its value is highly doubtful and because of its side effects, such as loss of balance, tinnitus, intense pain, and severe headaches (e.g., Roche 1991).

Power strategies than those of the diversity movements. Even so, the rhetoric of self-worth performs a necessary function that enables the movement to work for the internal building of community and eventually toward a multicultural society.

Creating an Internal Foundation for Community Building

Within the family of cultural diversity strategies, the rhetoric of self-worth moves the social movement to a higher plane of challenging dominant discourses through themes that seek greater ownership of the dominated community. African-centered curriculums and other multicultural practices illustrate. The Gallaudet movement embodied the ownership theme in the protestors' confrontation with patriarchal forces that had dominated the campus for years. The contemporary movement capitalizes on this theme by expanding it as a strategy to declare greater ownership within a multicultural framework.

One of the themes that characterized the rhetoric of Black Power was that the African American community was occupied: white people ran the community, administering it for those who lived there (Carmichael and Hamilton 1967). A central strategy in the post-Gallaudet movement has been the declaring of Deaf ownership of their community. The movement to place Deaf people in positions of authority in the community is illustrative of this strategy. The Gallaudet protest was a step forward in this direction. The theme of declaring ownership was exemplified at the Gallaudet protest in its demand for a Deaf president as well as its demand for a 51 percent deaf board composition. The successful launch of these demands at Gallaudet has paved the way for similar ventures elsewhere.

To ensure that the Gallaudet protest would not be a one-time thing, the Deaf social movement took advantage of the impetus to spread the discourses of Deaf ownership throughout the Deaf community. A particular venue for the strategy of Deaf ownership has been to point to the prevailing pathological practices within the educational establishment. Some Deaf people have argued that such practices are best illustrated by the meager numbers of educators—popularly quoted as between 10 and 20 percent—who are themselves deaf (e.g., Bahan 1989b; Coyne 1991).

The rhetoric of Deaf ownership is illustrated in Ben Bahan's (1989b) proposal that the Deaf movement demand that for the next ten years, educational programs for the deaf be restructured to accommodate a quote of at least 50 percent Deaf educators. The discourse of Deaf ownership has expanded from the call for an increased number of deaf people on the outside (e.g., the board) to that on the inside (e.g., a greater number of deaf teachers).

The call for more Deaf teachers has been transformed into several rallies across the nation for increased Deaf ownership. The contemporary Deaf movement has also capitalized on the success of the Gallaudet protest by adopting rallies as occasions for communicating their demands. A recent illustration of this practice was a protest held at the Wisconsin School for the Deaf. The Wisconsin school protest bore resemblance to the Gallaudet protest in demands that the hearing dean of students be replaced with a Deaf person; that the present hearing superintendent be replaced with a Deaf person upon the anticipated retirement of the incumbent in 1993; that the school establish a goal to hire enough Deaf people to compose a 51 percent deaf staff; and that the students face no reprisals after the protest (Moering 1991a).

These strategies explicitly convey the promotion of Deaf ownership. More implicit is the relationship between Deaf ownership and access to the language of the Deaf community—ASL. The superintendent at the school, John Shipman, however, picks up on this connection:

> In the deaf community in general, there's a movement toward a bilingual and bicultural approach that also carries with it a belief that there should be a larger percentage of deaf employees. This thinking is developing, and our school is not the only place where that thinking is going on. (cited in "Deaf Students," 1991, 1B)

Indeed, the newer Deaf social movement has turned toward the strategy of other diversity movements to establish more control over their own community as a means to seek acceptance as a diverse culture with its own language.

The protestors at the Wisconsin school movement gained momentum by capturing the attention of the state department of education that has jurisdiction over the Wisconsin School for the Deaf. Assistant Superintendent of Schools Victor Contrucci, in representing the state department, legitimized the protestors' efforts to focus attention on their cultural and linguistic needs. Contrucci announced that his department was in contact with the state Department of Employment Relations to ask that civil service tests for candidates to the school incorporate consideration for users of ASL, as tests typically were given in standard English, presenting a potentially discriminatory situation against Deaf people. Further, affirmative action efforts would be examined to encourage the recruitment of more Deaf personnel to the school (Moering 1991b).

The protest at the Wisconsin school is illustrative of the practice adopted by the Deaf social movement to target educational institutions as places to promote Deaf ownership. As places that foster the cultural community of Deaf people, educational institutions symbolize the home of Deaf people. And to ensure that these "homes" truly belong to Deaf people, it is necessary to establish ownership by placing them firmly under the control of Deaf people.

But administrative control is not the only characteristic of ownership that has caught the current movement's attention. In addition, an old theme is back with increased intensity: the effort for full recognition of ASL as the language of the Deaf community. Where previously, ASL was legitimized as a language outside the classroom, the newer movement brought it into the classroom in a fashion consistent with the multiculturalism cluster of rhetorical strategies. Consider, for example, the recent strategy to promote ASL through the rhetorical demand for a shift from "communication" to "language" policies in schools. Virtually every educational institution for Deaf students has communication policies that dominant discourses have long enforced, based on the premise that such policies serve as a guiding force for classroom communication. The movement's stress on language policy effectively shifts the focus of debate. No longer is the question: How will communication with the Deaf student in the classroom be best facilitated? Instead the question is: How will the language of the Deaf student be best facilitated?

The movement from communication to language policies has become a strategy to implement bilingual and bicultural approaches in the education of Deaf students. While the discourse of bilingualism promotes Deaf ownership, it also challenges the dominant society to take on a multicultural framework. In keeping with this strategy of the other diversity movements, Gallaudet students, two years after the Gallaudet protest, established an "ASL Now" campaign to rally for the recognition of ASL at Gallaudet. The students petitioned the Gallaudet faculty senate to "develop a language policy that officially recognizes American Sign Language and English as two official languages of Gallaudet University."

Specifically, "we want Gallaudet to be a bilingual university" (cited in Nye 1990, 5).

The push for language policies validates the bilingual and bicultural identity of Deaf people and condemns communication policies as a password or a "veiled term" (Valli 1990, 130) to legitimize the prevailing normalizing practices of Deaf people. This rhetorical move differs from the previous co-optative stance on total communication[9] policies. The earlier struggle illuminated the acceptance of total communication as a way out from oralism even while it retained the theme of integration. The newer movement has brought the struggle into a different context. The shift to communication versus language policies creates a battle between integration and the preservation of cultural identity.

To support the argument that communication policies are normalizing practices, those making these arguments marshal evidence such as survey results that demonstrate that many teachers of Deaf students use sign and speech in the classroom, rather than adopting the tenets of the total communication philosophy (Woodward and Allen 1987). Others depict a "Tower of Babel" scenario to illuminate total communication as a ridiculous practice. Bahan (1989c), for one, marshals support for a language policy with such a rhetorical strategy:

> Imagine a teacher going over this sentence: George Washington never chopped down a cherry tree. Seven times for each child's need, using oral method, Rochester method (fingerspelling all the words in the sentence), SEE 2, writing, simultaneous method, drawing, and, if necessary for a child, Morse code. When the teacher finally finishes her sentence seven different times, it might be time for the child to go to another class. (P. 119)

Deaf people point to policies that enforce the use of speech as granting teachers permission to order signing Deaf students to "sit on your hands." Even more "flexible" communication policies validate practices that require a conformity to the norm of speech. Simultaneous communication, for example, requires one to speak and sign at the same time.

9. Total communication is a philosophy rather than a method that endorses individual communication rights. In other words, any and all modes of communication, including sign language, speech and lipreading, reading and writing, among others, may be used in the instruction of Deaf children.

An editorial in the student newspaper at Gallaudet University illuminates how normalizing practices have been implicitly enforced by prevailing values placed on speech skills:

> I find it strange that in the course of my school career, virtually all of the teachers and people that ask me to use my voice while signing are the ones who really suck dead dogs in sign language. These are the ones who ask me to speak for their _____ing benefit, while they don't make the slightest effort to improve THEIR signing. (Whetter 1989, 4)

Communication policies however, not only promote normalizing practices of enforcing the standard modality and language on deaf children, they have also become a strategy to legitimize discrimination against Deaf people. Deaf teachers who do not speak face employment discrimination, especially in earlier grades where policies stipulate the need for teachers to train Deaf children to speak.[10] Many Deaf people have also related tales that illustrate practices by educators to give lower grades to students who do not speak. Consequently, by ridiculing communication policies such as total communication, the movement targets language policies as a strategy to legitimize ASL in the classroom. Thus, language policies that recognize both ASL and English validate Deaf people's bilingual and bicultural status. Such policies encourage the acknowledgment and respect of the cultural uniqueness of the Deaf community in keeping with the discourse of the diversity movements.

Further, this type of policy presents a rhetorical statement to the dominant society that Deaf people, as a distinct culture, should not be expected to function as the hearing people they are not. A language policy thus creates the distinction between pathological and cultural practices. The Indiana School for the Deaf makes such a distinction:

> The concept of bilingual/bicultural education for Deaf students is founded on a cultural perspective of Deaf life. This differs greatly from previous educational approaches that have been founded on a medical or pathological view of Deaf people, thus a bilingual/bicultural pro-

---

10. Beverly Hanyzewski (1989), for instance, was denied an internship at a preschool program for the Deaf because, according to the principal of the school, "[employees] must have good vocal skills, listening skills for evaluation of vocal skills" (p. 3).

gram represents a major shift in educational philosophy and attitude. ("Bilingual/Bicultural" 1990, 3)

The rhetoric of language policy, rather than communication policy, has begun its transformation into institutional practice at a few pioneer programs. Both the Indiana School for the Deaf and the Learning Center in Massachusetts have established bilingual and bicultural programs. Other schools are currently exploring ways to facilitate this approach. A significant move by Gallaudet toward this end has been the establishment of a Deaf Studies program.

Strategies that promote Deaf ownership foster a strengthened internal foundation for community building. To this end, the Deaf movement adopts the strategy of institutional rather than individualized integration as presented by the diversity movements. Even though Deaf ownership illuminates separatist rhetoric, as the diversity proponents have argued, creating a discourse of self-worth and building a healthy foundation of ownership are actually necessary attributes for challenging dominant discourses of inequality. Declaring ownership is thus a strategy to invalidate discourses of inequality and, consequently, to promote a rhetoric of multiculturalism in the dominant society.

Transforming the Internal Foundation to the External: Participation in Public Life

The Deaf-as-good phenomenon and the move toward greater control of the Deaf community serve the function of validating the self-defined perception of Deaf people as equal to their hearing peers. And by establishing a rhetoric of equality, Deaf people assert their right along with their hearing counterparts to full participation in the public sphere. However, a rhetorical dilemma is faced by diversity movements, along with the Deaf social movement, when dominant discourses posit the marginalized in a status of inequality.

For the Deaf community, a discourse of inequality has been created in the rhetoric of "it's a hearing world." Jane Bassett Spilman, chair of the Gallaudet board of trustees in 1988, said it with the purported infamous line that Deaf people are not ready to function in the hearing world. Educators of the deaf also prescribe the importance of speech skills and fluency in English based on its being a hearing world. This rhetoric legitimizes a standard based on the norm of hearing people. Discrimination against Deaf people who do not speak or possess nativelike fluency in English is based on the premise that they do not fit into a hearing world. By accepting the ideological "it's a hearing world out there," Deaf people are placed in a subordinate position. To counter this dominant practice, the Gallaudet protest adopted a strategy of reversal; that is, protesters responded with assertions that Elisabeth Zinser (the board's first choice for president) was not ready to function in the Deaf world. The post-Gallaudet movement has moved to a higher plane, however. Rhetoric such as "Hell, it's our world, too!" (Bahan 1989a, 47) illustrates this newer strategy.

In line with multicultural rhetoric, the slogan of "it's our world, too" explicitly asserts the right of Deaf people to fully participate in public life. The integrationist position that adapting to societal norms is the only way for Deaf people to acquire full accommodation is challenged by Bahan (1989a), who insists that such an approach "will never work" (p. 48). As some of the protestors of the Wisconsin protest point out, it will never work because: "Your [dominant society] world revolves around sound, ours revolves around sight—and that is why our language is so important to us. . . . You can learn our language, but we can never learn to hear" (Karlecke et al. 1991, 11). The strategy of "it's our world, too," thus insists that society accommodate the Deaf community in the move toward a multicultural society because it will not work the other way around.

As a strategy to induce society to accommodate the Deaf community, the rhetoric of "communication violence" (J.E. Tucker, conversation with author, 5 November 1991) has surfaced.[11] As Tucker explains, the rhetoric of communication violence is a charge against dominant practices that do not fully accommodate the Deaf community. This includes a wide spectrum from the inability to communicate with nonsigning family members to the nonavailability of ttys[12] at most telephone booths, to nonaccess

11. James Tucker coined the term on an inspiration from the Reverend Jesse Jackson, who frequently speaks of a rhetoric of "diversity." Jackson had employed the term "economic violence" to refer to the failure of the government to distribute equally to its constituents. He argued that all Americans should have, at the very minimum, basic health care, as the present system affords the best health care to those who can afford it. As a result, innocent children suffer from this practice, hence, the institution of "economic violence."

to intercoms and radios (Tucker, conversation with author). The rhetoric of communication violence is thus a strategy to awaken both the consciousness of the Deaf community and the sensibilities of the dominant society.

More significantly, however, strategies such as communication violence reject minimal accommodation and demand full participation. Bilingual proponents argue that it is language access that Deaf students need, not merely communication access. Accordingly, the rhetoric of communication violence is a demand for equal and total participation in the public sphere.

Consequently, some Deaf people have chosen to target the telephone as the symbol that obstructs access to public participation. For years, the telephone has legitimized discriminatory practices against Deaf people, especially in employment. Even in Deaf establishments, virtually every institution has made it a practice to hire at least one hearing employee to answer voice calls. Such a practice focuses on what Deaf people cannot do rather than on what they can do.

The choice of the telephone as a symbol is a bold strategic move. With the Gallaudet movement, the rhetoric of Deaf ownership was played out in the strategy of claiming turf that should officially have belonged to the Deaf community. The newer strategy of the telephone, on the other hand, is a brazen move to turn an object held dear by the dominant society into an object that legitimizes discriminatory practices against deaf people. The telephone is singled out as a symbol of obstruction to participation in the public sphere since the practice of hiring hearing people to answer voice calls sends the message that there are indeed some things Deaf people are not able to do, even within their own establishments. And if they cannot perform these functions in their own community, then employers outside Deaf establishments are justified in not hiring Deaf people because they cannot accomplish these crucial operations.

As such, declaring the telephone as a symbol of discrimination has prompted Deaf people such as Jack Levesque (1991) to propose that programs and services for Deaf people enact policies to accept only tty calls.

12. A tty is the original abbreviation for a device used by Deaf people to communicate over the telephone. It is possible to communicate with another party only if the other party also possesses a tty. A tty carries messages that are typed back and forth on the screen between the two parties.

This proposal would require voice callers to access establishments with such a policy via a telephone relay system and would thus place the telephone, which has long legitimized employment discrimination against Deaf people, into a subordinate position.[13]

The proposal to ban voice calls would also alter the technology of communication, opening up very different rhetorical possibilities. By reversing the roles, with non-tty callers at the receiving end having to adopt unfamiliar technologies, this strategy serves to place these callers in a subordinate role. Most of these callers, presumably hearing people, will then experience what Deaf people go through every day of their lives in placing calls to people who do not have ttys. In this vein, the condemnation of the telephone promotes self-worth by validating the Deaf-as-good motif and establishes participation in public life, thus creating an environment for greater tolerance of cultural diversity.

This strategy of the newer Deaf movement appears to create a paradox: seeking greater public access by refusing to communicate in the dominant technology of the very society the community is trying to access. However, this strategy illustrates the power of cultural diversity strategies—marginalized groups reject the practice of acquiring access on terms that deny their identity. The conversion of self-worth and the strong community into public participation is built with bridges to diversity rather than with access as inferior members—marginal members of the broader public community. Rather than seeking integration, as exemplified by the practice of accommodating on society's terms, this strategy demands access for the Deaf on their own terms. Such a strategy also mocks an old nemesis—Alexander Graham Bell—recaptured in a different mode.

For the Deaf social movement, demands that society adapt to Deaf people are also tempered by an invitation to work together to achieve that goal. The movement to officially recognize American Sign Language (ASL) as a language across the nation is such a strategy. As Bahan (1989a) contends, since Deaf people cannot conform to society, the dominant so-

13. Telephone relay systems refer to the process by which Deaf people communicate with people who do not have access to a tty, and vice versa. The consumer of this service can call either via a tty or voice call, and "operators" are the third party that translates conversations between the caller and the person called. It was not until recently that legislation mandated the establishment of telephone relay systems in the United States.

ciety can and should accommodate the Deaf community. One way to make this possible is to teach them ASL.[14]

Diversity movements share the theme that offering a multicultural education will enable the dominant society to better understand and thus respect various cultures. Accordingly, teaching ASL as a recognized language—analogous to foreign languages such as Spanish, common in our English-dominant society—is a strategy to create a pluralistic society. For the Deaf social movement, the official recognition of ASL throughout the country would validate its bilingual and bicultural status. Consequently, success in officializing ASL would promote a humanistic image of the Deaf community as a cultural and linguistic entity and put to rest the predominantly pathological view of Deaf people. The movement to officialize ASL promotes an environment that is willing to accommodate diversity and is then a strategy to create a pluralistic America.

CONCLUSION

Traditionally, rhetorical studies become focused on describing the full diffusion and effects of rhetorical strategy. The strategies discussed in this paper are contemporary strategies. They have not expanded to their full potential, nor have the effects of their power been universally witnessed. Nevertheless, the rhetorical scholar can see their usefulness and their relevance in the service of the Deaf movement and community as well as their relevance to other marginalized groups.

For instance, a dilemma that has just begun to be addressed by the Deaf social movement is: What is the balance between separatism and assimilation? Is there even a need for such a balance? As separatist rhetoric argues, total assimilation will not work because it deprives the cultural individual of his or her cultural identity. For Deaf people, full assimilation is additionally not possible since society does not accommodate the very basic communication needs of Deaf people. On the other

14. A poll in *Deaf Life* magazine suggests overwhelming support (96 percent) for hearing people to learn ASL. Among the comments were these: "More barriers between the hearing and nonhearing communities will fall." "Hearing people [would gain] a better understanding of the Deaf, [besides] they see the Deaf more often than foreigners." And, "DEFINITELY! Then more hearing people will feel comfortable talking to and [sic] meeting Deaf people" (Readers' Viewpoint 1989).

hand, integrationists contend that total separatism is not possible for eco-nomic survival. As the three proposed attributes for community build-ing indicate, a solution would appear to be a fusion of the best elements of each faction.

This theory is substantiated by Killian and Grigg (1964), who discuss a similar dilemma in regard to the assimilation of African Americans into society. They argue that for assimilation to work, African Americans need to have a psychologically and mentally healthy regard for themselves so that white people will be dealing with people who have a positive sense of their history and themselves as whole beings.

Killian and Grigg's evaluation need not be restricted to African Americans. Such a diagnosis can extend to Deaf Americans and other marginalized groups. In societies that deem certain groups such as Deaf people as not normal, strategies are needed to modify dominant percep-tions. As this paper has illustrated, a positive sense of self-worth, inter-nal community building, and participation in public life have become strategies for maintaining a distinctive cultural identity.

As with the other contemporary diversity movements, the Deaf move-ment has created new strategies to address prevailing themes. The newer strategies exemplify a strengthened rhetoric of self-assertion as evident in the transformation of jokes, the condemnation of the fixation on the ear, and mockery of the pathological labelling of Deaf people. These strat-egies pose a stark contrast to earlier co-optive practices. The increased rhetoric of self-assertion lends credence to arguments that social move-ments pave the way toward empowerment among the membership evi-dent in their break from traditional patterns and move to create further changes (e.g., King 1987).

This study of the rhetorical shaping of empowerment for the cultural identity of the Deaf movement illuminates the position taken by the Black Power advocates. Creating a sense of self-worth gives the marginalized group a sense of self-pride and thus generates an increased cycle of as-sertive rhetoric among the membership. With this healthy regard for them-selves as a cultural entity, members become empowered to establish a greater stake in their territory, which in turn further increases their self-worth and pride. In turn, staking out a greater territory emboldens and empowers the members to approach the dominant society from an equal rather than a marginal standpoint. Since the dominant society has cre-ated the rhetoric of pathology, demeaning marginalized groups, empowerment must come from within. Black power takes this position, as do the contemporary diversity movements. As this study illustrates, the Deaf movement has begun to move in this direction as well.

The strategy of retaining a separate cultural identity not only creates the basis for a healthy foundation, it also presents a means by which the cultural group can participate in the dominant society as equals, rather than subordinates. That is the strategy of multiculturalism: to promote a strong foundation by which cultural groups retain their identity and at the same time gain respect as exactly that while being extended the invitation to become an equal partner in society.

REFERENCES

Bahan, B. 1989a. It's our world too! In *American deaf culture*, ed. S. Wilcox, 45–48. Silver Spring, Md.: Linstok Press.

Bahan, B. 1989b. The war is not over. In *American deaf culture*, ed. S. Wilcox, 189–192. Silver Spring, Md.: Linstok Press.

Bahan, B. 1989c. Total communication: A total farce. In *American deaf culture*, ed. S. Wilcox, 117–120. Silver Spring, Md., Linstok Press.

Bilingual/bicultural education: Philosophy statement. 1990. *Bi-Cultural News*, April-May, 1–3.

Bookman, A., and S. Morgen, eds. 1988. *Women and the politics of empowerment*. Philadelphia: Temple University Press.

Campbell, K.K. 1971. The rhetoric of radical black nationalism: A case study in self-conscious criticism. *Central States Speech Journal* 22:151–160.

Carmichael, S., and C.V. Hamilton. 1967. *Black power: The politics of liberation in America*. New York: Vintage Books.

Cochlear implants in children: Position paper of the National Association of the Deaf. 1991. *NAD Broadcaster*, March, 3.

Coyne, J. 1991. No more voice calls? Letter to the editor. *DCARA News*, March-April, 13.

Deaf students push for change. 1991. *Janesville Gazette*, 18 November, 1B.

Douglas, M. 1968. The social control of cognition: Some factors in joke perception. *Man* 3:361–376.

Fine, G.A. 1983. Sociological approaches to the study of humor. In *Handbook of humor research*, ed. P.E. McGhee and J.H. Goldstein, 159–181. New York: Springer-Verlag.

Foucault, M. 1977. *Discipline and punish: The birth of the prison*, trans. A. Sheridan. New York: Pantheon Books.

Hanyzewski, B. 1989. Too bad to be true: Deaf teacher unqualified to teach deaf pre-schoolers. *TBC News*, June, 3–4.

Harrington, W. 1991. Black and white and Spike all over. *Washington Post Magazine*, 2 June, 11–27.

Karlecke, J., R. Karlecke, S. Kelly, and D. Kelly. 1991. In support of WSD superintendent response to protest. Letter to the editor. *The Delavan Enterprise and the Delavan Republican*, 28 November, 10, 11.

Karlen, N. 1989. Louder than words. *Rolling Stone*, 23 March, 134–140.

Killian, L.M., and C. Grigg. 1964. *Racial crisis in America*. Englewood Cliffs, N.J.: Prentice-Hall.

King, A. 1987. *Power and communication*. Prospect Heights, Ill.: Waveland Press.

Klima, E., and U. Bellugi. 1979. *The signs of language*. Cambridge, Mass.: Harvard University Press.

Levesque, J. 1991. No more voice calls at DCARA? *DCARA News*, 2 February, 2.

Martineau, W.H. 1972. A model of the social functions of humor. In *The psychology of humor*, ed. J.H. Goldstein and P.E. McGhee, 101–125. New York: Academic Press.

Moering, H. 1991a. WSD students protest lack of deaf on staff. *The Delavan Enterprise*, 19 November, Tuesday edition, 1, 7.

Moering, H. 1991b. Dean reassigned, WSD protest ends. *The Delavan Enterprise and The Delavan Republican*, 21 November, 1, 16.

Nye, E. 1990. Student's signature. *ASL Now Newsletter*, 23 April, 5.

Readers' Viewpoint. 1989. *Deaf Life*, 31.

Rosen, R. 1991. The president signs on. *The NAD Broadcaster*, February, 3.

Rutherford, S. D. 1989. Funny in deaf-not in hearing. In *American deaf culture*, ed. S. Wilcox, 65–81. Silver Spring, Md.: Linstok Press.

Scott, R. L., and W. Brockriede. 1969. *The rhetoric of black power*. New York: Harper and Row.

Stokoe, W. C., Jr. 1960. Sign language structure: An outline of the visual communication system of the American deaf. In *Studies in linguistics: Occasional paper 8*. New York: University of Buffalo.

Stratiy, A. 1989. The real meaning of "hearing impaired." *TBC News*, November, 1.

The future society of the deaf. 1990. *TBC News*. September, 1.

Valli, C. 1990. A taboo exposed: Using ASL in the classroom. In *Communication issues among Deaf people: Deaf American monograph-1990* 40:129–131.

Whetter, D. 1989. Speaking with both hands in mouth. *Buff and Blue*, 4.

Wilkins, R. 1966. Excerpts from a speech by R. Wilkins. *New York Times*, 6 July, 14.

Woodward, J. 1973. Implicational lects on the deaf diglossic continuum. Ph.D. diss., Georgetown University, Washington, D.C.

Woodward, J. 1974. Implicational variation in ASL: Negative incorporation. *Sign Language Studies* 5:20–30.

Woodward, J., and T. Allen. 1987. Classroom use of ASL by teachers. *Sign Language Studies* 54:1–10.

Index

Acceptance of deafness in Spanish-speaking families, 228, 237–38

ACEDHH. *See* Association of College Educators of the Deaf and Hard of Hearing

Adjectives
DEAF as, study of variables and constraints, 19–21
Quebec Sign Language, initialization in, 53

Advisory Committee on Education of the Deaf. *See* Babbidge Report

African Americans
cultural diversity and, 309–11, 315, 326–27
white vs. African American signing, 6–7

AGBAD. *See* Alexander Graham Bell Association for the Deaf

Agent-beneficiary directionality, 7–8

Alexander Graham Bell Association for the Deaf (AGBAD), 112–13, 133–34, 144–47

Allen, T. E., and Karchmer, M. A., 165

Alternate sign language used by persons already competent in spoken language, 77–83
history of, 79–82
primary system used by Deaf members of community, adoption as, 81–82, 101–2

American Indians
conversational style, 277
history of sign language as alternate to spoken language, 79–82
Navajo family use of sign language, 77–106

American Sign Language (ASL)
constructed dialogue and constructed action in, 255–71 (*see also* Constructed dialogue and constructed action in ASL)
Council on Education of the Deaf task force on, 143–48
DEAF, study of variables and constraints, 10–21 (*see also* DEAF, study of variables and constraints)
Deaf social movement and, 317–21, 324–25
Filipino use of, 274–76
fingerspelling, 63–64
Hispanic deaf children, exposure to, 222, 226, 236, 244
initialized signs, 32–34
as language policy vs. communication policy, 318–21
movement to officially recognize as language, 324–25
Navajo family not using during study, 103
Quebec Sign Language, links with, 48
role playing, 255–71 (*see also* Constructed dialogue and constructed action in ASL)
structure, 8–9
use of, in education of Deaf children, 109–63 (*see also* Education of Deaf children)
use of, to teach reading, 196, 198–211
variables and constraints, 9–10 (*see also* Variation, in ASL)
location as variable, 3–25

American Sign Language (ASL)
(*continued*)
study of formation of DEAF, 10–
21
Anderson, Tom, 127
Aramburo, A., 7
Argyle, M., and Cook, M., 278
ASL. *See* American Sign Language
Association of College Educators of
the Deaf and Hard of
Hearing (ACEDHH), 112,
136, 143, 144–46, 147
Audism, 114, 120–22, 135, 137, 148
Australia
aboriginal use of sign language in,
81–82
sign families in Australian Sign
Language, 47

Babbidge Report, 117, 130–31
Bahan, Ben, 316, 319, 322, 324
Baker, C., 278–79, 299
Baker, C., and Padden, C., 278
Ballin, A., 126
Battison, R., 31–33, 38, 52, 54–55, 63
Battison, R., Markowicz, H., and
Woodward, J., 5, 10
Bell, Alexander Graham, 82
Bellugi, U., and Newkirk, D., 33
Bennett, A. T., 225, 242
Bilingual policies
Deaf social movement advocating,
317–21
in Spanish-speaking families. *See*
Spanish-speaking families
with deaf children
Black Power, 310–11, 315, 327
Blacks. *See* African Americans
Body shifts in ASL constructed
dialogue and constructed
action, 256
Borrowing, lexical, 30–31, 49, 57–59
Bright, W., 274
British Sign Language (BSL), 32–33
Burnes, Byron B., 133

CAID. *See* Convention of American
Instructors of the Deaf
Campbell, K. K., 310
Cap College of the Deaf, 280
CEASD. *See* Conference of
Educational Administrators
Serving the Deaf
CED. *See* Council on Education of the
Deaf
Celebrezze, Anthony J., and Babbidge
Report, 130–31
Christensen, Kathee, 113, 144, 146–
47, 245
Class differences, effect of, on
sociolinguistic variation, 4
vertical variation, as, 6
Cochlear implants, 112, 124, 314–15
Code-switching (*see also* Borrowing,
lexical)
in Spanish-speaking families with
deaf children, 240, 244
Commission on Education of the Deaf
(COED), 117, 131–32
Communication violence, 322–23
Conference of Educational
Administrators Serving the
Deaf (CEASD), 112, 133–34,
144–45, 147
Constructed dialogue and constructed
action in ASL, 255–71
body shifts, 256
conclusions of study, 265–66
co-occurrence of constructed
dialogue and constructed
action, 261–62
direct action to reconstruct events,
262–63
eye gaze, 256, 263–64, 266
facial expression changes, 256
findings of study, 258–65
frequency of constructed dialogue
and constructed action, 260–
62
indirect action to reconstruct
events, 263–64

Filipinos (*continued*)
Turn-taking in sign conversations
of deaf Filipinos (*continued*)
discussion of study, 293–96
gender differences, 294, 296,
301
literature review, 276–77
methodology of study, 280–81
overlap and simultaneous
signing, 272, 281–86, 293–
96, 302
results of study, 281–86
Fingerspelling
borrowing from spoken language,
31–32
Navajo family use of, 103
Quebec Sign Language and
initialization, 31–32, 54–56
Rochester Method, 111, 128
use of, by deaf parents with their
deaf daughter, 62–73
analysis of results, 70–72
findings by age of child, 66–68
methodology, 64–65
partial phrase or sentence, 68
parts of speech, 68
sandwiching phrases, 65, 68–70
Foreign languages
French language and initialization
in Quebec Sign Language,
29–61
Italian conversation style, 277, 296
Pilipino, 273
Spanish-speaking families with
deaf children, 221–52
Tagalog, 273–74
Foreign sign languages
Australian (*see* Australia)
Canadian (*see* Quebec Sign
Language)
initialized signs in, 32–34
lexical variation in, 7
Norwegian Sign Language, 279
Philippine Sign Language (*see*
Filipinos)

Spanish-speaking families with
deaf children, 243, 247
Foucault, M., 308
Frishberg, N., 98–99

Gallaudet, Edward Miner, 121
Gallaudet Research Institute, Culture
and Communication Studies
Program, 62
Gallaudet University
"ASL Now" campaign, 318–20
"Deaf President Now" protest,
308–9, 311
Deaf Studies program, 321
Garretson, Mervin, 147
Gee, James, 208
Geertz, C., 196
Gender differences
effect on sociolinguistic variation,
7
eye gaze in sign conversation, 272,
297, 299
turn-taking in sign conversations,
294, 296, 301
Geographical variation, 4
horizontal variation, as, 6
Giroux, H., 116
Goldin-Meadow, S., and Mylander,
C., 97
Groce, Nora, 82
Guggenheim, L., 7
Guy, G., 10

Hand vs. elbow signs, 6
Haugen, E., 30, 58
Hearing aids, 112, 313–14
Hearization, 122–25, 135, 148
Hispanic families speaking Spanish
with deaf children. *See*
Spanish-speaking families
with deaf children
Home-sign systems, 98–101
Horizontal variation in signing, 6
Humor, as a coping strategy, 313–14
Humphries, Tom, 120, 247

Pilipino, 273
Poplack, S., Sankoff, D., and Miller, C., 30, 58
Pronoun usage, 8
Puerto Rican families with deaf children. *See* Spanish-speaking families with deaf children

Quebec Sign Language (LSQ), initialization in, 29–61
   adjectives, 53
   ASL, links with LSQ, 48
   based on existing signs, 45–46, 48
   borrowing from spoken language, 30–31, 49, 54–56
   data analysis, 39–43
   fingerspelling, 31–32, 54–56
   form, and relationship to meaning, 44–48
   frequency of initialized signs, 49–51
   hybrid creation, 58
   idiosyncratic initialized signs, 51
   integration
      linguistic, 52–54
      phonological, 56–57
      sociolinguistic, 49–52
   literature review, 32–34
   loanwords, loanblends, and loanshifts, 30, 54, 58
   methodology of study, 34–39
   movement, 39, 40–42, 43
   nonce borrowing, 30, 58
   nouns, 53
   place of articulation, 39–40, 42, 43
   sign families, 46–48
   status of initialized signs, 49–59
      hypotheses on, 57–59
   verbs, 54

Regional variation, 4
   horizontal variation, as, 6
Reported speech in ASL, 256

Rhetoric
   of communication violence, 322–25
   of cultural diversity movements, 309–311, 321, 322
   of deaf social movement, 311
      to declare Deaf ownership of Deaf community, 316–21
      to establish sense of self-worth, 311–14, 315, 321, 326
      as a strategy to demand shift from communication policy to language policy, 318–21
   of inequality, 321–22
   of pathology, 314, 315, 326–27
   strategies of, 325–27
Rickford, J., 16
Rochester Method, 111, 128
Role playing in ASL, 255–71 (*see also* Constructed dialogue and constructed action in ASL; Discourse analysis, role playing in ASL)
Romaine, S., 101
Rosen, Roslyn, 118, 314
Roy, C. B., 256
Ruiz, Richard, 113–14, 118–19
Rutherford, Susan, 313
Rutter, D. R., 278

Sacks, H., et al., 277
Sankoff, D., Poplack, S., and Vanniarajan, S., 58
Schieffelin, B. B., 123
Schreiber, Frederick C., 127–28
Scott, Hugh Lennox, 80–81
Scott, R. L., and Brockriede, W., 310
Scouten, Edward L., 111–12, 157–58
Seale, J., 276
Sebeok, T. A., and Umiker-Sebeok, J., 82
Second International Congress (Milan, Italy), 121, 125, 308
SEE. *See* Signing Exact English
Seeing Essential English, 128–29

Self-worth, effect of Deaf social
movement on, 311–16 (*see
also* Rhetoric, to establish
sense of self-worth)
Shaneyfelt, W., 274, 275
Shipman, John, 317
Shroyer, E., and Shroyer, S., 6
Signed English, 128–29
Signing Exact English (SEE), 128–29,
172, 198, 275
Signing in English word order, 198–
203, 210 (*see also*
Simultaneous
communication; Total
communication)
Sign languages and systems (*see also
specific sign languages and
sign systems*)
taxonomy, 83–86
Silverman, S. Richard, 134
Simmons de Garcia, J., 223
Simultaneous communication (*see also*
Total communication)
in education, 116–17, 128–29,
165–66, 194–97
limitations of, 168, 168–69 n, 170,
192, 193, 198–203
in Spanish-speaking families with
deaf children, 236
Singleton, J., and Newport, E., 97
Skutnabb-Kangas, T., 242
Smith, James L., 125
Spanish-speaking families with deaf
children, 221–52
academic achievement of children,
222
acceptance of deafness by, 228,
237–38
accommodation of deafness, 238–
39
advice of school to families, 245
ASL, exposure of children to, 222,
226, 236, 238, 244
code-switching, 227, 240, 244
communication strategies, 238,
240–41

conclusions of study, 243–45
delayed diagnosis of deafness, 229
demographic changes, 222
families studied, 228–35
foreign sign languages, 243, 247
home-based assessments, 244
language choice decisions, 240
language proficiency, 235–37
limitations of study, 249
methodology of study, 224–28
perspective of deaf child dealing
with family, 239–41
perspective of family dealing with
deaf child, 235–39
position of child in family, 240
recommendations for school's role,
246–49
school's views of families and
linguistic diversity, 241–43
recommendations for changes,
246–49
signing in, 226, 230–36, 238–41
spoken English in, 226, 236–37
trilingual classes to teach sign
language, 245
use of visual/gestural language,
238–41, 243–45
Spilman, Jane Bassett, 321
Spoken language. *See also* English
language; Foreign languages
influence on initialization in
signing, 54–56
sign language used instead of, by
hearing persons, 77–83
Stokoe, William C., 8–9, 32, 56, 255
Stratiy, A., 315
Streeck, J., and Hartge, U., 280
Supalla, S. J., 32–33
Swisher, M. V., and McKee, D., 33

Tagalog, 273–74
Tannen, D., 256–60, 266, 277
Tarra, Abbé Guilio, 121
Taxonomy
constructed dialogue and action in

Taxonomy (*continued*)
  ASL, 258–60, 270–71
  of sign languages, 83–86
Teachers of the Deaf. *See also*
    Education of Deaf children
  analysis of teacher graduate
    education, 136–48
  discrimination against deaf
    teachers, 320
  multicultural issues in education
    of, 248–49
  quota for deaf teachers, demand
    for, 317
  training and certification, 134
Telephones, 323–24
Thibeault, A., 272–73, 280, 294–95,
    302
Thumb extension in signing, 5, 10, 21
Total communication philosophy, 115
  shift from, as part of Deaf social
    movement, 319
TTY calls, 323–24
Tucker, J. E., 322–23
Turn-taking
  in sign conversations of deaf
    Filipinos, 272–306
  conclusions, 301–2
  discussion of study, 293–96
  gender differences, 294, 296,
    301
  literature review, 276–77
  methodology of study, 280–81
  overlap and simultaneous
    signing, 272, 281–86, 293–
    96, 302
  results of study, 281–86
  in sign language discourse,
    generally, 278

University of Arizona, Sign Language

Research Lab, 89

Van Uden, A., 115
Varbrul computer analysis of
    variation in language, 5, 13–
    14
Variables and constraints in ASL, 9–
    21. *See also* American Sign
    Language, variables and
    constraints; DEAF, study of
    variables and constraints
Variation, in ASL, 3–25
  of DEAF, 10–21
  face-to-face, 5–6
  lexical, 6–7
  morphosyntactic, 7–8, 10
  research on, 5–8
  socioeconomic status and, 4
Veditz, George, 77, 125
Verbs
  in Quebec Sign Language,
    initialization of, 54
  reduplication, 7–8
  teaching of, in episode structure in
    stories, 182, 185, 188, 190
Videotaping, effect on studies, 16, 300
Voegelin, C. F., 80

Washabaugh, W., 99
West, La Mont, 80, 81–82
Winston, E., 257, 266
Wisconsin School for the Deaf, 317,
    322
Wolfram, W., 10, 19
Woodward, J., 7–8, 32–33, 128
Woodward, J., and De Santis, S., 5, 7
Woodward, J., Erting, C., and Oliver,
    S., 5

Zinser, Elisabeth, 322